W9-BLF-705

always up to date

The law changes, but Nolo is on top of it! We offer several
ways to make sure you and your Nolo products are up to date:

Nolo's Legal Updater

We'll send you an email whenever a new edition of this book is
published! Sign up at **www.nolo.com/legalupdater**.

Updates @ Nolo.com

Check **www.nolo.com/update** to find recent changes
in the law that affect the current edition of your book.

Nolo Customer Service

To make sure that this edition of the book is the most
recent one, call us at **800-728-3555** and ask one of
our friendly customer service representatives.
Or find out at **www.nolo.com**.

please note

We believe accurate, plain-English legal information should help you solve many of your own legal problems. But this text is not a substitute for personalized advice from a knowledgeable lawyer. If you want the help of a trained professional—and we'll always point out situations in which we think that's a good idea—consult an attorney licensed to practice in your state.

NOLO

Lower Taxes in 7 Easy Steps

By Attorney Stephen Fishman

FIRST EDITION	NOVEMBER 2006
Editor	DIANA FITZPATRICK
Book Design	TERRI HEARSH
Proofreading	SUSAN CARLSON GREENE
Index	THÉRÈSE SHERE
Cover photography	TONYA PERME (www.tonyaperme.com)
Printing	DELTA PRINTING SOLUTIONS

Fishman, Stephen.
  Lower taxes in 7 easy steps / by Stephen Fishman
    p. cm.
  ISBN 1-4133-0550-4 (alk. paper)
  1. Tax planning--United States--Popular works. 2. Income tax--Law and
  legislation--United States--Popular works. I. Title. II. Title: Lower taxes in 7 easy
  steps.

  KF6297.Z9F57 2006
  343.7305'2--dc22

                                                          2006048284

Quantity sales: For information on bulk purchases or corporate premium sales, please contact
the Special Sales Department. For academic sales or textbook adoptions, ask for Academic
Sales. 800-955-4775, Nolo, 950 Parker Street, Berkeley, CA 94710.

Acknowledgments

Many thanks to:

Diana Fitzpatrick for her outstanding editing

Terri Hearsh for the excellent book design, and

Thérèse Shere for the helpful index

About the Author

Stephen Fishman is a San Francisco-based attorney who has been writing about the law for over 20 years. He received his law degree from the University of Southern California in 1979. After time in government and private practice, he became a full-time legal writer in 1983. His Nolo publications include:

- *Consultant & Independent Contractor Agreements*
- *Deduct It! Lower Your Small Business Taxes*
- *Every Landlord's Tax Deduction Guide*
- *Home Business Tax Deductions: Keep What You Earn*
- *How to Safely & Legally Hire Independent Contractors*
- *Nondisclosure Agreements: Protect Your Trade Secrets & More*
- *The Public Domain: How to Find Copyright-Free Writings, Music, Art & More*
- *Tax Deductions for Professionals*
- *Web & Software Development: A Legal Guide*
- *What Every Inventor Needs to Know About Business & Taxes*
- *Working for Yourself: Law & Taxes for Independent Contractors, Freelancers & Consultants*
- *Working With Independent Contractors*

Table of Contents

4 Delaying the Pain: Deferring Income and the Tax It Brings

5 Count Every Penny: Reducing Taxable Income With Deductions

Index

Winning the War on Taxes

W e've all heard that death and taxes are inevitable. Well, death may be inevitable, but taxes are not. With some planning, you can minimize the taxes you pay each year. However, many people don't do even the most basic planning to save on taxes and they end up paying more to the IRS than they need to. You don't want to be one of these people. This book shows you—in seven easy steps—ways you can reduce your taxable income and the amount of taxes you will owe each year.

The tax planning strategies discussed in this book are the tried-and-true techniques for reducing taxes that every taxpayer should be familiar with. There's nothing in here about offshore bank accounts or convoluted tax shelters. We cover the basics—strategies that are not difficult to understand or put to use, and are most likely to save you—the average taxpayer—money. You may even find it fun to learn, particularly when you see how much you can save with a little knowledge and planning.

Is Tax Planning for You?

Tax planning means figuring out ways to minimize the taxes you have to pay each year. Tax planning is perfectly legal and makes sense for anyone who pays taxes. It's not tax evasion which is cheating on your taxes—for example, not reporting all your income to the IRS. Tax evasion is illegal and, if you're caught, you'll have to pay the IRS all the taxes you owe, plus interest and penalties. In some cases, you could even go to jail. Look at what happened to the winner of the first *Survivor* television series, Richard Hatch. He was sentenced to 51 months in jail for tax evasion after he failed to report his $1 million winnings to the IRS.

You might think tax planning is just for rich people who use high-priced tax and accounting professionals to help them. This isn't true. People with modest incomes can benefit from tax planning too, and often can do it themselves. There are many ways to lower your taxes that are simple to understand and implement yourself—for example, opening an IRA or hiring your children to work in your business. Others are more complex and may require the help of a tax professional, such as tax-free exchanges of business property.

The important thing is to have an understanding of your options. A surprisingly large number of taxpayers fail to take even the most basic steps to reduce their income taxes, even though it would save them hundreds or thousands of dollars each year. You owe it to yourself to learn the basics. Then you can rest assured that you are not one of the many people paying too much money to the IRS.

A Quick Look at the Seven Steps

Here's a quick look at seven steps you can take to reduce your taxable income and the taxes you will owe. Each step is covered in one of the chapters that follows. The steps that are likely to save you the most taxes are listed first, but you don't need to implement them in any particular order. You probably won't be able to use all seven tax-saving strategies each year—for example, you may not qualify for tax-free income or have anyone to shift income to. And which steps you can use may change year to year. That's fine. Just keep in mind that the more of these tax-saving tips you put into practice each year, the less taxes you'll owe.

Step 1: **Maximize Tax-Free Income.** Certain types of income aren't subject to income tax at all. The single best way to avoid taxes is to earn as much tax-free income as possible. (See Chapter 2.)

Step 2: **Take Advantage of Tax Credits.** Obtaining a tax credit is the next best thing to paying no taxes at all because it reduces your taxes dollar for dollar—something a deduction does not do. Thus, tax credits are always better than deductions. There are many different types of tax credits. Doing something as simple as adding insulation to your home can qualify you for a tax credit. (See Chapter 3.)

Step 3: **Defer Taxes.** You'll have to pay income tax on your taxable income sooner or later, but you'll usually be better off if you pay it later. Deferring payment of taxes to a future year is like getting a free loan from the government. There are many ways to do this, from postponing an employer bonus to investing in IRAs and other retirement accounts. (See Chapter 4.)

Step 4: **Maximize Your Tax Deductions.** Perhaps the most well-known way to reduce taxable income is to take tax deductions. The more deductions you have, the less tax you'll pay. All individual taxpayers are entitled to either take a specified standard deduction or itemize their deductions. People in business may also deduct their business expenses. There are many ways to increase your tax deductions. (See Chapter 5.)

Step 5: Reduce Your Tax Rate. Federal income tax rates can vary dramatically, from as low as 5% to as high as 35%. You can benefit from the lowest rates available if you earn income from investments like stocks, bonds, mutual funds, and real estate. (See Chapter 6.)

Step 6: Shift Income to Others. If you're in a high tax bracket, you can save substantial taxes by shifting your income to someone in a lower tax bracket—for example, your children. This process is called income shifting or income splitting. Recent changes in the tax law make this harder to do than it was in the past, but it's still a viable planning tool for many taxpayers. (See Chapter 7.)

Step 7: Take Advantage of Your Filing Status and Tax Exemptions. Few people give much thought to their tax filing status, but it can have a big effect on the taxes you pay. All individual taxpayers are entitled to tax exemptions. Those with dependent children or other dependents may be entitled to many. (See Chapter 8.)

This book is not a guide on how to fill out your income tax forms. By then, it will be too late to implement many of the tax-saving techniques you will learn by reading this book.

Income Tax 101: How the System Works

You will need a basic understanding of how the income tax system operates to figure out which tax-saving strategies work best for you. Cheer up! This isn't that hard to understand.

As the name implies, with income tax, you are paying tax on your income—for example, the salary you earn from a job or interest income you earn on savings. However, you don't have to pay income tax on all your income—not by a long shot. The amount of your income that is subject to income tax is called your taxable income. The idea behind tax planning is to use all legal means available to keep your taxable income for the year as low as possible. There are all sorts of ways

When to Start Tax Planning

People often wait until December to start thinking about ways they can reduce their taxes for the year (if they think about it at all). This is a mistake. You should start doing serious tax planning no later than the beginning of the fourth quarter of the year—that is, October. But earlier in the year is usually better.

Start by making a projection of what your taxes will be for the year assuming you don't take any of the steps outlined in this book. To do this, you take your income and expenses to date and add your anticipated income and expenses for the rest of the year. This can be done easily with tax preparation software such as *TurboTax*. There are also several online calculators you can use (www.hrblock.com/taxes/, for example), but they don't provide as much information as *TurboTax*. If you like hard work, you can do it yourself with paper and pencil.

If you're happy with your projected tax bill, you don't need to do any more tax planning. But, if you want to reduce your taxes, look at the tax-saving steps in this book and use as many of them as you can.

Keep in mind that it's usually better to act earlier in the year with tax-planning strategies. For example, the beginning of the year is the best time to establish and/or contribute to tax-deferred accounts because you'll get a whole year's worth of tax-deferred income. So, don't wait until the end of the year to read this book.

to reduce your taxable income. One way, for example, is by taking deductions. These are expenses you're allowed to subtract from your income. But deductions are just one way to lower your taxable income; there are many others you'll read about in this book.

In a nutshell, here's how income taxes work:

- **Start with all your income.** First, you start with all the income you earn or receive each year, regardless of the source—salary, interest, net business income, investment income, and anything else. If you're married and file jointly, as the great majority of married couples do, you include your spouse's income as well.

- **All Income – Exclusions = Gross Income.** Certain items are excluded from all your income to arrive at your gross income. (It's not called this because it's disgusting; here, gross means the totality of your income, minus some important exclusions.) These exclusions include such things as gifts, life insurance proceeds, up to $500,000 in profits from the sale of your home if certain requirements are met, interest earned on municipal bonds, and several others. (These exclusions are covered in Chapter 2.)

- **Gross Income – Adjustments to Income = Adjusted Gross Income.** Next, certain adjustments to income are subtracted from your gross income to determine your adjusted gross income (AGI). (These adjustments are often called "above the line deductions," because they go before the line for AGI on your tax return.) These adjustments include contributions to deductible IRAs and self-employed retirement plans, contributions to health savings accounts, health insurance payments by the self-employed, moving expenses if you change jobs, and several others.

- **Adjusted Gross Income – Deductions and Exemptions = Taxable Income.** You then subtract from your AGI (1) your deductions, and (2) your tax exemptions to determine your taxable income. You may take a specified standard deduction or itemize your deductions. If you itemize, you deduct expenses for such things as mortgage interest, state and local taxes, charitable contributions, medical expenses, and unreimbursed employee expenses. (These deductions are often called "below the line deductions" because they go after the AGI line on your tax return.) (Deductions are covered in Chapter 5.) Your exemptions consist of specified amounts you may deduct for yourself, your spouse, and your dependents (if any). (Exemptions are covered in Chapter 8.)

- **Taxable Income x Tax Rates = Tax Liability.** You multiply the amount of your taxable income by the tax rates set forth in IRS tax tables or schedules to determine your tax liability. The tax rates vary according to the amount of your taxable income, from a low of 10% to a high of 35%. (These brackets are listed in Chapter 6.)
- **Tax Liability – Tax Credits = Tax Due.** Finally, you subtract any tax credits you're entitled to, if any, from your tax liability. You may obtain tax credits for such things as buying a hybrid car, paying for higher education or child care expenses, or making your home more energy efficient. (Tax credits are covered in Chapter 3.) The total is the amount you owe the IRS.

EXAMPLE: Ron and Rachel Smith are a married couple, with two young children, who file a joint income tax return. In 2006, Ron earns $70,000 in salary from his job, Rachel earned $20,000 from a part-time home, the couple earned $5,000 in interest income, and they received a $5,000 gift from Rachel's grandfather. Their total itemized deductions are $12,000, which exceeds their $10,000 standard deduction. Here's how they compute their taxes:

Total Income	$ 100,000
Minus: Exclusions to Income	− 5,000 gift
Gross Income	$ 95,000
Gross Income	$ 95,000
Minus: Adjustments to Income	0
Adjusted Gross Income	$ 95,000
Adjusted Gross Income	$ 95,000
Minus: Itemized Deductions	− 12,000
Minus: Exemptions (4 x $3,300)	− 13,200
Taxable Income	$ 69,800
Tax Liability (25% tax bracket)	$ 10,565
Minus: Tax Credits	− 0
Tax Due	$ 10,565

Could the Smiths have reduced their income tax by implementing one or more of the seven tax-planning steps outlined above? Do you really need to ask? Here are just a few ways the Smiths could have reduced their 2006 tax bill through tax planning:

- **Defer taxes.** The Smiths could have deferred part of their income taxes to future years by opening an IRA and contributing the $8,000 maximum. Rachel could have put off collecting part of her business income until 2007—$8,000 for example.
- **Take advantage of tax credits.** The family could have taken advantage of tax credits and made their home more energy efficient by purchasing a solar water heater.
- **Maximize tax deductions.** The Smiths could have increased their 2006 tax deductions by making a $1,000 contribution to their favorite charity. Rachel could have purchased a new $2,000 computer for her business.

Had the Smiths done these things, here is what their 2006 taxes would have looked like instead:

Total Income	$ 92,000	(100,000 – $8,000 of deferred income)
Minus: Exclusions to Income	– 5,000	gift
Gross Income	$ 87,000	
Gross Income	$ 87,000	
Minus: Adjustments to Income	8,000	(IRA contribution)
Adjusted Gross Income	$ 79,000	
Adjusted Gross Income	$ 79,000	
Minus: Itemized Deductions	– 15,000	($1,000 more for charitable contribution and $2,000 for business computer)
Minus: Exemptions (4 x $3,300)	– 13,200	
Taxable Income	$ 50,800	
Tax Liability (15% tax bracket)	6,865	
Minus: Tax Credits	– 2,000	(solar water heater credit)
Tax Due	$ 4,865	

Too bad Mr. and Mrs. Smith didn't buy and read this book. They could have paid $4,865 in taxes instead of $10,565.

AMT: The Stealth Tax System

You may be surprised to learn that the United States actually has two separate or parallel tax systems. One is the regular tax system described above. The other is the Alternative Minimum Tax, or AMT for short. The AMT is designed to force taxpayers to pay a minimum amount of tax, even if they are required to pay less, or no tax at all, under the regular tax system. If you're required to pay the AMT, you pay it in addition to your regular income taxes.

You're most likely to be subject to the AMT if you have a high income (over $100,000 for singles and $150,000 for married couples) and have many exemptions and deductions that are not allowed for the AMT. For example, you:

- have lots of children—each one provides a $3,300 dependency exemption not allowed for with the AMT
- live in a state with high income taxes like New York or California
- have substantial miscellaneous itemized deductions, such as unreimbursed employee expenses or investment expenses
- have a very large medical expense deduction
- pay substantial interest on a home equity loan and don't use the money to improve your home or buy or improve a second home, or
- receive stock options from your employer.

The IRS has an AMT Assistant on its website (www.irs.gov) that you can use to see if you might be subject to the AMT.

Planning for the AMT can be extremely complicated and many of the usual tax-planning techniques covered in this book would not be applicable. Tax software like *TurboTax* can be a big help with the AMT; but, if you are facing a substantial AMT liability you should see a tax pro.

This book is about the regular tax system, not the AMT. The AMT is so complicated it would take an entire book to explain it in any detail. Fortunately, there is such as book: *The Alternative Minimum Tax*, by Harold S. Peckron (Sphinx Publishing).

Most States Have Income Taxes Too

This book focuses on the federal income tax—the tax administered by the Internal Revenue Service (IRS). However, 43 states have their own income taxes. The seven states with no income tax are Alaska, Florida, Nevada, South Dakota, Texas, Washington, and Wyoming. Fortunately, state income taxes are much lower than federal rates (you can find a list of all state income tax rates at www.taxadmin.org/FTA/rate/ind_inc.html). State income tax laws generally track federal law, so the tax-planning techniques covered in this book will help lower your state income taxes as well. For more information on state income taxes, refer to your state tax department's website. A handy directory of links to these sites can be found at www.taxsites.com/state.html.

Icons Used in This Book

 This icon alerts you to a practical tip or good idea.

 This is a caution to slow down and consider potential problems.

 This refers you to other sources of information about a particular topic covered in the text.

 This icon lets you know when you may need the advice of a professional, usually a lawyer or tax professional.

 This icon refers you to related information in another place in the book.

The Best Tax Is No Tax: Income That's Tax Free

Ordinarily, when you earn income, you have to pay income taxes. This is true regardless of where the income comes from—wages, bonuses, or benefits from a job; interest or dividends from investments; business or rental income; withdrawals from retirement accounts like IRAs and 401(k)s; or profits you earn by selling assets like real estate and stocks. There are exceptions, however. Certain types of income are not included in your gross income so you don't pay any taxes on it.

Everyone knows that paying less taxes is a great way to save money. Obviously, paying no taxes is the best tax-saving strategy of all. For a person whose combined federal and state top tax rate is 40%, every dollar of tax-free income is equal to $1.67 in taxable income. That adds up to incredible savings—the trick is figuring out how to earn tax-free income.

Congress exempted certain types of income from taxes because it wanted to encourage people to engage in certain activities. Almost anyone can earn at least some tax-free income. In fact, there's a good chance you're earning some now without even being aware of it—for example, if your employer gives you fringe benefits like health insurance.

Some of the most common ways to earn tax-free income are:
- selling your home
- saving money for your children's education
- investing in municipal bonds
- contributing to a health savings account
- receiving health insurance and certain other employee benefits from your employer
- spending some of your salary on out-of-pocket health costs instead of taking it in cash, or
- giving some investments to your children.

The tax on retirement accounts is deferred. The income earned on money placed in retirement accounts such as 401(k)s, traditional IRAs, and SEP-IRAs is not tax free. Rather, the tax is deferred until retirement. That is, the money grows tax free while in the account, but income tax must be paid on it when it is withdrawn upon retirement. However, withdrawals from Roth IRAs and Roth 401(k)s are tax free. Retirement accounts are covered in Chapter 4.

Selling Your Home With No Income Tax

For most people, the largest tax break they'll ever get is when they sell their home. If you meet the requirements for the home sale tax exclusion, you don't have to pay any income tax on up to $250,000 of the gain from the sale of your principal home if you're single, or up to $500,000 if you're married and file a joint return.

> **EXAMPLE:** Ed and Eve are married and file jointly. They purchased their home in 1990 for $200,000. They sold it in 2006 for $600,000. Their gain (profit) on the sale is $400,000. If they qualify for the $500,000 exclusion, they don't have to pay any income tax on this gain. If they don't qualify, they would have to pay a 15% long-term capital gains tax on their gain, for a tax of $60,000 (15% x $400,000 = $60,000).

If you qualify for the exclusion, you may do anything you want with the tax-free proceeds from the sale. You are not required to reinvest the money in another house. But, if you do buy another home, you can qualify for the exclusion again when you sell that house. Indeed, you can use the exclusion any number of times over your lifetime as long as you satisfy the requirements discussed below. If you're a homeowner. this is the one tax law you need to thoroughly understand.

Forget the Old Law

The $250,000/$500,000 home sale exclusion came into effect in 1997. Before then, there were two different tax breaks for homeowners who sold their principal homes. One allowed homeowners to avoid (defer) any tax on their profits from a home sale if they purchased a new home within two years that cost as much as or more than their old home. Another law allowed taxpayers who were at least 55 years old to exclude one time, and one time only, up to $125,000 in profit when they sold their home. You can forget about these old laws. They are no longer in effect. If you meet the requirements discussed below, you may take advantage of the $250,000/$500,000 exclusion even if you previously used one or more of the old laws to avoid taxes on a home sale.

The Two-Year Ownership and Use Rule

Here's the most important thing you need to know: To qualify for the $250,000/$500,000 home sale exclusion, you must own and occupy the home as your principal residence for *at least two years before you sell it*. Your home can be a house, apartment, condominium, stock cooperative, or mobile home fixed to land.

> **EXAMPLE:** Jack and Jill are joint filers who purchased their first house and moved in on July 1, 2005. If they sell the house on July 1, 2007, they will qualify for the $500,000 exclusion.

If you meet all the requirements for the exclusion, you can take the $250,000/$500,000 exclusion any number of times. But you may not use it more than *once every two years*.

> **EXAMPLE:** Sean buys a condo for $200,000 and uses it as his primary home for two full years—2003 and 2004. In 2005, he buys a house and uses the house as his primary home instead. In 2007, he sells the condo for $300,000. Because the condo was his primary house for two years, he qualifies for the $250,000 exclusion for single taxpayers and doesn't have to pay any income tax on his $100,000 profit from the sale. He then sells his house in 2008, earning a $50,000 profit. Because he took the exclusion for his condo in 2007, less than two years before he sold the house, he doesn't qualify for the exclusion even though he used the house as his primary home for more than two full years. Had he waited another year to sell the house, he would have qualified.

The two-year rule is really quite generous, since most people live in their home at least that long before they sell it. (On average, Americans move once every seven years.) By wisely using the exclusion, you can buy and sell many homes over the years and avoid any income taxes on your profits.

EXAMPLE: Nicole and Nick, a married couple who file jointly, purchased their first house for $200,000 in 1998. They sold it for $300,000 in 2001. They owed no tax on their $100,000 profit from the sale because they qualified for the $500,000 exclusion. They used the money to purchase a $400,000 house in 2001, which they sold for $600,000 in 2004. Again, they qualified for the $500,000 exclusion, so they owed no income tax on their $200,000 profit. They used the money to purchase an $800,000 house in 2004 that they sold for $1 million in 2006. They owed no tax on their $250,000 profit because they qualified for the $500,000 exclusion. They then purchased a $1 million house in 2006 that they plan to sell in 2008 for $1.5 million. Their $500,000 profit will still be tax free because they can use the $500,000 exclusion. From 1998 to 2008, Nicole and Nick will earn a total profit of $1 million on the sales of their four homes. But, because they use the exclusion for each sale, they won't have to pay any taxes on these profits.

One aspect of the exclusion that can be confusing is that ownership and use of the home don't need to occur at the same time. As long as you have at least two years of ownership and two years of use during the five years before you sell the home, the ownership and use can occur at different times. The rule is most important for renters who purchase their rental apartments or rental homes. The time that a purchaser lives in the home as a renter counts as use of the home for purposes of the exclusion, even though the renter didn't own the home at the time.

EXAMPLE: Jackie rented the condo she lived in for five years—2001 through 2005. In 2006, she purchases the unit from her landlord and continues to live in it. In 2007, she gets a new job out of state and rents out the condo. In 2008, she sells it. Does Jackie qualify for the $250,000 exclusion? Yes. During the five years before the 2008 sale, she has two full years of ownership—2006 and 2007; and more than two years of use—2004 through 2006. Although she lived in the condo as a renter during 2004 and 2005, it still counts as use for purposes of the exclusion.

If You Are Not Living in the Home

To qualify for the home sale exclusion, you don't have to be living in the house at the time you sell it. Your two years of ownership and use may occur anytime during the five years before the date of the sale. This means, for example, that you can move out of the house for up to three years and still qualify for the exclusion.

This rule has a very practical application: It means you may rent out your home for *up to three years* prior to the sale and still qualify for the exclusion. Be sure to keep track of this time period and sell the house before it runs out.

> **EXAMPLE:** Connie purchases a one-bedroom condo on February 1, 2004 and lives in it for two full years. She then moves to another state to take a new job. Rather than sell the condo, she elects to rent it out. If she sells the condo by February 1, 2009, she'll qualify for the $250,000 home sale exclusion because she owned and used the condo as her principal home for two years during the five-year period before the sale. If she waits even one more day to sell, she will get no exclusion at all.

The Home Must Be Your Principal Residence

To qualify for the exclusion, you must have used the home you sell as your principal residence for at least two of the five years prior to the sale. Your principal residence is the place where you (and your spouse, if you're filing jointly and claiming the $500,000 exclusion for couples) live.

You don't have to spend every minute in your home for it to be your principal residence. Short absences are permitted—for example, you can take a two-month vacation away from home and count that time as use. However, long absences are not permitted. For example, a professor who is away from home for a whole year while on sabbatical cannot count that year as use for purposes of the exclusion.

You can only have one principal residence at a time. If you live in more than one place—for example, you have two homes—the property you use the majority of the time during the year will ordinarily be your principal residence for that year.

EXAMPLE: Alvin owns two condos, one in New York and one in Florida. From 2001 through 2006, he lives in the New York condo for seven months and the Florida condo for five months of each year. The New York condo is Alvin's principal residence. Alvin would be eligible for the $250,000 exclusion if he sold the New York condo, but not the Florida condo.

If you have a second home or vacation home that has substantially appreciated in value since you bought it, you'll be able to use the exclusion when you sell it if you use that home as your principal home for at least two years before the sale.

Partial Exclusions for Partial Compliance

What if you have to sell your home even though you don't comply with all the requirements for the exclusion? This would occur, for example, if you sell before you have lived in the home for two years, or if you have already used the exclusion for another home less than two years prior to this sale. If this happens, you may still qualify for a partial exclusion if you have a good excuse for selling the property. Good excuses include:

- a change in your place of employment
- health problems that require you to move, or
- circumstances you didn't foresee when you bought the home that force you to sell it—for example, a death in the family, losing your job and qualifying for unemployment, not being able to afford the house anymore because of a change in employment or marital status, a natural disaster that destroys your house, or you or your spouse have twins or other multiple birth.

A change in the place of employment for you, your spouse, any co-owner of the property, or any other person who uses your home as his or her principal residence is always a valid excuse if the location of the new job is at least 50 miles away from your old home. This is the same distance rule that applies for the moving expense deduction. Moves of fewer than 50 miles could also qualify depending on the circumstances.

Health problems are a valid excuse if a doctor recommends that you move for health reasons—for example, you have asthma and your doctor tells you that living in Arizona would be better for you than

Maine. The health problems can belong to you, your spouse, any co-owner of the property, any other person who uses your home as his or her principal residence, or a close family member of any person in the prior categories—for example, a child or parent. Thus, for example, you can move if you need to be closer to an ill parent. If you want to use the health exception, be sure to get a letter from your doctor stating that the move is for health reasons and what they are. Keep the letter with your tax files.

If you have a valid excuse for not complying with all the requirements for the exclusion, you'll get a partial exclusion—not the whole $250,000/$500,000. The amount is ordinarily limited to the percentage of the two years that you fulfilled the requirements. For example, if you own and occupy a home for one year (50% of two years) and have not excluded gain on another home in that time, you may exclude 50% of the regular maximum amount—up to $125,000 of gain for a single taxpayer and $250,000 for married couples who meet the requirements for the married couples' $500,000 exclusion discussed below. The percentage may be figured by using days or months.

$500,000 Exclusion for Married Couples

There are certain additional requirements you must meet to qualify for the $500,000 exclusion. Namely, you must be able to show that *all* of the following are true:

- you are married and file a joint return for the year
- *either* you or your spouse meets the ownership test
- *both* you and your spouse meet the use test, and
- during the two-year period ending on the date of the sale, neither you nor your spouse excluded gain from the sale of another home.

If either spouse does not satisfy all these requirements, the exclusion is figured separately for each spouse as if he or she was not married. This means they can each qualify for up to a $250,000 exclusion. For this purpose, each spouse is treated as owning the property during the period that either spouse owned the property.

EXAMPLE 1: Emily sells her home in June 2006. She marries Jamie later in the year. She meets the ownership and use tests, but Jamie does not. Emily can exclude up to $250,000 of gain on a separate or joint return for 2006.

EXAMPLE 2: The facts are the same as above, except that Jamie also sells a home in 2006. He meets the ownership and use tests on his home. Emily and Jamie can each exclude up to $250,000 of gain.

For joint owners who are not married, up to $250,000 of gain is tax free for each qualifying owner.

EXAMPLE: Melinda and Mel were married for 20 years and owned a house together. Their divorce became final in 2005. They both moved out of the house and rented it out in December of that year. In 2006, they sold their house for a $400,000 profit and split the proceeds. They are each entitled to a $250,000 exclusion on their separate tax returns, so neither need pay tax on their $200,000 individual gain.

Calculating Your Gain

If you qualify for the $250,000 or $500,000 exclusion and your profit from the sale of your home is less than that amount, you're sitting pretty. You'll owe no income tax on the sale. Indeed, *you don't even have to report the sale on your income tax return.*

On the other hand, if the profit you earn from the sale of your home exceeds the applicable exclusion amount, you'll have to list the excess profit as taxable income on your tax return and pay income tax on it. If you owned the home for at least 12 months, you'll be taxed on your gain at the long-term capital gains rate, which is currently 15% for most people. That rate could change after 2008 (the rate is 5% for taxpayers in the two lowest tax brackets).

It is very important to understand that it is not the total amount of money you receive for the sale of your home, but the *amount of gain* on the sale over and above your cost (basis) that determines whether your profit exceeds the $250,000 or $500,000 exclusion amount.

To know how much gain you earn from selling your home, you must first know the property's tax basis. The tax basis of property is the value (dollar figure) from which the IRS determines gain or loss on a sale. When you purchase property, its basis is generally its cost. In fact, basis is often referred to as cost basis.

When you figure your tax basis, use the full purchase price you paid for the home as your starting point. You may also add certain fees and other expenses you paid when you bought the property, such as attorney fees, escrow fees, title insurance fees, recording fees, transfer taxes, and other expenses of the sale. Most of these fees should be listed on the closing statement you receive after escrow closes. However, some may not be listed there, so be sure to check your records to see if you've made any other payments that should be added to your property's basis.

In addition, if you make major (capital) improvements to your home, you may add those costs to your property's basis. For example, if you spend $10,000 to install a new deck for your home, you may add $10,000 to your home's basis. This will help reduce the amount of gain you receive from the sale. Be sure to keep copies of bills, checks, receipts, and other documentation showing the work that was done on your home and how much you paid for it.

> **EXAMPLE:** Jim and Jennifer purchased their home in 1980 for $100,000, including fees and other expenses. During their years of ownership, they spent $50,000 adding on a new bedroom and garage. Their tax basis is $150,000. They sold the house in 2006 for $800,000. Their gain on the sale is $650,000 (the purchase price minus their basis). They qualify for the $500,000 exclusion, so they owe income tax on $150,000 of the sale proceeds.

If the equity in your home is approaching the applicable exclusion amount ($250,000 or $500,000), you can sell it and take advantage of the exclusion so you won't owe any income tax on your profit. You can then buy a new home with all or part of the money and use the exclusion again when you sell that home (provided you live in it for at least two years). This is one way to create tax-free income for yourself.

If You Don't Qualify for the Exclusion

If you don't qualify for the home sale exclusion at all, you'll have to pay income tax on all the gain you earn from the sale of your home. If you owned the home for at least one year, you'll at least qualify for the long-term capital gains rate, which is currently 15% for most taxpayers. If you owned the property for less than one year, you'll have to pay tax at the short-term capital gains rate which is the same as for ordinary income— up to a 35% tax, depending on your income tax bracket. Obviously, you should wait at least one year to sell if you can.

If you'll have a substantial taxable gain if you sell your home, you may want to consider doing something other than selling the property. One possibility would be to convert the home into a rental property and exchange it for another rental property. Recent changes in the law make this a more attractive option than ever. Now, when you exchange a home that you've converted into a rental property, you can combine the exclusion with the exchange. You use the exclusion to pocket $250,000 or $500,000 in cash and then use the exchange rules to defer payment of tax on any remaining capital gain (or depreciation recapture where you've had a home office).

> **EXAMPLE:** Phil owns a condo in Manhattan worth $1 million, and has $500,000 in equity. He's lived in the unit for five years and, as a single taxpayer, qualifies for the $250,000 exclusion. If he sold the condo now he'd have to pay capital gains tax on his $250,000 profit above the exclusion amount. Instead, he moves out of the unit and rents it to a tenant. After one year, he has converted it from his principal home to a rental property. He then exchanges it for another condo worth $750,000 plus $250,000 in cash. He uses his $250,000 exclusion to pay no tax on the cash payment. The $250,000 profit he obtained by exchanging his old condo for the new condo is tax deferred—he need pay no tax on it until he sells the new condo. He must rent out the new condo for at least 12 to 18 months to qualify for exchange treatment. After this, he can move into the unit. He'll qualify to use the $250,000 exclusion again after he has owned the unit for five years.

See Chapter 4 for a detailed discussion of tax-free real property exchanges.

Another approach is to sell the home in an installment sale. In such a sale the buyer pays you the purchase price over several years instead of all at once. You still need to pay tax on the profit you obtain over your applicable exclusion, but need only pay a little at a time each year as you receive your installment payments. (See Chapter 4 for more on installment sales.)

Alternatively, you may choose not to sell the home at all. You could continue to live in it or rent it out. When you die, your home's value for tax purposes is "stepped up" to its fair market value. As a result, no tax would ever be paid, by you or your heirs, on the appreciation your home earned while you were alive.

> **EXAMPLE:** Ernie and Edna purchased their home in 1950 for $50,000. In 2007, it is worth $1 million. If they sold the house in 2007, they would have a $950,000 gain, far in excess of their $500,000 home sale exclusion. Instead, they decide continue to live in it. Assume they both die in 2010, leaving the home to their daughter Edwina. At their death, the home is worth $1.3 million—this becomes its value in Edwina's hands for tax purposes. If Edwina later sells the home, her taxable gain will only be the amount she earns in excess of the home's $1.3 million tax basis.

If You Have a Home Office

Even if you qualify for the home sale exclusion, you'll owe some tax if you had an office in your home and took the home office deduction in prior years. Part of the home office deduction is an amount allocated for depreciation of the portion of your home used as your office. You'll have to pay a 25% income tax on all the depreciation deductions you took after May 6, 1997 on the office.

> **EXAMPLE:** Steve, a writer, used 10% of his home as a home office during 2000 through 2007. During that time he took $10,000 in depreciation deductions as part of his home office deduction. He sells his home in 2007 for a $200,000 profit. He qualifies for the $250,000 exclusion, so he doesn't have to pay any income tax on his profit. But he must pay a 25% tax on his home office depreciation deductions—$2,500.

Things don't work out nearly as well if you use a separate building as an office (instead of having an office inside your home). In this event, the separate building is treated as a commercial property separate from your home. You must allocate the gain on the sale of your property between your home and this separate property, and the exclusion may only be used for the gain earned from the sale of your home.

> **EXAMPLE:** Stephanie, a writer, owns a three-bedroom house and uses a separate one-bedroom guest house on her property as her office. She sells the entire property for a $300,000 gain. She figures that the guest house accounts for 20% of the total sale proceeds, so she must allocate her gain $240,000 for the principal house and $60,000 for the guest house. She may use the home sale exclusion for the gain she earned from her principal house, but not the separate guest house. Thus, she must pay income tax on the $60,000 gain she earned from the guest house.

The Minor Advantage: Tax-Free Income for Children

It doesn't seem right, but children have to pay taxes on their income, just like everybody else. Fortunately, a certain amount of income earned by a child is tax free—how much depends on the child's age.

Giving Investments to Your Children

Parents, grandparents, and other relatives love to give children things like stocks, bonds, mutual funds, and savings accounts. Such property generates investment income—interest, dividends, and profits from asset sales. Investment income is also called "unearned income" because it is obtained without working at a job or business.

No Income Tax on Gifts

The person who receives a gift or inheritance never has to pay any income tax or gift tax on its value. However, the person or estate that makes the gift might have to pay a gift tax. This applies only to the well-off: A person must give away more than $1 million in money or property while they're alive for their estate to be subject to any gift taxes. Moreover, there are ways to give away even more than $1 million and still incur no gift taxes. For more information on gifts, see *Plan Your Estate*, by Denis Clifford and Cora Jordan (Nolo).

The person who owns investment property is the one who must pay tax on the income—even if it was received as a gift. This means that your children, no matter how young, can be taxpayers in their own right if you give them ownership of an investment like stocks or bonds. How a child's investment income is taxed depends on his or her age—the rules differ for children under 18 years of age and those over 18 (at the end of the tax year).

Giving your under 18-year-old children income-producing investments can result in a modest amount of tax-free income because they do not have to pay any tax on the first $850 of their unearned income for the year. The income is tax free because the minimum standard deduction for children and other dependents is $850. The income does not need to be reported to the IRS.

However, if a child under 18 years old earns more than $850 in investment income during the year, he or she will become subject to the "kiddie tax." The kiddie tax requires that investment income from $851 to $1,700 be taxed at the child's tax rate—usually the lowest income tax rate which is currently 10%. Any investment income over $1,700 is taxed at the parent's highest income tax rate, which can be as high as 35%.

There is no kiddie tax for children 18 and over. These children are taxed like adults—all their income is taxed at their own income tax rates, not their parents' rates. If a child doesn't work, he or she will have the $850 standard deduction (just like children under 18) and won't have to pay any tax on that amount of income. Any income over $850 will be taxed at his or her own tax rates, which are usually lower than those of the parents.

(See Chapter 7 for a detailed discussion of transferring property to children.)

> ⚠ **Do you really want to give your children investment property?**
> Think twice about giving your children investment property like stocks and bonds because there can be significant drawbacks down the line. First of all, you must give up ownership of the property. Such gifts are most often made through custodial accounts—either a Uniform Gift to Minors Act (UGMA) or Uniform Transfers to Minors Act (UTMA) account. You can control the funds as custodian of the account until the child reaches age 18 or 21 years of age, depending on your state. Then the child takes over control of the account and can do anything he or she wants with it.

Also, the more money a child has in his or her name, the less financial aid will be available. (See "Know Financial Aid Rules," below.)

Children Who Work

Children who work receive earned income—salaries, wages, tips, and other amounts as pay for work actually done. All earned income is subject to taxation at the child's income tax rates, no matter what his or her age. There is no kiddie tax for a child's earned income.

A child who works can have a much larger standard deduction than a child who just has investment income. A larger standard deduction means a greater opportunity for tax-free income because tax is owed only on income above the standard deduction amount. A working child gets a standard deduction that is the *larger* of:

- $850, or
- the amount of the child's earned income for the year plus $250 (but this amount can't be more than the standard deduction for single adults).

EXAMPLE: Phillipa, a 17-year-old, earned $2,000 from babysitting during the year and had $500 in interest income. Her standard deduction is limited to the greater of $850, or her earned income ($2,000) plus $250. Since $2,250 is larger than $850, her standard deduction is $2,250. Phillipa need only pay tax on $250 of her income ($2,500 total income minus $2,250 standard deduction = $250).

A child can have a standard deduction of as much as $5,150 in 2006 (the deduction for adult single taxpayers), provided that the child had at least $4,900 in earned income from a job.

> **EXAMPLE:** Burt, a 16-year-old boy, earned $5,000 from a summer job during 2006 and had $1,000 in investment income from some stocks his grandparents gave him. His standard deduction is $5,150 (the standard deduction for single adults because his earned income plus $250 exceeds this amount). He need pay income tax on only $850 of his $6,000 total income.

A child can get even more tax-free income by opening an IRA and deducting the contribution to the account. If the maximum $4,000 annual contribution is made, up to $9,150 could be earned tax free ($5,150 standard deduction + $4,000 IRA contribution = $9,150). If the child is over 14, this may be both earned and unearned income. However, as described above, children under 18 must pay a kiddie tax on all unearned income over $850 (but not on earned income).

If you have a business, whether full- or part-time, a great way to give your child earned income is to hire him or her to work as your employee. He or she can earn up to the standard deduction ($5,150 in 2006) free of income tax. Moreover, you need not pay Social Security or Medicare taxes for your child under the age of 18 who works in your unincorporated business or your partnership, if it's owned solely by you and your spouse. But such taxes must be paid if your business is incorporated. (See Chapter 8.)

Any amount earned by a child over the standard deduction is taxed at the child's income tax rates, but these will usually be lower than the parents'. This makes hiring children a good way to shift income to lower-taxed taxpayers. This is discussed more fully in Chapter 7.

Renting Your Home at No Tax Cost

A little-known tax rule allows homeowners to rent out their vacation homes or principal homes for a limited time and pay no tax on the rental income they receive. That's right—tax-free income! This is true, no matter how much you earn.

To qualify for this tax-free treatment, during the year you must:
- rent out your home for *fewer than 15 days*, and
- personally use the home for *15 days or more*. (IRC Sec. 280A(g).)

The home can be a vacation home, second home, or your principal home. This rule can provide you with a real windfall if you own a home in a desirable area where people are looking for short-term rentals.

> **EXAMPLE 1:** Sam lives full-time in a condo on the beach in Hawaii. He leaves for a trip to Europe and rents out his condo for two weeks to some vacationers, earning $2,000. He doesn't have to pay income tax on this rental income.

> **EXAMPLE 2:** Claudia rents her Florida beachfront condominium for 14 days during the summer for $3,000. She lives in the condo herself for two months during the year. She doesn't owe any income tax on the rental income.

The home is treated as a personal residence for tax purposes, so you may not deduct any operating expenses you incurred while it was rented out, or depreciation. You don't file Schedule E—the tax form landlords file to report their income and expenses—because your home is not a rental property. However, you may continue to deduct your home mortgage interest and real estate taxes.

To obtain this tax-free treatment, you must make sure your personal use and rental use fall within the time limits. If you rent the home for more than 14 days or live in it fewer than 15 days, you'll have to pay taxes on your rental income. How much you pay and what deductions you get depends on how much you rent the home out and how much you live in it during the year. Complex IRS rules apply. To learn more about them, refer to *Every Landlord's Tax Deduction Guide*, by Stephen Fishman (Nolo).

Bonds and Other Tax-Free Investment Income

Ordinarily, you have to pay tax on the income you earn on your investments each year. For example, if you have a savings account and earn $1,000 in interest, you must add it to your taxable income and pay tax on it. However, some types of investments are wholly or partly tax free—that is, you don't pay tax on the interest or other income you receive from the investment. Bonds issued by state and local governments are the longtime mainstay of tax-free investing (U.S. government bonds and notes have some tax-free attributes as well). However, muni bonds aren't the only tax-free game in town. Specialized accounts intended to be used to save money for a child's college education can also be a major source of tax-free investment income. Roth IRAs and Roth 401(k)s are the latest tax-free investment vehicles.

Bonds

Issuing bonds is one of the main ways that corporations and governments raise money. When you purchase a bond, you are essentially loaning money to the bond issuer for a period of time. The issuer promises to make regular interest payments at a preestablished interest rate (called the coupon rate) and to repay the face amount of the bond when it comes due. The interest you are paid by a bond issuer is ordinarily taxable income, but some types of bonds are wholly or partly tax free.

Municipal bonds. As the name indicates, municipal bonds are used by state, city, or local governments, and by other government entities such as water and sewer districts or turnpike authorities. The money raised from these bonds may be used to fund regular government activities, or to pay for specific projects, such as building roads, sewer systems, schools, or hospitals.

Interest earned from municipal bonds is ordinarily exempt from federal tax. The federal government does this to help state and local governments raise money more cheaply. Municipal bonds are also exempt from state tax if the bond purchaser lives in the state that issued the bond.

> **EXAMPLE:** Art, an Illinois resident, purchases a municipal bond issued in Michigan. He must pay Illinois state income tax on the interest he earns on this out-of-state bond.

Muni bonds are exempt from local taxes as well if the purchaser lives in the city, county, or other locality that issued the bond.

The moral: Buy muni bonds issued in your home state, or your locality.

If you sell a municipal bond at a profit (called a capital gain), you must pay federal and state tax on the amount. However, most of the money earned from bonds comes from the interest they pay, not capital gains.

Because municipal bonds are tax free, they pay lower interest than bonds whose interest is taxable. But, depending on your top tax rate, municipal bonds can provide a greater after-tax return than taxable bonds. For example, if you're in the 28% tax bracket, a muni bond earning 4% interest would end up paying you as much as a taxable bond earning 5.56% after you pay the taxes on the interest. The higher your tax bracket, the better will be your total return (yield) from a tax-free municipal bond. This makes muni bonds most attractive for wealthy people who pay high taxes.

For more information, see the website www.investinginbonds.com. It contains a calculator you can use to compare the returns from municipal bonds with those from taxable bonds.

U.S. Government bonds, notes, and bills. The federal government in Washington, D.C. needs to borrow money—quite a bit of money. To accomplish this, it issues its own bonds. These are long-term Treasury bonds, and shorter-term Treasury bills and notes. Interest income from Treasury bills, notes, and bonds is subject to federal income tax, but is exempt from all state and local income taxes. Both notes and bonds generally pay interest every six months and you usually report this interest for the year paid. For more information, see the U.S. Treasury web page at www.publicdebt.treas.gov.

Roth IRAs and Roth 401(k)s

Roth IRAs and Roth 401(k)s are retirement accounts in which you can place various types of investments—stocks, bonds, mutual funds, and money market funds. They are like other retirement accounts, with one big difference—all the profit you earn on your investment while it is in the account is tax free. Unlike most other retirement accounts, you get no tax deduction when you deposit money in a Roth IRA or 401(k) and in return, you pay no taxes when you withdraw the money. However, whether Roth accounts are better than traditional retirement accounts is not always clear. See Chapter 4 for more information on these retirement accounts.

⚠ **Tax-free investments and regular retirement accounts don't mix.** Do not place tax-free investments like municipal bonds in tax-deferred retirement accounts such as 401(k) plans and traditional IRAs. You must pay taxes at ordinary income rates when you withdraw money from the account after you retire. Even if all or part of that money comes from muni bonds or other tax-free investments, you would have to pay tax on it. So you'll end up paying income tax on your tax-free investments. Keep tax-free investments like municipal bonds in a taxable account, such as a brokerage account. (See Chapter 4.)

Tax-Free Income From Education Accounts

Paying for college has grown incredibly expensive—far outstripping the rate of inflation. According to the College Board, a student entering college in the year 2020 will pay more than $85,000 at a public university for a four-year education, and a whopping $225,000 at a private college.

That's a lot of money. The government has created two types of special tax-free accounts that parents can use to help accomplish the Herculean financial task of getting a kid through college: Coverdell ESAs and 529 savings plans. Contributions to these accounts are not tax free, but the money in the accounts grows tax free and withdrawals used for educational purposes are tax free. Thus, so long as the money is used for educational purposes, the income earned on it is tax free.

Coverdell ESAs and 529 savings plans each have their pros and cons. However, they are not an either-or proposition. You can contribute to both a 529 plan and an ESA for the same beneficiary in the same year. In addition, the Hope tax credit or Lifetime Learning credit can be claimed in the same year the beneficiary takes a tax-free distribution from a Coverdell ESA or 529 plan, as long as the same expenses are not used for both benefits. (See Chapter 7 for a discussion of education tax credits.)

Coverdell ESAs and 529 savings plans are not the only way to save for a child's college education. Other options include savings bonds, prepaid tuition plans, and custodial accounts.

The following websites contain a mountain of information on Coverdell ESAs and 529 plans:

- www.collegesavingsfoundation.org
- www.nasd.com, and
- www.savingforcollege.com.

Also, refer to IRS Publication 970, *Tax Benefits for Education*.

Know Financial Aid Rules

If you want your child to qualify for financial aid to help pay college expenses, pay careful attention to how you invest his or her college money.

Colleges and universities expect students to spend at least 35% of all assets in their name on their college expenses. The more money in a child's name—for example, in a custodial account—the less financial aid he or she will qualify for to attend college. If a child's savings are substantial, he or she may not qualify for financial aid at all.

It's better to keep as much money as possible in the parents' names because only 5.6% of parents' assets are factored into determining how much the family is expected to contribute for their child's education. Assets in the parents' names include Coverdell ESA and 529 savings plans they establish for their children.

Money parents hold in retirement accounts is not considered at all in determining a child's eligibility for financial aid. So you should first fully fund your IRA before putting any money in an education account or giving gifts to your children. You can withdraw money from an IRA free of penalty each year to pay for a child's college education. For more information, see *IRAs, 401(k)s, & Other Retirement Plans*, by Twila Slesnick and John C. Suttle (Nolo).

For more information on college financial aid, see the Department of Education's website at http://studentaid.ed.gov.

Coverdell ESA: The Education IRA

Coverdell ESAs (short for Education Savings Accounts) are named after a late U.S. senator who helped create the program. These accounts used to be called Education IRAs. A Coverdell ESA is much like a Roth IRA except that it is used only for education expenses. Here's how it works.

- You open an account with a bank, brokerage, or mutual fund company that offers Coverdell ESAs (not all do, so you may have to shop around). The account is a trustee or custodial account like an IRA, with a person below age 18 named as beneficiary—this can be your child, grandchild, or anyone else. You decide how the money in the account should be invested. As with IRAs, there is a wide array of investment choices.

- Up to $2,000 per year can be deposited, in cash, into a Coverdell ESA for the beneficiary, until he or she reaches age 18. There can be many Coverdell ESAs for the same child, but the total of all their contributions can't exceed $2,000 each year. You can have an ESA for each of your children and each can receive $2,000 in contributions every year.

- Anyone can make contributions if they meet the income test: Contributions may only be made by people whose adjusted gross income for the year is less than $110,000 ($220,000 for individuals filing joint returns). If your income is between $95,000 and $110,000 (between $190,000 and $220,000 if filing a joint return), the $2,000 limit for each designated beneficiary is gradually reduced to zero. You have until April 15 to make contributions for the prior year.

- Contributions are *not* tax deductible, but the funds in the account grow tax free.

- The money in the account may be withdrawn at any time and is tax free to the child and parents as long as it is used for "qualified education expenses." These include tuition, fees, books, supplies, and equipment to attend an accredited college. There is no minimum enrollment requirement to withdraw money tax free for these purposes—taking a single course at a college or university would do. Room and board may also be paid from an ESA, but in this event, the student must attend college at least half-time. Qualified education expenses also include expenses to attend elementary or secondary school—for example, a private high school or parochial school. This is a unique feature of the Coverdell ESA.

- If the money taken from a Coverdell ESA is used for noneducational purposes, the account earnings are taxed to the beneficiary at ordinary income rates, plus a 10% penalty is imposed.
- When the beneficiary reaches age 18, he or she takes over control of the account.
- The money in a Coverdell ESA must be spent by the time the beneficiary reaches age 30. There are three options if any funds are left in the account when the beneficiary reaches 30: (1) The money can be paid out to the beneficiary, in which event the account earnings are taxable; (2) the beneficiary can name a new member of his or her family under age 30 as beneficiary of the account; or (3) the account can be rolled over (transferred tax free) into a Coverdell ESA for another member of the family under age 30.

EXAMPLE: Irving and Ida establish a Coverdell ESA at a brokerage firm for their daughter Irene when she is 12 years old. They contribute $2,000 into the account every year. They get no tax deduction for their contributions, but the money in the account grows tax free. When Irene reaches 18, she takes control of the account, which is now worth $18,000. She withdraws the money to pay for her tuition and room and board at Dartyard University. Neither she nor her parents have to pay taxes on these withdrawals.

Some Coverdell ESA benefits are scheduled to expire in 2011 unless Congress acts to extend them. If Congress doesn't act:

- elementary and secondary school expenses will no longer qualify for tax-free ESA withdrawals
- the annual ESA contribution limit will be reduced to $500 per year, and
- ESA withdrawals will not be tax free in any year in which a Hope tax credit or Lifetime Learning credit is claimed for the beneficiary.

Most tax experts believe that Congress will act to avoid these changes in ESA benefits, but there is no guarantee of this. Even if some ESA withdrawals are taxed after 2010, however, the tax would be paid at the child-beneficiary's tax rate, which is usually low.

What If You Exceed the Coverdell ESA Income Limits?

If you exceed the income limits, you are not allowed to contribute to a Coverdell ESA. There is an easy way around this limitation, however. Have the child's grandparents or other relatives contribute to the ESA in their own names and repay them. This is perfectly legal and will avoid the income limits if the grandparents or other relatives' incomes are below the income ceiling.

529 Savings Plan

529 savings plans are named after Section 529 of the tax code—the provision that establishes them. They are also called Qualified Tuition Programs or QTPs for short. 529 savings plans are more complicated then Coverdell ESAs, but you can contribute much more money to them. They have become very popular with parents in recent years, but you should do careful research before you invest in one.

529 savings plans are very different from Coverdell ESAs. First of all, unlike other tax-advantaged accounts, 529 plans must be sponsored by state governments or state agencies. Every state has some type of 529 plan; some have several. However, the states do not actually run the plans. Instead, they enter into agreements with investment companies to operate them—these firms manage the investments in the plan. You must pay annual management fees to the investment company—part of which goes to the state—which makes 529 plans a big moneymaker for state governments. Well-known investment firms such as Fidelity Investments, Vanguard Group, and TIAA-CREF all operate 529 plans for various states.

You may open a 529 account in any state. However, there can be tax advantages to having a plan sponsored by the state where you live. You can find a directory of, and links to, all the state 529 plans at www. collegesavings.org.

Here's how 529 savings plans work:
- You open a 529 account with the investment company that operates the plan you want to invest in. Anyone can open a 529 account, in any state. Unlike Coverdell ESAs, there are no income restrictions on the individual contributors.

- A 529 account is a trust account—you are the owner of the account and the child (or other person) for whom it is established is the beneficiary. Unlike Coverdell ESAs or custodial accounts, however, the beneficiary does not gain control of the money when he or she becomes an adult (usually 18 or 21 years old). The account owner always controls the money. In addition, you can change the beneficiary to another member of your family.

- There are no annual limits on how much you can contribute to a 529 plan (although there are overall contribution limits). Annually, you can contribute far more than to a Coverdell ESA. However, contributions to a 529 account are considered to be a gift to the beneficiary for gift tax purposes. You'll avoid gift taxes if you contribute no more than the annual gift tax exclusion for the year. This means that in 2006 you can contribute $12,000 ($24,000 if both you and your spouse make contributions). In addition, you can make a one-time contribution equal to five years' worth of gift-tax exclusions—$60,000 at 2006 gift tax exclusion rates, $120,000 if both spouses make gifts.

- There is an overall limit on how much money can be in a 529 account for the same beneficiary. The limits vary from state to state, ranging from $200,000 to over $300,000. In most states, this limit includes all the income the money in the account earns.

- The money you contribute is invested by the investment company on your behalf. It manages the money in the account, not you. This differs from Coverdell ESAs where you have total control over the investments. Each 529 plan has a predetermined menu of investment choices, typically including stock mutual funds, bond mutual funds, and money market funds, as well as age-based portfolios that automatically shift toward more conservative investments as the beneficiary gets closer to college age. Investments in college savings plans that invest in mutual funds are not guaranteed by state governments and are not federally insured.

- Contributions to a 529 account are not deductible from your federal taxes. However, over half the states allow a state income tax deduction if the account owner is a state resident. If you live in a high tax state like California or New York, this can save you some money. You don't get this state tax deduction if you open a 529 plan in a state where you don't live.

- The money in 529 account grows tax free. Withdrawals are tax free as well if they are used for qualified educational expenses—tuition, fees, books, supplies, and equipment required for enrollment at an accredited college, university, or vocational school. Room and board may also be paid for if the student attends school at least half-time. However, unlike a Coverdell ESA, 529 plan money may not be used to pay for elementary or secondary school expenses—for example, you can't use it to send your child to a private high school or parochial school.
- In most states, there is no age limit or time limit for when the money in a 529 plan must be used. In contrast, money in a Coverdell ESA must be used by the time the beneficiary is 30.
- If you withdraw money from a 529 plan and do not use it on an eligible college expense, you generally will be subject to income tax and an additional 10% federal tax penalty on the earnings from the account.

EXAMPLE: Tony and Carmella are a married couple who live in New Jersey. They open a 529 account for their daughter, Meadow, with a 529 plan sponsored by their home state. Over ten years they deposit $100,000 in the plan. Their contributions are not deductible from their federal income taxes. However, they are able to deduct them from their New Jersey state taxes. By the time Meadow is 18, the account has grown to $150,000. Meadow enters Columbia University and her parents withdraw $20,000 to pay her tuition and room and board. The $20,000 withdrawal is tax free. The parents also withdraw $2,000 that Meadow uses for personal spending money. This withdrawal is not tax free. It is income for Meadow on which she must pay regular income tax, plus a 10% penalty.

One problem people have found with 529 plans is that the management fees are often extremely high, which can really eat away at earnings. These fees vary from state to state. You should carefully investigate the fees before opening any 529 account. Most people open 529 accounts through brokers, but the fees will be lower if you buy directly from the investment company that manages the plan you want. In some states, only state residents can do this. In addition, 529 plans often have a very narrow range of investment choices—some offer more choices than others. The only way you can change your investments is to change plans. You can roll over (transfer tax free) the money from your 529 plan to another state's plan once a year.

You can compare the fees and other attributes of all 529 plans at the website www.morningstar.com. (Click on the "Personal Finance" button on the home page, and then on "529 Data.")

Other Tax-Free Education Options

There are several other ways you can obtain tax-free treatment for income you use to pay for education expenses.

U.S. savings bonds. United States savings bonds may not be as sexy as 529 plans or Coverdell ESAs, but they can be a good way to save for college. The interest earned on U.S. savings bonds is not subject to state or local taxation, but it ordinarily is subject to federal income tax. If you do not include the interest in income in the years it is earned, you must include it in your income in the year in which you cash in the bonds.

Certain bonds issued under the Education Savings Bond Program—Series EE and Series I—may be cashed in without paying any federal or other tax on the interest if the money is used to pay tuition and fees to enroll yourself, your spouse, child, or other dependent at any accredited college, university, or vocational school. Only Series EE bonds purchased after 1989 qualify for tax-free treatment (Series I bonds are not subject to this rule). The bond must be issued either in your name (as the sole owner) or in the name of both you and your spouse (as co-owners). The bond owner must be at least 24 years old before the bond's issue date. The issue date is printed on the front of the savings bond.

In addition, there is an income limit to qualify for tax-free treatment of the interest. If you are married and filing jointly or a qualifying widow(er) you cannot take the deduction if your adjusted gross income is $124,700 or more in 2006. The amount of your interest exclusion is phased out if your AGI is between $94,700 and $124,700. If you're a single filer or married and filing your taxes separately, you cannot take the deduction if your AGI is $76,200 or more. Your interest exclusion is phased out if your AGI is between $63,100 and $78,100. These limits are adjusted each year for inflation.

Savings bonds can be purchased online or at most banks, credit unions, or savings institutions.

For more information see:

- www.savingsbonds.gov, or
- www.publicdebt.treas.gov/sav/sav.htm.

529 prepaid tuition plans. Another type of state-sponsored education savings plan involves prepaying a child's tuition at a specific college or university. The tuition is paid for at current rates, and is all that you must ever pay even if tuition costs more when the child attends the school. The prepaid tuition is not tax deductible, but plan earnings are tax free when used to pay tuition.

These plans are mostly used for state universities and colleges, but some private schools have them too. Participation is often limited to state residents or alumni of state colleges and universities.

One obvious problem with these plans is how to know which college or university you should prepay your tuition to. As a general rule, having a prepaid tuition account does not improve your child's chances of getting into a particular college. If he or she does not get into the school you've chosen, the plan will be useless. You might be able to transfer your money to another school; if not, you'll have to have it refunded to you or change the plan beneficiary to another family member. Some plans only refund the amount of your original contribution, without any interest. If your child decides not to go to college, you'll also either have to change beneficiaries or get a refund.

Another big drawback is that prepaying tuition severely limits a child's eligibility for financial aid. Prepaid tuition is treated the same as a scholarship for financial aid purposes.

For more information, refer to: www.collegesavings.org/faq/529prepaid.htm.

Custodial account. You can also open a custodial account for your child at a financial institution and use the money for college. But this has some serious drawbacks (see "Do you really want to give your children investment property?" above).

Tax-Free Scholarships and Fellowships

If your child is fortunate enough to win a scholarship (only one in 15 do), or a fellowship, the money is tax free if:

- the child is enrolled in a degree program at an accredited college or university, and
- the money is used to pay "qualified education expenses"—tuition and fees and course-related costs, such as books and supplies.

Scholarship or fellowship funds used to pay for other education expenses—for example, room and board—are taxable to the student. Also taxable is scholarship money a student earns by working at a college job ("work study" programs).

Health Savings Accounts: The Triple Tax Break

Health savings accounts (HSAs), which first became available in 2004, are a great way to avoid taxes on part of your income and pay for your and your family's health expenses. If you're not happy with the health coverage you currently have, or have no coverage, think about getting an HSA.

What Are Health Savings Accounts?

The HSA concept is very simple: Instead of relying on health insurance to pay small or routine medical expenses, you pay them yourself. To help you do this, you establish a health savings account with a health insurance company, bank, or other financial institution.

In case you or a family member gets really sick, you must also obtain a health insurance policy with a high deductible—at least $1,000 for individuals, and $2,000 for families. The money in your HSA can be used to pay this large deductible and any copayments you're required to make. The premiums for your high-deductible health insurance policy should be lower than those for traditional comprehensive coverage policies or HMO coverage.

What Are the Tax Benefits?

HSAs combine three great tax benefits. First, you can deduct HSA contributions made with your personal funds as a personal deduction on the first page of your IRS Form 1040. You deduct the amount from your gross income, just like a business deduction. This means you get the full deduction whether or not you itemize your personal deductions.

> **EXAMPLE:** Martin, an actuary, establishes an HSA for himself and his family with a $2,000 deductible. Every year, he contributes the maximum amount ($2,000) to his HSA account. Because he is in the 25% federal income tax bracket, this saves him $500 in federal income tax each year.

Second, you don't have to pay tax on the interest or other money you earn on the money in your account. If you don't tap into the money, it will keep accumulating free of taxes.

> **EXAMPLE:** Over five years Martin (from the above example) deposited $10,000 in his HSA account. In addition, the account earned $2,000 in interest. Martin doesn't have to pay tax on this interest.

Finally, if you or a family member needs health care, you can withdraw money from your HSA to pay your deductible or any other medical expenses. You pay no federal tax on HSA withdrawals used to pay qualified medical expenses. Qualified medical expenses are broadly defined to include many types of expenses ordinarily not covered by health insurance—for example, dental or optometric care. This is one of the great advantages of the HSA program over traditional health insurance

> **EXAMPLE:** Martin withdraws $1,000 from his HSA to pay for health expenses. He doesn't need to pay tax on the $1,000.

Note that Martin from the above example got to deduct the $1,000 he deposited in his HSA, he earned interest on it tax free, and he didn't have to pay any tax when he withdrew the money for medical expenses. No other account provides both front-end and back-end tax breaks. With IRAs, for example, you must pay tax either when you deposit or when you withdraw your money.

If you withdraw funds from your HSA to use for something other than qualified medical expenses, you must pay the regular income tax on the withdrawal plus a 10% penalty. For example, if you were in the 25% federal income tax bracket, you'd have to pay a 35% tax on your nonqualified withdrawals.

Once you reach the age of 65 or become disabled, you can withdraw your HSA funds for any reason without penalty. If you use the money for nonmedical expenses, you will have to pay regular income tax on the withdrawals. Withdrawals you use for health expenses remain tax free.

When you die, the money in your HSA account is transferred to the beneficiary you've named for the account. The transfer is tax free if the beneficiary is your surviving spouse. Other transfers are taxable.

If you enjoy good health while you have your HSA and don't have to make many withdrawals, you may end up with a substantial amount in your account that you can withdraw without penalty for any purpose once you turn 65. You can also withdraw it completely tax free to pay for health expenses. This feature can make your HSA an extremely lucrative tax shelter—a kind of super IRA.

Who Can Establish an HSA?

Anyone under 65 not covered by a health plan may establish an HSA. You may individually establish an HSA for yourself and your family and pay for your health insurance with personal funds.

Many employers are also providing HSAs for their employees. This is an attractive option for them because it usually costs less than providing employees with traditional health insurance. Any business, no matter how small, may participate in the HSA program. The employer purchases an HSA-qualified health plan for its employees, and they establish their own individual HSA accounts. The employer can pay all or part of its employees' insurance premiums and make contributions to their HSA accounts. Employees may also make their own contributions to their individual accounts. The combined annual contributions of the employer and employee may not exceed the limits listed below.

Another great thing about HSAs is that they are portable when an employee changes employers. Contributions and earnings belong to the account holder, not the employer. So an employee doesn't have to stay on a job just to keep health insurance.

HSAs are not for everybody. You could be better off with traditional comprehensive health insurance if you or a member of your family has substantial medical expenses. When you are in this situation, you'll likely end up spending all or most of your HSA contributions each year and earn little or no interest on your account (but you'll still get a deduction for your contributions). Of course, whether traditional health insurance is better than an HSA depends on its cost, including the deductibles and co-payments you must make.

In addition, depending on your medical history and where you live, the cost of an HSA-qualified health insurance plan may be too great to make the program cost-effective for you. However, if your choice is an HSA or nothing, get an HSA.

HSA Nuts and Bolts

To participate in the HSA program, you need to have two things:
- an HSA-qualified health insurance policy, and
- an HSA account.

HSA-qualified health insurance policy. First, you need to obtain a bare-bones, high-deductible health plan that meets the HSA criteria (is "HSA qualified"). You may obtain coverage from an HMO, PPO, or traditional plan. If the coverage is for only for you, your plan must have a $1,050 minimum annual deductible. If the coverage is for you and your family, your plan must have a $2,100 minimum deductible.

In the case of families, the deductible must apply to the entire family, not each family member separately. With such a per-family deductible, expenses incurred by each family member accumulate and are credited toward the one family deductible. For example, a family of four would meet the $2,100 deductible if $525 in medical expense were paid for each family member during the year (4 x $525 = $2,100). This is a unique feature of the HSA program.

You can have a deductible that is larger than the minimum amount if you wish. However, keep in mind that there are limits on how much money you can contribute to your HSA account each year. To be on the safe side, you don't want your deductible to exceed these limits or your account may not have enough money in it to cover the deductible if you become seriously ill—particularly if you develop a chronic illness that will require payments year after year. In 2006, the maximum annual contribution to an HSA was $2,700 for individuals and $5,450 for families. These amounts are adjusted each year for inflation.

You can obtain an HSA-qualifying health plan from health insurers that participate in the program. The following websites contain directories and contact information for insurers providing HSAs: www. hsainsider.com and www.hsafinder.com. The U.S. Treasury has an informative website on HSAs at www.treas.gov/offices/public-affairs/hsa. You can also contact your present health insurer.

HSA account. Once you have an HSA-qualified health insurance policy, you may open your HSA account. An HSA must be established with a trustee. The HSA trustee keeps track of your deposits and withdrawals, produces annual statements, and reports your HSA deposits to the IRS.

Health insurers can administer both the health plan and the HSA. However, you don't have to have your HSA administered by your insurer. You can establish an HSA with a bank, insurance company, mutual fund, or other financial institution offering HSA products.

Look at the plans offered by several companies to see which offers the best deal. Compare the fees charged to set up the account, as well as any other charges (some companies may charge an annual service fee, for example). Ask about special promotions and discounts. And find out how the account is invested.

Contribution Limits

When you have your HSA-qualified health plan and HSA account, you can start making contributions to your account. There is no minimum amount you are required to contribute each year; you may contribute nothing if you wish.

There are, however, maximum limits on how much you can contribute to an HSA each year.

- If you have individual coverage, the maximum annual contribution is the amount of your annual deductible or $2,700, whichever is less.
- If you have family coverage, the maximum annual contribution is the amount of your annual deductible or $5,450, whichever is less.

These maximum amounts are for 2006. They are adjusted for inflation each year.

Optional, tax-free catch-up contributions can be made to HSAs for individuals who are 55 to 65 years old. The amounts are shown in the following chart. This rule is intended to compensate for the fact that older folks won't have as many years to fund their accounts as younger taxpayers. If you're in this age group, it's wise to make these contributions if you can afford them, so your HSA account will have enough money to pay for future health expenses.

HSA Catch-Up Contributions	
Year	Maximum Annual Catch-Up Contribution
2005	$600
2006	$700
2007	$800
2008	$900
2009 and later	$1,000

HSA contributions may be invested just like IRA contributions, which means you can invest in almost anything: money market accounts, bank certificates of deposit, stocks, bonds, mutual funds, Treasury bills, and notes. However, you can't invest in collectibles such as art, antiques, postage stamps, or other personal property.

Every year, you may roll over up to $500 of unused funds in your HSA into an Individual Retirement Account (IRA) without paying tax on the money.

Employee Fringe Benefits: Don't Miss These Tax Savings

If you and/or your spouse is employed, the salary, bonus, and any other pay you receive from your employer is income on which you must pay taxes. These consist of federal income tax, your employee's share of Social Security and Medicare taxes (a 7.65% tax up to an annual ceiling), and, in most states, state income tax.

> **EXAMPLE:** Ralph, a married man, is employed by BigTech and earned $90,000 in salary and bonus in 2006. His top federal income tax rate is 28%, plus he must pay 7.65% in Social Security and Medicare taxes. To add insult to injury, he also owes a 6% state income tax. On his last dollar of salary income, he's paying over 40% in taxes.

Wouldn't it be great if employees could avoid paying taxes on at least part of their pay? Well guess what, they can.

There is one big exception to the rule that you have to pay tax on anything your employer gives you as payment for your services: You don't pay any taxes on the value of tax-qualified fringe benefits your employer provides. These fringe benefits can include such things as health insurance, medical expense reimbursements, dental insurance, education assistance, day care assistance, and transportation allowances.

When we say tax free, we mean it: Tax-qualified benefits are totally free of federal and state income tax, *and* Social Security and Medicare taxes. The savings extend not just to the employee, but to the employer as well because it doesn't have to pay the 7.65% employer's share of Social Security and Medicare taxes on the value of the benefits.

These tax savings can make employee fringe benefits so attractive that in many cases you'd be better off forgoing part of your salary to obtain them.

> **EXAMPLE:** Remember Ralph from the above example? He needs health insurance for himself and his family. He can pay for it out of his own pocket (which will cost $6,000 per year) or he can enroll in BigTech's group health insurance plan. To obtain coverage for

his family, he'll have to allow BigTech to deduct $6,000 per year from his salary. In effect, he must give up $6,000 in salary to obtain health insurance as an employee fringe benefit. Which option should he choose? The salary reduction. The $6,000 in salary is taxable income. Before Ralph can use it to buy health insurance or anything else, he must pay a combined state and federal tax of 41% on it—an annual tax of $2,460. In contrast, Ralph pays no tax on the $6,000 BigTech deducts from his salary for health insurance. So Ralph effectively saves $2,460 in income taxes by having part of his salary converted into a tax-free employee fringe benefit.

Of course, you won't be better off if you contribute part of your salary to obtain an employee benefit you don't really want or need. But there are plenty of benefits that most people, including you, probably do want.

Employers have enormous flexibility as to employee benefits. Your employer may offer all, some, or no benefits. There is no federal law requiring employers to give employees any benefits. However, most employers provide at least some employee benefits. Unfortunately, many employees fail to take full advantage of them—a lost opportunity for tax savings.

Types of Tax-Qualified Employee Fringe Benefits

Only certain types of employee fringe benefits are tax qualified and receive tax-free treatment. Employees must pay tax on the fair market value of any benefits they receive that are not tax qualified—for example, a company car they use for personal driving.

Tax-free employee fringe benefits include:

Health benefits. Health benefits are by far the single most important tax-qualified employee fringe benefit. Health benefits include providing employees with health, dental, and vision insurance, and paying for uninsured health-related expenses.

Except in Hawaii and Massachusetts, businesses aren't required to provide health benefits for employees, but most companies provide some type of health benefits. Employers have many choices: They can purchase a group policy to cover all employees, or have each employee purchase his or her own policy and be reimbursed all or part of the cost. Employers can also fully or partly fund a health savings account (HSA) instead of providing traditional health insurance. Moreover, employers can require employees to pay part or even all of the premiums. Employers can also choose to pay for uninsured health-related expenses by providing their employees with health reimbursement accounts.

Long-term care insurance. This insurance covers expenses such as the cost of nursing home care. Premiums paid for such insurance are not taxable. However, benefits received under the insurance may be partly taxable if they exceed limits set by the IRS.

Group term life insurance. A company may provide up to $50,000 in group term life insurance to each employee tax free. If an employee is given more than $50,000 in coverage, the employee must pay tax on the excess amount. However, this tax is paid at very favorable rates.

Disability insurance. If an employer pays disability insurance premiums for an employee (and the employee is the beneficiary), the premiums are excluded from the employee's income. However, the employee must pay income tax on any disability benefits received under the policy. There is an important exception, however: Disability payments for the loss of a bodily function or limb are tax free.

Educational assistance. Employers may pay employees up to $5,250 tax free each year for educational expenses such as tuition, fees, and books.

Dependent care assistance. Up to $5,000 in dependent care assistance may be provided to an employee tax free. For example, the company could help pay for day care for an employee's child. However, working parents may also be able to obtain a tax credit for child and dependent care. Unfortunately, you can either take the credit or the employee benefit, not both. Which is better? The one that saves you the most taxes, which depends on your overall child care expenses, your household income, and tax filing status.

Transportation benefits. Employers may also pay up to $205 per month for employee parking or up to $105 per month for mass transit passes for those employees who don't drive to work.

Working condition fringe benefits. Working condition fringes are anything your employer provides or pays for that you need to do your job—for example, local and long distance travel for business,

business-related meals and entertainment, professional publications, and company cars used for business driving.

Other fringe benefits. Other tax-free employee fringe benefits include employee stock options, employee discounts (up to 20% off), moving expense reimbursements, meals provided for the employer's convenience, adoption assistance, achievement awards, and retirement planning help, employee gyms, and free services provided to employees. Other de minimis (minimal) benefits can also be provided. These are things that cost very little, like occasional parties or picnics for employees and occasional tickets for entertainment or sporting events.

Cafeteria Plans and Flexible Spending Accounts

An employer may pay for any or all of the benefits listed above out of its own pocket. But, as you doubtless know, the trend is to require employees to pay for more and more benefits themselves. This is usually done through cafeteria plans and flexible spending accounts (FSAs).

A cafeteria plan (also called a "Section 125 Plan") is a written plan established by an employer that allows employees to choose between receiving cash salary (which is taxable) and certain tax-qualified employee fringe benefits (which are tax free). For example, an employee might be able to choose between receiving health insurance coverage or an additional $5,000 in salary. He'd have to pay tax on the salary, but not the employee health benefit. As explained above, the benefit can be worth much more than the salary because it is tax free.

These plans are called cafeteria plans because the process is similar to choosing a meal among the many selections in a cafeteria. The tax-free benefits that may be provided under a cafeteria plan include:
- group health, dental, and vision insurance (but not medical savings accounts or long-term care insurance)
- prescription drug benefits
- long-term disability insurance
- adoption assistance
- dependent care assistance
- 401(k) plan contributions, and
- group term life insurance coverage.

Employers choose which of these benefits to include in their plans. Health benefits are, of course, the most important for most employees.

Many cafeteria plans are used just for premiums for medical, dental, and other insurance. These are often called premium-only plans, or POPs for short.

Cafeteria plans often include flexible spending accounts (FSA), although FSAs can also be provided outside a cafeteria plan. FSAs can be used by employees to pay for out-of-pocket medical and dental expenses they incur during the year. Such expenses typically include co-payments, deductibles, nonprescription drugs, and many expenses not covered by a health plan, such as eyeglasses and contact lenses, laser eye surgery, fertility treatments, chiropractic care, doctor-recommended weight loss programs, and prescription and nonprescription drugs. Separate FSAs can also be used to pay for day care for employees' children and other dependents.

An FSA is like a savings account you fund from your salary. But, unlike your salary or money in a regular savings account, the money in your FSA is not taxed. Each year you decide how much you want to contribute to your account and your employer withholds the necessary amounts from your paychecks to fund your account. For example, if you elect to have $1,200 in your FSA and are paid monthly, your employer would withhold $100 from each of your 12 monthly paychecks during the year. Since they are completely free of tax, the amounts deducted from your paychecks are not counted when your employer determines how much tax to withhold from your paycheck.

If your employer offers it, you may have a regular FSA and another FSA just for child care expenses (such expenses can't be paid from a regular FSA). The IRS does not impose any limit on how much money can be put in a regular FSA each year, but most employers impose their own annual limits. FSAs used for child and dependent care are limited by the IRS to $5,000 per year.

Throughout the year, you use your FSA funds to pay for uninsured medical or dental expenses (or child care expenses). You either submit your bill to your employer for reimbursement from your FSA, or your employer pays it directly. You can't add any additional funds when you use up what you elected to contribute to your account. You can use your entire annual draw at any time, even though you fund your account from paycheck reductions throughout the year.

FSAs have one serious drawback that discourages some people from using them: They are use-it-or-lose-it accounts. Any money left unspent in an FSA at the end of the year is forfeited to your employer. You can't roll it over to the following year. However, the plan can provide for a grace period of up to 2½ months after the end of the plan year. If there is a grace period, any qualified medical expenses incurred in that period are treated as having been incurred during the previous year and can be paid from any amounts left in the account at the end of that year. Your employer is not permitted to refund any part of the balance to you.

> **EXAMPLE:** Ralph (the BigTech employee in the earlier examples) has an FSA plan that he decides to use. Before the start of the year, he elects to reduce his salary by $200 a month in exchange for contributions of that amount to his FSA. BigTech does not count these $200 monthly contributions as salary Ralph must pay taxes on. This saves Ralph $928 in taxes (the sum of a 25% federal income tax, 7.65% Social Security and Medicare tax, and 6% state income tax). He may use the funds from his FSA to pay for medical and dental expenses not covered by his insurance. His total draw, which must be available at the start of the year, is limited to $2,400 (the sum of his monthly contributions for the year). If all $2,400 is used the first nine months, for example, he cannot replenish the account until the next year. Any amount in the Ralph's FSA that remains unspent after 14½ months is forfeited to BigTech.

You need to decide how much money to put in an FSA during your plan's open enrollment period. These periods vary from employer to employer, but they are usually in the fall. You should make this decision with care since you don't want to put too much in your account and end up losing it.

Use your records to estimate what you'll need for out-of-pocket health and/or dependent day care expenses for the coming year. Divide this amount by the number of paychecks you receive yearly. This is the amount your employer should deduct from each check. You can change or revoke your salary reduction amount only if there is a change in your employment or family status that is specified by the plan—for example, a divorce or death in the family reduces your health care expenses for the year.

FSAs are a great deal, and you should definitely use one if your employer offers it. Unfortunately, only about 36% of eligible employees participate in the FSA plans offered by their employers. If you're one of the nonparticipating 64%, talk to your employer about starting an account right away.

Employee Benefits for Business Owners

If you're a business owner—whether a sole proprietor, partner in a partnership, member of a limited liability company, or an over 2% shareholder in an S corporation—you don't qualify for any tax-free employee fringe benefits (except for working condition fringes). If your business provides you with such benefits, you'll have to pay tax on their fair market value.

So what do you do about health insurance? Luckily, people with their own businesses may deduct 100% of the health insurance premiums they pay for themselves and their families (including dental and long-term care coverage) as a special personal income tax deduction. But this deduction is limited to the business's annual profit each year—no profit, no deduction.

If you really want to enjoy tax-free employee fringes, there are a couple of ways you can get them.

First, you can legally organize your business as a regular C corporation and work as its employee. You'll then qualify for tax-free fringes just like any other employee. You'll also have to be treated like an employee for all tax and other purposes—for example, have income and employment taxes withheld from your pay, and possibly be covered by workers' compensation insurance.

If you're married, another option is to hire your spouse as your employee and provide employee benefits to him or her. These benefits, such as health insurance, can cover your spouse, you, your children, and other dependents as well. For this to work though, your spouse must be a real employee—that is do real work—and be paid a reasonable salary on which taxes are withheld.

If you or your spouse work as your business's legitimate employee, your business can deduct the cost of any tax-qualified fringes it provides and you or your spouse need pay no tax on them.

> **EXAMPLE:** Joe, a self-employed consultant, hires his wife, Martha, to work as his full-time employee assistant. He pays her $25,000 per year and provides her with a health insurance policy covering both of them and their two children. The annual policy premiums are $6,000. Martha doesn't pay tax on the value of the insurance because it is a tax-qualified employee fringe benefit. Moreover, Joe may deduct the $6,000 as a business expense for his business, listing it on his Schedule C.

However, the total compensation you pay your spouse-employee must be reasonable—that is, you can't pay more than your spouse's services are worth. For example, you can't pay your spouse at a rate of $100 per hour for simple clerical work. Total compensation means the sum of the salary, plus all the fringe benefits you pay your spouse, including health insurance and medical expense reimbursements.

Social Security Benefits: Tax Free Until They're Not

Social Security benefits are tax free unless you earn too much income during the year. To know whether you might be subject to such taxes you have to figure your "combined income." This is actually quite easy: Simply add one-half of the total Social Security you received during the year to all your other income, including any tax-exempt interest (for example, interest you earned from tax-exempt bonds).

You'll have to pay tax on part of your benefits if your combined income exceeds these thresholds:

- $32,000 if you're married and file a joint tax return (as most couples do), or
- $25,000 if you're single.

If both members of a married couple file their taxes separately, the threshold is reduced to zero—they always have to pay taxes on their benefits. The only exception is if they did not live together at any time during the year; in this event the $25,000 threshold applies.

How much of your Social Security benefits will be taxed depends on just how high your combined income is.

Individual filers. If you file a federal tax return as an individual and your combined income is between $25,000 and $34,000, you have to pay income tax on up to 50% of your Social Security benefits. If your income is above $34,000, up to 85% of your Social Security benefits is subject to income tax.

Joint filers. If you file a joint return, you have to pay taxes on up to 50% of your benefits if you and your spouse have a combined income between $32,000 and $44,000. If your income is more than $44,000, up to 85% of your Social Security benefits is subject to income tax.

> **EXAMPLE:** Betty and Bruno are a retired married couple who file jointly and both work at part-time jobs. Betty earned $12,000 from her job and Bruno earned $18,000 from his. They also had $10,000 in investment income, including $5,000 in interest from tax-exempt municipal bonds. They received $20,000 in Social Security benefits during the year. Their combined income is $50,000 ($30,000 in wages + $10,000 investment income + (50% x $20,000 Social Security benefits) = $50,000.) Because this is more than the $44,000 ceiling, they must pay income tax on 85% of their Social Security benefits. Of course, they must also pay tax on the income from their part-time jobs.

If you earn enough money for your benefits to be taxable, you could end up paying the highest income taxes in the country. Here's why: Every dollar you earn over the 85% threshold amount will result in 85 cents of your benefits being taxed, plus you'll have to pay tax on the extra income. So for every dollar you earn over the 85% threshold, you'll end up paying tax on $1.85. If you're in the 28% bracket, this works out to a 52% tax rate (28% x 1.85 = .518).

Calculating the exact amount of tax that must be paid on Social Security benefits can be quite complicated. IRS Publication 915, *Social Security and Equivalent Railroad Retirement Benefits*, contains detailed instructions and a worksheet you can use.

If you plan to work after the normal retirement age, you should consider putting off claiming your Social Security benefits. If you wait until after your full retirement age to claim Social Security retirement benefits, your benefit amounts will be permanently higher. Your benefit amount is increased by a certain percentage each year you wait up to age 70. After age 70, there is no longer any increase, so you should claim your benefits then, even if they will be partly subject to income tax.

Once you start receiving Social Security benefits, to keep your income below the applicable threshold, or at least as low as possible, you should:

- put off taking money out of retirement accounts like traditional IRAs, and 401(k)s. You don't have to take any money out until you reach age 70.5.
- choose investments that don't generate a lot of taxable income during the year—for example, stocks that don't pay dividends, or tax-managed mutual funds that have low or no taxable distributions (see Chapter 2).
- put your retirement money in Roth IRAs and Roth 401(k)s. Your earnings are not subject to any tax if you hold the account at least five years and are over 59.5 years old. If you have a traditional IRA, you can convert it into a Roth IRA (see Chapter 4).
- consider reducing your income by giving income-producing assets to your children or other relatives, or to charities (see Chapter 8).

The tax laws encourage retired people to "live in sin"—that is, without benefit of marriage. A couple increases the amount of income they can earn without being taxed on their Social Security benefits if they aren't married and file their taxes separately. Each will be entitled to earn $25,000 in combined income without paying tax on their benefits, for a total of $50,000 of income without extra taxes. In contrast, a married couple can earn no more than $32,000 in combined income without paying extra taxes. However, a married couple can get the same treatment as singles if they live apart part of the year and file their taxes separately.

For more information on Social Security, refer to *Social Security, Medicare & Government Pensions: Get the Most Out of Your Retirement & Medical Benefits*, by Joseph L. Matthews and Dorothy Matthews Berman (Nolo).

Live and Work Abroad and Avoid U.S. Taxes

One way to earn income free of U.S. taxes is to live and work outside the U.S. You'll undoubtedly have to pay income tax on the money you earn in the foreign country, but you can get a break on your U.S. taxes. The foreign-earned-income exclusion was created so that Americans who earned income abroad wouldn't be taxed twice on the same income—once by the country where they live and again by the U.S. Under the exclusion rule, up to $82,400 in income need not be counted as U.S. taxable income if:

- The income is earned income—salary, wages, or professional fees you were paid for your work—but not interest, dividends, or other money earned from foreign investments.
- You earned the income for performing personal services outside the U.S.—it's fine if you worked for a U.S. company abroad, but you can't have worked for the U.S. government.
- The income was for services you performed while either (1) you were physically outside the U.S. for at least 330 days out of any 12 consecutive months, or (2) you were a resident of a foreign country for at least a full calendar year.
- Your tax home is in a foreign country—your tax home is the place of your principal place of employment.

You can see that for the exclusion to apply you must live and work in a foreign country long-term—at least about 11 months (330 days). Starting in 2007, the amount of the exclusion will be adjusted each year for inflation.

If your employer pays for your foreign housing, you can also exclude part of the payments from your U.S. taxable income. The amount of this exclusion was reduced starting in 2006. You may only deduct housing costs that exceed $13,184 in 2006; and the maximum amount of the exclusion is capped at $11,536.

If you qualify for the exclusion, you'll likely qualify for the foreign tax credit as well. It allows you to deduct the amount of the foreign taxes you paid from your U.S. taxable income. You can use the credit in addition to the exclusion. (See Chapter 3.)

For more information, refer to IRS Publication 54, *Tax Guide for U.S. Citizens and Resident Aliens Abroad*.

Don't Overlook These Other Types of Tax-Free Income

Other forms of tax-free income include:

- property received as a gift or inheritance
- life insurance proceeds received because of the death of an individual
- child support payments
- welfare benefits
- accident and health insurance proceeds
- veteran's benefits
- worker's compensation benefits for an occupational sickness or injury, and
- death gratuity benefits paid to survivors of deceased armed forces members for deaths occurring after September 10, 2001.

For more information about gifts, inheritances, and life insurance, see *Plan Your Estate*, by Denis Clifford and Cora Jordan (Nolo). For more on all forms of tax-free income, see IRS Publication 525, *Taxable and Nontaxable Income*.

How to Win the Nobel Prize Tax Free

If you win the Nobel Prize, Pulitzer Prize, or a similar award that comes with a cash payment, you'll ordinarily need to pay income tax on the amount. The Nobel Prize comes with a cash award of 10 million Swedish kroner—about $1.3 million—so you could have a hefty tax bill. But there is a way to collect a Nobel tax free: Immediately donate the cash payment to a tax-exempt charity. As long as you don't use the award before it is transferred, you need not include it in your income. This tax rule applies not only to well-known awards like Nobels or Pulitzers, but to any prize awarded to you in recognition of your accomplishments in religious, charitable, scientific, artistic, educational, literary, or civic fields.

The Dollar-for-Dollar Advantages: Tax Credits

Obtaining a tax credit is the next best thing to paying no taxes at all. A tax credit is a sum of money that you directly deduct from your taxes—for example, a $1,000 tax credit reduces the amount of taxes you pay by $1,000. This is much better than a $1,000 tax deduction, which only reduces your taxable income. If you're in the 28% income tax bracket, a $1,000 tax deduction will save you only $280 in taxes (28% x $1,000 = $280). A person in the 28% tax bracket would need $3,571 in tax deductions to save $1,000 in income taxes.

Credits Versus Deductions	
Credits	**Deductions**
Tax credits are subtracted directly from your tax liability. Credits reduce tax liability dollar for dollar.	Tax deductions are subtracted from your total income to compute your taxable income. Deductions reduce tax liability by the amount of the deduction times the tax rate.
$1,000 credit = $1,000 tax reduction	**$1,000 deduction x 28% tax rate = $280 tax reduction**

So, how do you get these wonderful tax credits? Congress hands them out as rewards to taxpayers who do things it approves of or wants to encourage. Take, for example, John and Jenny Jones. Their combined taxable income in 2005 and 2006 was $100,000 per year. They paid $20,000 in income taxes in 2005 but owed only $13,500 in 2006. They owed less in 2006 because of tax credits they received for certain things they did that year. The activities that resulted in a tax benefit to them included:

- having their first child ($1,000 credit)
- purchasing a hybrid car ($2,000 credit)
- adding new insulation to their home ($500 credit)
- installing a solar water heater in their home ($2,000 credit)
- incurring child care expenses so that they could both work ($500 credit), and
- paying for night classes for John at the local college ($500 credit).

They received a total of $6,500 in tax credits for these activities, which meant they owed $6,500 less in taxes that year.

Congress has taken a great liking to tax credits in recent years and is adding new ones all the time. For example, in 2005 it created new tax credits for hybrid cars and home energy improvements.

Each tax credit is different, with its own eligibility rules and amounts. Most credits are based on the amount you spend, but some have specified maximum annual amounts you can't exceed. Several credits have income limits and are reduced or not available to people whose income exceeds the limits. You claim tax credits on the second page of your Form 1040. First, you figure out your taxes due without any credits, then you deduct from this amount the total of all your credits—a highly enjoyable bit of subtraction. You'll also need to include with your return a special tax form for each credit you claim—there are different forms for different credits.

A tax credit ordinarily will defray only part of a covered expense, so there's no point in buying something you don't really need or want just to get a tax credit. For example, don't buy a hybrid car to get a tax credit if you really don't want one. But, if you do need or want the item, the credit will help pay for it by reducing your income taxes.

Tax Credits Come and Go

Some tax credits have been around for years and are more or less permanent—the child care credit and low-income housing credit, for example. Others have been created more recently and have scheduled phaseout dates. Congress can, and often does, extend credits that are scheduled to end. The research and experimentation, work opportunity, welfare to work, and Indian tax credits, have been extended one year at a time for several years. However, there is no guarantee that Congress will extend a tax credit, so it's wise to act before the expiration date if you want to use a tax credit that is scheduled to expire.

Below are tax credits with expiration dates:

Credit	Expiration Date
Hybrid car	December 31, 2010
Homeowner energy efficiency	December 31, 2007
Solar power for homes and businesses	December 31, 2007
Build energy efficient homes	December 31, 2007
Work opportunity	December 31, 2006
Welfare to work	December 31, 2006
Indian tax credit	December 31, 2006
Research and experimentation	December 31, 2006

Hybrid Cars: New Wheels and a Tax Break, Too

High gas prices got you down? Are you considering buying one of the new hybrid cars? These vehicles, such as the popular Toyota Prius, are powered by both an internal combustion engine and a rechargeable battery, and get incredibly good gas mileage—up to 60 miles per gallon or more. However, hybrid cars are more expensive than similar cars with ordinary internal combustion engines. To encourage people to purchase these cars and reduce the country's dependence on foreign oil, Congress enacted a hybrid vehicle tax credit that took effect on January 1, 2006. Prior to 2006, there was a $2,000 tax deduction available for purchasers of hybrid vehicles. The deduction ended on December 31, 2005.

The tax credit is available to anyone who purchases a new hybrid vehicle between January 1, 2006, and December 31, 2010, provided the hybrid model has been certified by the IRS. The IRS publishes a list of certified hybrids on its website (www.irs.gov). You get no credit if you lease a hybrid car.

Just how much is the tax credit? Good question. Unfortunately, there is no easy answer. The size of the credit is determined using a complex formula based on each hybrid vehicle's fuel efficiency, so different model hybrids qualify for different credit amounts. The credit consists of two parts: (1) a fuel economy amount that is based on the car's fuel consumption; and (2) a conservation credit based on the estimated lifetime fuel savings of the vehicle. The maximum allowable credits are listed in the chart below.

Type of Hybrid Vehicle	Maximum Tax Credit
Passenger cars and other hybrid vehicles weighing less than 8,500 pounds	$3,400
Trucks and other hybrid vehicles weighing 8,500–14,000 pounds	$3,000
Trucks and other hybrid vehicles weighing 14,001–26,000 pounds	$6,000
Trucks and other hybrid vehicles weighing more than 26,000 pounds	$12,000

It appears that few, if any, hybrid cars will qualify for the maximum credit. The following chart—current as of mid-2006—shows all the hybrid models the IRS has certified and their applicable tax credit amounts.

Vehicle Year, Make, and Model	Credit
2006 Ford Escape Hybrid Front WD	$2,600
2006 Ford Escape Hybrid 4WD	$1,950
2006 Mercury Mariner Hybrid 4WD	$1,950
2005 Toyota Prius	$3,150
2006 Toyota Prius	$3,150
2006 Toyota Highlander 2WD and 4WD Hybrid	$2,600
2006 Lexus RX400h 2WD and 4WD	$2,200
2007 Toyota Camry Hybrid	$2,600
2007 Toyota Lexus GS 450h	$1,550
2005 Honda Insight CVT	$1,450
2006 Honda Insight CVT	$1,450
2005 Honda Civic Hybrid MT and CVT	$1,700
2006 Honda Civic Hybrid CVT	$2,100
2005 Honda Accord Hybrid AT and Navi AT	$650
2006 Honda Accord Hybrid AT w/updated calibration and Navi AT w/updated calibration	$1,300

Another factor complicates things even further. Congress didn't want to allow too many tax credits for hybrids, so once a hybrid manufacturer sells 60,000 vehicles, the credit will be phased out over the following 15 months for all hybrids produced by that company. The phaseout times and percentages are show in the following chart.

Hybrid Tax Credit Phaseout	
Calendar Quarter	**Percentage of Full Credit**
Until manufacturer's total hybrid sales reach 60,000	100%
1st quarter after	100%
2nd quarter	50%
3rd quarter	50%
4th quarter	25%
5th quarter	25%
6th quarter and later	No credit

Toyota announced that it reached the 60,000 car limit during the second quarter of 2006. Thus, the tax credit for all Toyota hybrids will be gradually reduced to zero over the next fifteen months. (Lexus hybrids are included with Toyota sales because Toyota manufactures the Lexus.) The full $3,150 credit was only available until the end of the following calendar quarter (September 30, 2006). The credit was then reduced by 50% for the next two quarters (October 1, 2006, through March 31, 2007), and by 75% for the two quarters after that (April 1, 2007, through September 30, 2007.) Thereafter (after October 1, 2007), no credit will be available for the purchase of any Toyota or Lexus hybrid.

Clearly, you should act quickly if you want to purchase a popular hybrid model and get the full credit. Hybrid manufacturers are required to provide the IRS with quarterly sales reports showing where each manufacturer stands as to the 60,000 vehicle limit; this information is also available on the IRS website. Be sure to check these reports before you buy any hybrid; otherwise, you could be surprised to discover you'll get no tax credit.

The credit is scheduled to end on December 31, 2010, for hybrids produced by manufacturers that never sell 60,000 vehicles.

Tax Credits Are Available for Other Fuel-Efficient Vehicles

Tax credits are also available for fuel cell vehicles and alternative fuel vehicles. The same formulas used for hybrid vehicles are used to determine the tax credit for these vehicles.

Fuel cell vehicles are powered by one or more cells that convert chemical energy to electricity by combining oxygen with hydrogen fuel. The maximum allowable credit for fuel cell vehicles is $8,000, but greater credits are available for heavier vehicles.

Alternative fuel vehicles include those fueled by compressed natural gas, liquefied natural gas, liquefied petroleum gas, hydrogen, and any liquid that is at least 85 percent methanol. The maximum allowable credit for alternative fuel vehicles weighing less than 8,500 pounds is $2,500.

Pain-Free Reduction of Energy and Your Tax Bills

Home gas and electricity bills have been skyrocketing. A good way to lower your bills is to make your home more energy efficient. You'll not only save on your utility expenses, but you may also qualify for a brand new tax credit.

Home Energy Tax Credits

Tax credits are available to homeowners who buy certain energy-efficient products during 2006 and 2007. The following chart shows the tax credits that are available. However, the total combined credit you can get for all tax years is $500, and no more than $200 of the credit can be for windows. The credit is equal to 10% of your costs for windows, thus, you'll reach the $200 ceiling when you spend $2,000. The items must be purchased new and placed in service in your main home (which must be in the United States) between January 1, 2006, and December 31, 2007.

Home Energy Tax Credits			
Product Category	**Product Type**	**Energy Savings Requirements**	**Tax Credit**
Windows	Exterior windows	Must satisfy year 2000 International Energy Conservation Code (IECC) requirements (most ENERGY STAR windows qualify)	10% of cost up to $200
	Skylights	Must satisfy 2000 IECC requirements (most ENERGY STAR skylights qualify)	10% of cost up to $200
	Exterior doors	Must satisfy 2000 IECC requirements (most ENERGY STAR doors qualify)	10% of cost up to $500
Roofing	Metal roofs	Must have pigmented coatings that meet ENERGY STAR requirements	10% of cost up to $500
Insulation	Insulation	Must satisfy 2000 IECC requirements	10% of cost up to $500

	Home Energy Tax Credits (continued)		
Product Category	**Product Type**	**Energy Savings Requirements**	**Tax Credit**
Heating and cooling systems	Central air conditioning	For a list of qualified products, check the Consortium for Energy Efficiency product directory at www.ceehvacdirectory.org	Up to $300 of cost
	Air source heat pump	Must be in the highest efficiency category set by Consortium for Energy Efficiency—15 SEER and 13 EER—and must have a heating seasonal performance factor (HSPF) of at least 9. Not all ENERGY STAR heat pumps qualify.	Up to $300 of cost
	Geothermal heat pump	Must meet current ENERGY STAR requirements	Up to $300 of cost
	Electric heat pump water heater	Must have an EF of at least 2.0	Up to $300 of cost
	Gas, oil, or propane water heater	Must have an EF of at least 0.80. Only some tankless water heaters currently reach this efficiency level. For a list of qualifying products check the Gas Appliance Manufacturing Association website at www.gamanet.org.	Up to $300 of cost
	Gas, oil, or propane furnace or hot water boiler	Must have at least a 95% annual fuel utilization efficiency (AFUE). For a list of qualifying products, check the Gas Appliance Manufacturing Association website at www.gamanet.org.	Up to $150 of cost
	Advanced furnace air circulating fan	Fan must account for no more than 2% of the total annual energy use of the furnace. For a list of qualifying products check the Gas Appliance Manufacturing Association website at www.gamanet.org.	Up to $50 of cost

EXAMPLE: During 2006, Margaret spends $2,000 on new ENERGY STAR-compliant storm windows for her home. She also buys a highly efficient tankless gas water heater for $2,000. She is entitled to a $200 tax credit for the windows and a $150 tax credit for the water heater. This amounts to $350 of her total $500 home energy credit, so she'll have $150 left to use in 2007.

You get the credit only if the items you buy meet the energy efficiency specifications established by law. Many of these specifications are quite stringent—for example, an electric heat pump water heater qualifies for the credit only if its energy efficiency is over twice as great as the current federal standard. Make sure the product you want to buy qualifies—don't take a salesperson's word for it. Some tax preparers have reported that salespeople have told taxpayers that they can get the credit for items that don't qualify—for example, wood or pellet furnaces. Only furnaces that use natural gas, oil, or propane qualify for the credit.

The best way to know whether a product qualifies for the home energy tax credit is to get written certification from the manufacturer stating that the item qualifies. Manufacturers are not required by law to provide consumers with such certification statements, but they are encouraged to do so. The certification statement should either be included with the product's packaging, or available to print out on the manufacturer's website. Make sure you get a copy and keep it with your tax records (you don't have to attach it to your tax return).

You don't need any kind of certification if you purchase an exterior window or skylight that bears an ENERGY STAR label. You'll qualify for the credit so long as the window or skylight is installed in the geographic region identified on the label.

Solar Power

More generous credits are available to homeowners who install solar water-heating or electric power systems in their homes. For these, you get a credit of:

- 30% of the cost of solar water-heating equipment, up to a $2,000 maximum each tax year, and

- 30% of the cost of solar panels and related equipment that generates photovoltaic electricity, up to a $2,000 maximum each tax year.

The solar equipment may not be used to heat a pool or hot tub. The equipment must be placed in service in your main home sometime between January 1, 2006, and December 31, 2007.

So, is it time for you to go solar? Maybe … maybe not. The cost of a solar water heater typically ranges from $3,500 to $6,000, which means a 30% tax credit saves you anywhere from $1,050 to $1,800. That is a big chunk of the expense. With heating bills going through the roof in many parts of the country, your investment could pay off quickly.

Solar panels to produce electricity for home use are a different story. Home solar panel electricity systems are expensive—they range from $16,000 to $64,000, depending on the size of the home. A $2,000 maximum credit won't defray much of that cost. However, several states have much more generous tax incentives. For example, California provides tax rebates equal to approximately 35% of the cost of installing solar panels, while New Jersey offers a tax rebate of approximately 60%. You can find out if your state offers any tax incentives by checking the Database of State Incentives for Renewable Energy at www.dsireusa.org.

Before making the decision to go solar, it's a good idea to figure out how long it will take you to recoup your investment. You will have to look at your cost (after federal and state tax credits and rebates) and your estimated utility savings. In some cases, it could take as many as 20 years to recoup the cost; in others, you might get back the total cost in just a few years. You can easily come up with your own cost estimate by using the solar estimator at www.findsolar.com.

Tax Benefits From Your Bundles of Joy

Children are an expensive, yet necessary, evil. Congress wants to encourage people to have kids by giving them special tax credits. There are two different tax credits available for taxpayers who support children:

- a child tax credit of $1,000 per child, and
- a child and dependent care tax credit of up to $2,100.

If you qualify, you can get both credits in the same year, and you can still get the tax exemption for children and other dependents (see Chapter 8). There is also a tax credit for people who adopt children. All these credits, however, are subject to limitations that can reduce or eliminate the benefit, depending on your circumstances.

Which Children Qualify You for Tax Credits?

The child tax credit and child and dependent care tax credit are only available if you have what the IRS calls a "qualifying child." A qualifying child is one for whom you can claim a dependency exemption. A qualifying child can be your son, daughter, stepchild, adopted child, foster child, brother, sister, stepbrother, stepsister, or a descendant of any of them—for example, your grandchild, niece, or nephew. (See Chapter 8 for a detailed discussion of which children are qualifying children.) The child tax credit may be claimed if you have a qualifying child under age 17. The child and dependent care tax credit may be claimed for qualifying children under age 13. If a child turns 17 or 13 during the year, you can get the applicable credit only for the part of the year the child was under the age limit.

Child Tax Credit

Before you get too excited about how much money Junior is going to save you on your taxes, read on. The child tax credit was created for low- and middle-income taxpayers. It is subject to an income threshold and the amount of credit you can take each year goes down as your income approaches that threshold amount. Here's how it works.

Everyone with a qualifying child starts out the tax year entitled to a $1,000 credit per child for the tax year. This credit is gradually phased out for taxpayers whose incomes rise up to and above the annual threshold amount specified for the year. For 2006, the income threshold is $110,000 for a married couple filing jointly, $55,000 for a married couple filing separately, an $75,000 for a single person, head of household, or widower.

The phaseout works like this: For each $1,000 that your modified adjusted gross income exceeds the income threshold level, the total child tax credit for a family (not the amount per child) is reduced by $50. If you make too much money, you won't get any credit at all. For example, a married couple filing jointly with one qualifying child gets no child tax credit if their adjusted gross income exceeds $130,000. The $1,000 credit they started the tax year with would be whittled down to zero by 20 $50 reductions.

If the great composer Bach were alive today and living in the United States, he'd be entitled to a $20,000 child tax credit because he had 20 children (with two wives, thankfully). But what if Bach owed only $9,000 in income taxes for the year? What happens to the remaining $11,000 in tax credits? Luckily, depending on his income, Bach could get all or part of the excess child credit amount paid to him by the IRS as a refund. Taxpayers in this situation are entitled to a refund equal to 15% of their earned income over a threshold amount ($11,300 in 2006). If, for example, Bach's earned income was $81,300 in 2005, he'd be entitled to a refund of $10,500 (15% x $70,000 = $10,500).

Child and Dependent Care Tax Credit

Unlike the child tax credit (which you get simply by having a qualifying child), you can use the child and dependent care credit only if you shell out money for child care so that you and your spouse, if any, can work. And, there is no income ceiling on the child and dependent care credit (which is also different from the child tax credit). However, people with higher incomes get a smaller credit than those with more modest incomes. Here's how it works.

You qualify for the credit if:

- You have a qualifying child or other dependent under the age of 13, or you have a child over 13 who is totally and permanently disabled.
- You incur child care expenses to enable you and your spouse, if any, to earn income.
- You and your spouse file a joint tax return (if you're married).
- You and your spouse, if any, both work either full- or part-time, unless you or your spouse is a full-time student or disabled. (Looking for work counts as being employed.)

The amount of the credit is based on a percentage of the child care expenses you incur on the days that you and/or your spouse work. The percentage ranges from 20% to 35% of expenses, depending on your income. Taxpayers with an adjusted gross income (AGI) of over

$43,000 use the 20% amount. Those with an AGI under $15,000 use the 35% amount. Those with AGIs between $15,000 and $43,000 use a percentage based on a sliding scale. However, there is an annual ceiling on the amount of child care expenses that can be taken into account for the credit. For 2005, the ceilings are $3,000 for one qualifying child and $6,000 for two or more.

> **EXAMPLE:** In 2006, John and Jane Smith had two qualifying children and $10,000 in child care expenses. Their AGI was $100,000 so they used the 20% percentage to figure their credit. Even though they had $10,000 in child care expenses, they can only take 20% of $6,000 because $6,000 is the annual ceiling for people with two or more children. They are entitled to a $1,200 credit for the year (20% x $6,000 = $1,200).

If you're fortunate enough to have an employer that reimburses you for child care expenses, you must deduct the reimbursed amount from your annual child care expenses.

Obviously, you need to keep track of everything you spend on child care during the year and be sure to keep receipts and cancelled checks. Child care expenses include expenses both in and outside your home, such as:

- babysitting
- day care center
- nursery school, and
- day camp (but not if the child sleeps overnight at the camp).

The costs of sending a child to school in the first grade or beyond are not included. Nor can you hire your spouse, child, or other dependent as a day care provider. If your child turns 13 during the year, you can only include those expenses you incur before his or her 13th birthday.

To claim the credit, you'll have to list on your tax return the name, address, and Social Security or Employer Identification number of the people you pay for dependent care, so be sure to get this information.

Adoption Tax Credit

There is a tax credit for people who adopt children. The credit is equal to 100% of adoption expenses up to an annual ceiling. The ceiling was

$10,960 per child in 2006. Any reasonable and necessary expenses for the adoption may be taken into account for the credit—for example, adoption agency fees, attorney fees, court costs, and traveling expenses (including meals and lodging).

However, there is an income limit on the credit and the credit is gradually phased out for taxpayers whose modified adjusted gross income exceeds an annual ceiling. In 2006, the ceiling was $164,410. Those with an AGI over $204,410 in 2006 get no credit at all.

> **EXAMPLE:** Burt and Betty decide they want to adopt a child. They spend $20,000 in attorney fees, adoption fees, and travel expenses in 2006 and adopt a Vietnamese child. Their adjusted gross income for the year was $120,000, so they qualify for the full $10,960 adoption tax credit.

Get Educated and Get a Tax Break

Congress figures that well-educated taxpayers will make more money and be able to pay more taxes so it has created two tax credits for expenses related to higher education:

- the Hope tax credit, and
- the Lifetime Learning credit.

You can't take both credits in the same year for the same person. However, both credits can be claimed on the same return for different students. For example, you could qualify for the Hope credit for a child enrolled in college and also take the Lifetime Learning credit for a work-related course you take.

If the total expenses involved are $7,500 or less, it's usually better to use the Hope credit if you have a choice. If your expenses are above that amount, it's better to use the Lifetime Learning credit because the Lifetime Learning credit is larger for expenses over the threshold amount.

 For more information about education tax credits, refer to IRS Publication 970, *Tax Benefits for Education*.

Hope Tax Credit

The Hope tax credit is designed to help low- and middle-income taxpayers pay tuition for the first two years of higher education. You can claim the credit for any tuition and related fees you pay an accredited college, university, vocational school, or other educational institution eligible to participate in the federal student aid program. The payments must be made on behalf of an eligible student, which includes any dependent child or children for whom you claim a tax exemption, your spouse, you, or any other dependents for whom you claim tax exemptions. The student must be in his or her first or second year of school, attending school at least half-time, and enrolled in the program to obtain a degree or other credential. Like the three child tax credits discussed above, the Hope tax credit is subject to an income threshold—if you earn over a certain amount, you can't use the credit.

The amount of the credit is the sum of:

- 100% of the first $1,100 of education expenses you pay for the eligible student, plus
- 50% of the next $1,100 of education expenses you pay for that student.

Thus, you can claim the full $1,650 for each eligible student for whom you paid at least $2,200 of education expenses. The credit can be claimed by a parent, spouse, or a dependent child on his or her own tax return, but not by more than one person for the same year.

The maximum credit you can claim per eligible student for 2006 is $1,550. The maximum amount of the credit is gradually reduced if your modified adjusted gross income (MAGI) is between $45,000 and $55,000 ($90,000 and $110,000 if you file a joint return). You cannot claim a Hope credit at all if your MAGI is $55,000 or more ($110,000 or more if you file a joint return). See IRS Publication 970, *Tax Benefits for Education*, for details on how the credit is reduced.

> **EXAMPLE:** Jon and Karen are married and file a joint tax return. For 2006, they claim an exemption for their dependent daughter on their tax return. Their MAGI is $70,000. Their daughter is in her sophomore (second) year of studies at the local university. Jon and Karen pay tuition and related fees of $4,300 in 2006. Jon and Karen

can claim the full $1,650 Hope credit in 2006. This is 100% of the first $1,100 of their education expenses, plus 50% of the next $1,100.

Remember, you can only get the Hope credit for the first and second years a student attends college. After that, you get no credit for that student. Thus, Jon and Karen from the above example will get no Hope credit for their daughter for her junior (third) and later years at college.

When you figure the amount of the credit, you can only take into account what you spend for tuition and any other related fees you pay the school (for example, student activity fees). You can't take into account personal expenses such as room and board, insurance, medical expenses (including student health fees), or transportation, even if you pay the school for them. The college or university will send each enrolled student an IRS Form 1098-T by January 31 of each year showing how much tuition and related fees were paid on behalf of that student for the prior year.

You can pay the education expenses in cash or borrow money to pay them. It makes no difference for purposes of the credit. You can take into account both expenses that you pay yourself and expenses that your dependent child pays—for example, you can include the amount of a student loan your child takes out to help pay for tuition.

Lifetime Learning Credit

The Lifetime Learning credit is subject to many of the same rules as the Hope credit. However, the Lifetime Learning credit is far more flexible because:

- the student does not have to be in his or her first or second year of school
- it can be used for nondegree education to acquire or improve job skills (for example a continuing education course), and
- there is no requirement that the student be enrolled at least half-time—it can be used for a single course.

If you qualify, your credit equals 20% of the first $10,000 of post-secondary tuition and fees you pay during the year for any eligible students, for a maximum credit of $2,000 per tax return. This differs from the Hope credit, which is figured per student. The credit is phased out and then eliminated at the same income levels as the Hope credit—

it begins to go down if your modified adjusted gross income is over $45,000 ($90,000 for a joint return) and you cannot claim the credit at all if your MAGI is over $55,000 ($110,000 for a joint return).

You can take this credit not only for a dependent child (or children) for whom you claim a tax exemption, but for yourself or your spouse as well (if you file jointly). And it can be taken any number of times.

> **EXAMPLE:** Bill and Jane are a jointly filing married couple with a MAGI of $100,000. In 2006, they spend $5,000 on tuition so that their dependent son Biff can attend his fourth year at the local state college. Bill, an attorney, also spends $1,000 on continuing legal education for himself. They have $6,000 in total education expenses that qualify for the Lifetime Learning credit. Their credit is $1,200 (20% x $6,000 = $1,200).

Save for Your Retirement—Another Tax Benefit

There is a retirement tax credit that is designed to benefit people with modest incomes who save for their retirement. You qualify for the credit only if:

- you were born before January 2, 1988
- you are not a full-time student
- no one else (such as your parents) claims an exemption for you on his or her tax return, and
- your adjusted gross income is not more than:
    - $50,000 if your filing status is married filing jointly
    - $37,500 if your filing status is head of household (with qualifying person), or
    - $25,000 if your filing status is single, married filing separately, or qualifying widow(er) with dependent child.

To get the credit, you must invest in a traditional or Roth IRA, 401(k) plan, SIMPLE IRA, or employee SEP. The actual amount of the credit depends on the amount of your contributions and your income level. The most a single person can get is $1,000, if he or she makes a $2,000 contribution and his or her AGI is below $15,000. The most a married couple filing jointly can receive is $2,000, if they each make a $2,000 contribution and their joint AGI is less than $30,000. People with higher incomes receive much less. As you can see, this credit is for taxpayers with very modest incomes.

This credit does not affect or reduce the tax deduction and deferral benefits of investing in traditional IRAs and tax-deferred retirement plans. (See Chapter 4.)

Tax Breaks for Good Corporate Citizens

There are many different types of tax credits just for businesses. If you don't have a business, you can't use them. If you are in business, you may qualify for one or more. However, many business credits are quite specialized and can be used only by specific types of businesses. They all tend to be complicated, so it's highly advisable to have a tax pro handle the details for you. We'll just look at the more commonly used credits. You can find information about all available business tax credits from IRS Publication 334, *Tax Guide for Small Business*.

To get a business credit, your business must do, or be involved in, something that Congress likes or views as socially beneficial. These types of activities that Congress views favorably enough to warrant a tax credit can be divided into a few broad categories:

- helping the disadvantaged or disabled
- improving the environment
- helping your employees, or
- investing in research and development.

You may be able to qualify for several different credits at the same time. However, there is an overall limit on total business credits you can take in a year which is based on your tax liability. If you exceed the limit, you can take the credits in future years or apply them to previous years' taxes—within limits.

Help the Disadvantaged or Disabled

Several tax credits are available if you help someone who is disadvantaged or disabled.

Hire them. A great way to help someone who is poor or disabled is to give that person a job. Several tax credits are intended to encourage this.

Work opportunity credit. This is a credit of up to $2,400 for the first year you hire people from targeted groups that have a particularly high unemployment rate or other special employment needs—for example, welfare and food stamp recipients, low-income ex-felons, disabled people, and high-risk young people. You can also get a $1,200 credit for giving disadvantaged youths summer jobs.

Welfare-to-work credit. This credit is similar to the work opportunity credit, but is larger—up to $15,000 over two years. You can get it when you hire long-term welfare recipients.

Empowerment zone employment credit. This is a credit of up to $15,000 ($3,000 per employee) when you hire someone to work in a federal "empowerment zone"—an area designated as economically disadvantaged.

Indian employment credit. You can get a credit of up to $20,000 ($4,000 per employee) for hiring Indian tribe members who live and work on a reservation.

For more information on these credits, see IRS Publication 954, *Tax Incentives for Distressed Communities.*

Make your business accessible. The Americans with Disabilities Act (ADA) prohibits private employers with 15 or more employees from discriminating against people with disabilities in the full and equal enjoyment of goods, services, and facilities offered by any "place of public accommodation"—this includes businesses open to the public. The disabled access tax credit is designed to help small businesses defray the costs of complying with the ADA. The credit may be used by any business with either:

- $1 million or less in gross receipts for the preceding tax year, or
- 30 or fewer full-time employees during the preceding tax year.

The credit can be used to cover a variety of expenses, including the cost to remove barriers that prevent a business from being accessible to disabled people. However, the credit may only be used for buildings constructed before November 5, 1990. The credit may also be used for equipment acquisitions and services such as sign language interpreters.

The amount of the tax credit is equal to 50% of your disabled access expenses in a year that exceed $250 but are not more than $10,250. Thus, the maximum credit is $5,000.

Improve the Environment

This is the largest group of business credits—for businesses that work to improve the environment. Most of these credits, however, are highly specialized and can only be used by a few types of businesses (probably not including yours). For example, there is a low-sulfur diesel fuel production credit for oil refineries and a reforestation credit for timber companies.

Solar power. One credit you may be able to use is the solar power credit. Businesses can get a credit of up to 30% of the cost of buying and installing solar equipment to generate electricity to heat or cool (or provide hot water for use in) a structure, or to provide solar process heat. Unlike the solar credit for homeowners, there is no dollar limit on this credit.

Energy-efficient new homes. If you're a building contractor who builds homes, there is a new tax credit just for you. Starting in 2006, you can get a credit of up to $2,000 for building an energy-efficient home that is sold anytime in 2006 through the end of 2007. The credit is available for all new homes, including manufactured homes, built after August 8, 2005. To meet the energy-saving requirements, a home must be certified to provide heating and cooling energy savings of 30% to 50% compared to a federal standard. For more information, see IRS *Form 8908, Energy Efficient Home Credit*, and IRS Notices 2006-27 and 2006-11.

Help Your Employees

There are a couple of credits you can get if you do some nice things for your employees.

Credit for employer-provided child care. This credit applies to expenses you pay for employee child care and child care resource and referral services. The credit is 25% of qualified expenses you paid for employee child care and 10% of qualified expenses you paid for child care resource and referral services. This credit is limited to $150,000 each year. For more information, see IRS Form 8882, *Credit for Employer-Provided Childcare and Services.*

Credit for small employer pension start-up costs. This credit applies to pension plan start-up costs. If you begin a new qualified defined-benefit or defined-contribution plan (including a 401(k) plan), SIMPLE plan, or simplified employee pension, you can receive a tax credit of 50% of the first $1,000 of qualified start-up costs. For more information, see IRS Publication 560, *Retirement Plans for Small Business.*

Invest in Research

The research and experimentation credit, also called the R & E credit, is intended to encourage businesses to invest in scientific research and experimental activities, including energy research. Any technological research qualifies, so long as it relates to a new or improved function, performance, reliability, or quality. The research must involve principles of the physical or biological sciences, engineering, or computer science. The credit is not available for research in the social sciences, including economics, business management, and behavioral sciences, arts, or humanities.

You can get the credit whether you do the research in-house or contract it out. The credit is generally 20% of the amount by which your research expenses for the year are more than a base amount based on an IRS formula or your business's gross receipts. This credit is complicated. For more information, see IRS Form 6765, *Credit for Increasing Research Activitie*s.

The Expatriate Advantage: Credit for Income Taxes Paid Elsewhere

If you earn income from a foreign country and pay income taxes on it in that country, you may qualify for a credit on your United States income taxes for all or part of the foreign tax. Congress created the foreign tax credit because it thought it wasn't fair for people to be taxed twice on the same income.

Only foreign income taxes, war profits taxes, and excess profits taxes (or taxes paid in lieu of such taxes) qualify for the credit. Thus, for example, no credit may be taken for foreign value-added taxes, sales taxes, or property taxes. You also can't count any foreign income taxes you paid on income that is excluded from U.S. income tax under the foreign-earned-income exclusion or the foreign housing exclusion. For more information, see IRS Publication 54, *Tax Guide for U.S. Citizens and Resident Aliens Abroad.*

The annual foreign tax credit is limited to the portion of your U.S. income tax attributable to your foreign income. This is equal to the *lesser* of:

- the amount of foreign income taxes paid, or
- an overall limitation based on an IRS formula.

Here's the formula:

$$\frac{\text{Foreign-source taxable income}}{\text{Worldwide taxable income}} \times \text{U.S. tax before foreign tax credit} = \text{Overall limit on credit}$$

It's easy to figure out. First, you divide your foreign income by your worldwide taxable income (foreign and U.S. taxable income, not including the amount of your U.S. personal and dependency exemptions). You then multiply this total by the amount of your U.S. income taxes before deducting any foreign tax credits. The total is the overall annual limitation on the credit.

> **EXAMPLE:** Andy, a geologist, earned $10,000 working in a foreign country during part of the year. His U.S. taxable income, not counting his personal and dependency exemptions, is $100,000. Thus, his worldwide taxable income is $110,000. His U.S income tax before taking any foreign tax credit is $20,000. He figures the limitation on his foreign tax credit as follows:
>
> $$\frac{\$10,000}{\$110,000} \times \$20,000 = \$1,818.$$
>
> The overall limitation on Andy's foreign tax credit is $1,818. He paid $3,000 in income taxes in the foreign country. Because the overall limitation is less than the foreign tax he paid, his credit is limited to $1,818, leaving $1,182 in foreign taxes he can't deduct that year ($3,000 − 1,818 = 1,182). He can take a credit for this amount during next five years, or he can use it to reduce his taxes for the prior two years by amending his tax returns for those years and claiming a refund. The credits he can take for these future or past years are subject to the same limitations as for the current year.

You may also qualify for a foreign tax credit if you own mutual funds that invest in foreign securities. But you may do this only if the fund elects to pass the credit for taxes paid to foreign governments on to its shareholders. If it does, your proportionate share of the foreign taxes paid by your fund will be shown in Box 6 of IRS Form 1099-DIV, *Dividends and Distributions*, the form the fund sends you and the IRS at the beginning of each year to report your annual dividends and other distributions for the prior year.

Instead of taking a credit for foreign income taxes, you can deduct them as an itemized deduction on your Schedule A. However, it is almost always better to take the credit instead. This is so, even though the itemized deduction is not subject to the dollar limitations for tax credits discussed above. Only in unusual cases will an itemized deduction for foreign taxes exceed the value of the foreign tax credit.

For more information, see IRS Publication 514, *Foreign Tax Credit for Individuals*

Credit to Rehabilitate an Old or Historic Building

The rehabilitation tax credit helps defray part of the cost of rehabilitating old buildings. It is intended to help preserve historic buildings and encourage businesses to stay in older, economically disadvantaged areas, such as many inner cities.

There are actually two different rehabilitation tax credits:
- a credit equal to 10% of part of the cost of rehabilitating non-historic buildings built before 1936 that are used for nonresidential commercial purposes, and
- a 20% credit of part of the cost for the rehabilitation of any certified historic structure—one listed on the National Register of Historic Places or located in a Registered Historic District and determined to be of significance to the historical district.

If the building is located in the area damaged by Hurricane Katrina and part of the Gulf Opportunity Zone, these credits are increased to 13% and 26% respectively until the end of 2008.

The two credits are mutually exclusive. Only one applies to a given project. Which credit applies depends on the building—not on the owner's preference.

The 20% credit can be obtained for commercial, industrial, agricultural, and residential rental buildings, but it is not available for property used exclusively as the owner's private residence. To get the 20% credit, the Secretary of the Interior must certify to the Secretary of the Treasury that the project meets their standards and is a "Certified Rehabilitation." You obtain this by filing a three-part application with the National Park Service. If your building is not already registered as historic, but you think it should be, you can nominate it for historical status by contacting your state historical officer.

No historic certification is needed to obtain the 10% credit. However, the building must be *depreciable*. That is, it must be used in a trade or business or held for the production of income. It may be used for offices, for commercial, industrial or agricultural enterprises, or for rental housing. It may not serve exclusively as the owner's private residence. Hotels qualify because they are considered to be in commercial use, not residential.

How Much Work Must You Do?

Before you start looking to buy an old building, keep in mind that to get either credit, your rehabilitation efforts must be substantial. Cosmetic improvements won't do. Your rehabilitation expenditures must *exceed* the greater of $5,000 or the adjusted basis of the building and its structural components. The adjusted basis is generally the purchase price, minus the cost of land, plus improvements already made, minus depreciation already taken.

Real estate pros call such extensive rehabilitation projects "gut rehabs." To spend this much money on a rehab, you'll usually have to purchase a building that is more or less a shell and restore it—a very substantial undertaking.

Collecting the Credit

You won't get the credit until the year the building is placed in service— that is, returned to use.

> **EXAMPLE:** In 2006, Beverly purchased a nonhistoric residential hotel built in 1930 for $100,000. The building's adjusted basis is $80,000. Beverly spends $90,000 in 2006 to restore the hotel and returns it to service in 2007. She'll get a $9,000 credit in 2007 (10% x $90,000 = $9,000).

To keep the full credit, you must hold the building for five full years after completing the rehabilitation. If you dispose of the building within a year after it is placed in service, 100% of the credit must be paid back. For properties held between one and five years, the amount to be paid back is reduced by 20% per year.

The following websites provide detailed information on the rehabilitation tax credit:

- National Trust for Historic Preservation at www.nationaltrust.org,
- National Park Service Heritage Preservation at www2.cr.nps.gov/tps/tax/index.htm.

Benefit From Investing in Low-Income Housing

Have you thought about making a real estate investment? If so, you may want to consider investing in low-income housing. Such investments can provide solid returns because of the generous federal tax credit for low-income housing.

The low-income housing credit was enacted by Congress to encourage new construction and rehabilitation of existing rental housing for low-income households. To spur investment, Congress authorized the states, within specified limits, to allocate tax credits to qualifying housing projects. The credit can be used to construct new or renovate existing rental buildings.

The Amount of the Credit

There are two tax credit rates: one for new construction and substantial rehabilitation projects that are not subsidized by the Federal government, and another lower rate for federally subsidized projects. Investors in unsubsidized projects get an annual tax credit of approximately 9% of project construction costs each year for ten years. Investors in subsidized projects receive up to a 4% credit for ten years.

There is no income limit on the credit and you can invest any amount. However, the credit for individuals cannot exceed an annual ceiling—generally the amount of tax you would owe on $25,000. For example, if your top tax bracket is 28%, the annual ceiling is $7,000.

In addition, to keep the full credit, you must invest in the property for at least 15 years. If you don't, you must pay back to the IRS part of the credits you received.

How You Get the Credit

To obtain the credit, you must invest in a low-income housing project that meets state and federal requirements and is chosen to participate in the low-income housing credit program. Typically, rents are restricted to 30% of the residents' annual incomes, and the tenants' incomes must be below the area's average.

Individual investors can get the credit by buying into limited partnerships or limited liability companies that are put together by syndicators to invest in low-income housing. These partnership or LLC interests can be purchased through brokers and financial planners. You may be able to buy in for as little as $5,000.

The investment is made at the beginning of the construction period, which may take a year or more, while the tax credits are paid only when the project is completed and the housing units rented. In order to attract investors, the amount you are required to invest to buy into the limited partnership or LLC is ordinarily less than the total value of the tax credits.

The low-income housing credit program is funded by the federal government, but operated by state tax credit allocation agencies. These state agencies choose which projects in their states receive the credit. Each state has only so many credits to hand out, based on its population. If you want more information, contact your state tax credit allocation agency. You can find a list at www.novoco.com/stcaa.shtml. Useful information can also be obtained from the National Housing & Rehabilitation Association website at www.housingonline.com.

Low-income housing projects are complex, long-term investments with risk. For example, a project could end up losing money if it fails to meet all the requirements for the credit or has trouble attracting tenants. Seek competent advice before making any investment in a low-income housing project.

Delaying the Pain: Deferring Income and the Tax It Brings

A basic tax-saving strategy is to put off paying taxes on your income for as long as possible. Deferring a tax on this year's income to a future year is like getting a free loan from the government. Just consider: If you pay $1,000 of tax today, it costs you $1,000. But if you postpone paying the $1,000 for five years, you can take that $1,000 and put it in the bank. In five years, it will be worth $1,200. You can pay the $1,000 tax with it and end up $200 ahead.

You need to exercise caution with this strategy though, because it won't always work to your advantage. If you defer paying your taxes and end up in a higher tax bracket when you pay, you may be worse off than you would have been if you had paid your taxes earlier when your tax rate was lower. Deferring payment works best if your top tax rate when you pay is almost the same as or is lower than it was at the time you deferred—something that can be difficult (at best) to predict.

There are various ways you can defer paying taxes you owe now to a future year. Some permit you to defer payment for only a year or two; others can allow you to defer payment for decades. Some of these strategies are extremely simple. Others are complex and can only be done with professional help. We'll look at the more common ones and also discuss ways to deal with the uncertainty of what tax bracket you'll be in when you do pay your taxes.

Everybody's Deferral Tool: Retirement Accounts

The most commonly used method to defer income tax is to contribute to a retirement account, such as an IRA, 401(k), or both. This is something anyone can do whether self-employed, retired, or an employee of a company. While plans and options differ, most offer you two types of tax deferral opportunities:

- You defer paying tax on the amount you (and/or your employer) contribute to the account.
- You defer paying income tax on the money your account earns until you withdraw the money (but withdrawals before age 59½ may be subject to tax penalties).

You defer tax on your retirement contributions because you can deduct the amount you contribute to a retirement account from your income taxes for the year (except for Roth IRAs, Roth 401(k)s, and nondeductible traditional IRAs). You have to pay income tax on the money when you withdraw it upon retirement, but this may be many years—even decades—into the future.

> **EXAMPLE:** Art and Agnes, a married couple who file jointly, contribute $8,000 this year to their traditional IRA. They deduct the entire amount from their personal income taxes for the year—that is, they deduct $8,000 from their gross income. Because they are in the 28% tax bracket, they save $2,240 in income taxes for the year (28% x $8,000), and they have also saved $8,000 toward retirement. They won't have to pay any income tax on their $8,000 contribution until they start withdrawing the money from their IRA.

The second type of tax deferral is for the income your retirement investments earn. When you earn money on an investment, you usually pay taxes on those earnings in the same year that you earn the money. For example, you must pay taxes on the interest you earn on a savings account or certificate of deposit in the year when the interest accrues. And when you sell an investment at a profit, you must pay income tax in that year on the gain you receive. For example, you must pay tax on the profit you earn from selling stock in the year that you sell it.

A different rule applies, however, for earnings you receive from a retirement account. You do not pay taxes on investment earnings from retirement accounts until you withdraw the funds. Over time, the money in a tax-deferred retirement account will grow much more quickly than the same amount of money in a taxable account because no money has to be taken out to pay taxes.

> **EXAMPLE:** Bill and Brian both invest in the same mutual fund. Bill has a taxable individual account, while Brian invests through a tax-deferred retirement account. They each invest $5,000 per year. They earn 8% on their investments each year and pay income tax at the 28% rate. At the end of 30 years, Brian has $566,416 and Bill has $272,869. Reason: Bill had to pay income taxes on the interest his investments earned each year, while Brian's interest accrued tax-free because he invested through a retirement account.

The following chart compares the annual growth of a tax-deferred retirement account and a taxable account. You can use the online calculator at http://www.ingfunds.com/v2/investor/content/resources/calculators to do your own comparisons between deferred and non-tax-deferred accounts for different time periods, amounts, and tax rates.

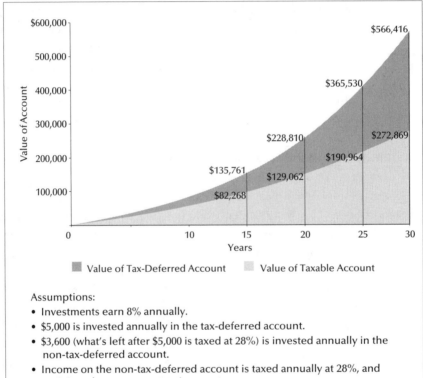

Assumptions:
- Investments earn 8% annually.
- $5,000 is invested annually in the tax-deferred account.
- $3,600 (what's left after $5,000 is taxed at 28%) is invested annually in the non-tax-deferred account.
- Income on the non-tax-deferred account is taxed annually at 28%, and recipient does not pay state income tax.

Of course, eventually you will have to pay income tax on the money in a retirement account—you have to make taxable withdrawals sooner or later. But, hopefully, this won't occur until you retire. For many people, their income tax rate at retirement is lower than the rate they were paying when they were making the contributions during their working years. If you're one of these people, you'll come out well ahead. You'll also be better off if your retirement tax rate is the same as when you worked.

However, it's possible that your tax rate will be higher when you retire than it is now. In historic terms, federal income taxes are quite low right now. The tax rates on dividends and long-term capital gains taxes are particularly low. (This is the tax on profits from sales of capital assets, like stocks and other securities, which you own for more than one year.) The top 15% tax rate on long-term capital gains is the lowest rate for capital gains since 1933. The 15% tax on dividends is the lowest since 1916. (See Chapter 6 for a detailed discussion of capital gains taxes.) You can't take advantage of these low rates when you place stock, mutual funds, or other capital assets in a retirement account—all your withdrawals are taxed at ordinary income rates (see "Which Investments Belong in Retirement Accounts?," below).

Many people believe taxes will have to be raised in the future to pay for the federal deficit, as well as Social Security and Medicare costs for the hordes of retiring baby boomers. Indeed, income tax rates are scheduled to increase in 2011 if the Bush tax cuts aren't extended—the maximum income tax rate will rise from 35% to 39.6%. If the top income tax rate you end up paying upon retirement is higher than your current rate, you might be better off keeping your money in a taxable account and paying tax on it today. Of course, this depends on how long you save your money, and if, when, and by how much, taxes are raised.

EXAMPLE: Jane puts $1,000 in a tax-deferred retirement account that earns 8% per year. At the end of 20 years, she would have $4,661 in the account. When she withdraws the money, she'll have to pay tax on it at her current tax rate. If, 20 years from now, her tax rate is 35%, she'd have to pay $1,631 in taxes if she withdraw all the money. That would leave her with $3,030. In contrast, if her top tax rate today is 25% and she put $1,000 in a taxable account that also earns 8%, she'd have to pay a 25% tax on her contribution and then pay income tax every year on her earnings at her applicable tax rate. Let's say Jane's top rate stays at 25% for ten years, then goes up to 35% because Congress raises income taxes to pay for the deficit. At the end of 20 years, she'd have $3,451—14% more than in the tax-deferred account. She can withdraw any or all of that money tax-free because she already paid taxes on it. The result could be even worse for a tax-deferred account if the time frame was shorter. If Jane left the money in the account for 10 years instead of 20, and her tax rate went up to 35% after five years, she'd have $2,159 in the tax-deferred account and $2,626 in the taxable account. After 10 years, the taxable account would be worth 22% more than the tax-deferred account.

Unfortunately, no one can predict the future, particularly where taxes are concerned. For most people, then, the best advice is to hedge your bets about future tax rates. By all means, contribute to tax-deferred retirement plans like a 401(k), especially if your employer will make a matching contribution—this is like found money, so you should always put enough money in to get the maximum employer match.

However, don't put all your savings in tax-deferred plans (which many people are now doing). Instead, keep some money in taxable accounts whose earnings will be taxed at your current tax rates. It's a particularly good idea right now to keep capital assets like stocks and mutual funds in taxable accounts because of the low capital gains tax rates. Also, take advantage of Roth IRAs and, if available, Roth 401(k)s. You don't get to deduct your contributions to these accounts, but you pay no taxes at all on withdrawals.

How much money should you keep in taxable versus tax-deferred accounts? Some investment advisors recommend a 50-50 split. However, this is an individual decision no book can make for you.

EXAMPLE: Eva and Eddie are a young married couple who file jointly. Eva works for Acme, Inc., and participates in its 401(k) plan. Eddie is self-employed and has no retirement plan. This year together they earned $100,000 and want to save $10,000 toward their retirement. How should they invest it? Acme, Inc., will match up to $5,000 of Eva's contributions to her 401(k), so she should put that much in her account. That leaves $5,000. Eddie should obtain a Roth IRA and contribute the $4,000 maximum. This leaves $1,000 which the couple put in taxable accounts consisting of stocks and municipal bonds

For additional information on the tax aspects of retirement, see:

- *IRAs, 401(k)s & Other Retirement Plans: Taking Your Money Out*, by Twila Slesnick and John C. Suttle (Nolo)
- IRS Publication 560, *Retirement Plans for the Small Business*, and

- IRS Publication 590, *Individual Retirement Arrangements*.

You also find excellent discussions of both the tax and investment aspects of retirement at the websites maintained by major mutual fund companies such as the Vanguard Group (www.vanguard.com) and Fidelity Investments (www.fidelity.com).

Which Investments Belong in Retirement Accounts?

If you have a retirement account other than a traditional lifetime employee pension, you'll have to decide how your money will be invested. (Remember, your investment options with an employer 401(k) plan may be quite limited.)

Here is a basic rule to follow: Keep investments subject to high taxes in a tax-deferred retirement account so you can defer the tax as long as possible. Keep investments subject to low taxes or no tax at all in taxable accounts. The following chart gives some examples:

Investments to Be Held in Tax-deferred Retirement Accounts	Investments to Be Held in Taxable Accounts
Corporate bonds	Municipal bonds
Certificates of deposit	Growth stocks
Treasury bills and notes	Dividend-paying stocks
Real estate investment trust (REIT) shares	U.S. savings bonds
	Tax-managed mutual funds
	Index funds
	Tax-deferred annuities

There are thousands of websites, hundreds of books, and several magazines about retirement investing. Two easy-to-understand guides on retirement investing are:

- *Get a Life: You Don't Need a Million to Retire Well*, by Ralph Warner (Nolo), and
- *Investing for Dummies*, by Eric Tyson (Wiley).

Retirement Accounts for Everybody—IRAs

The simplest type of tax-deferred retirement account is the individual retirement account, or IRA. An IRA is a retirement account established by an individual, not an employer or business. There are two different types: traditional IRAs and Roth IRAs.

You can have an IRA whether you're a business owner or an employee in someone else's business. Moreover, you can have an IRA even if you have other types of retirement plans. However, there are limitations on your deductions for, or contributions to, IRAs if you have other retirement plans and your income exceeds certain limits.

An IRA is a trust or custodial account set up for the benefit of an individual or his or her beneficiaries. The trustee or custodian administers the account. The trustee can be a bank, mutual fund, brokerage firm, or other financial institution (such as an insurance company).

IRAs are extremely easy to set up and administer. You need a written IRA agreement but don't need to file any tax forms with the IRS. Most financial institutions offer an array of IRA accounts that provide for different types of investments. You can invest your IRA money in just about anything: stocks, bonds, mutual funds, treasury bills and notes, and bank certificates of deposit. However, you can't invest in collectibles such as art, antiques, stamps, or other personal property.

You can establish as many IRA accounts as you want—both traditional and Roth IRAs—but there is a maximum combined amount of money you can contribute to all of your IRA accounts each year. This amount goes up every year through 2008 as shown in the chart below. After 2008, the limit will be adjusted each year for inflation in $500 increments.

Anyone at least 50 years old at the end of the year can make increased annual contributions of $500 per year in 2005, and $1,000 per year thereafter. This rule is intended to allow older people to catch up with younger folks, who will have more years to make contributions at the higher levels.

Annual IRA Contribution Limits		
Tax Year	Under Age 50	Age 50 or Over
2006–2007	$4,000	$5,000
2008 and later	$5,000	$6,000

If you are married, you can double the contribution limits. For example, a married couple in 2007 can contribute up to $4,000 per spouse into their IRAs, for a total of $8,000. (If they are 50 or older, they can contribute $5,000 each, for a total of $10,000.) This is true even if one spouse isn't working. To take advantage of doubling, you must file a joint tax return, and the working spouse must earn at least as much as the combined IRA contribution.

Traditional IRAs. Traditional IRAs have been around since 1974. Anybody who has earned income (income from a job, business, or alimony) can have a traditional IRA. As stated above, you can deduct your annual contributions to your IRA from your taxable income. If neither you nor your spouse (if you have one) has another retirement plan, you may deduct your contributions no matter how high your income is.

However, there are income limits on your deductions if you (or your spouse, if you have one) are covered by another retirement plan. For these purposes, being covered by another plan means your employer provides you with a qualified retirement plan, or you're self-employed and have one of the self-employed plans described in "Retirement Accounts for Business Owners," below.

If you're a single taxpayer with a retirement plan, your deductions start to phase out when your modified adjusted gross income exceeds $50,000. Once your modified adjusted gross income exceeds $60,000, you get no deduction at all. Your modified adjusted gross income is your adjusted gross income before it is reduced by your IRA contribution and certain other more unusual items.

Things are bit more complicated if you're married and file your taxes jointly, because each spouse's IRA contribution is separate. The phaseout income levels are shown in the following chart. The dollar figures represent a married couple's joint modified AGI.

IRA Deduction Phaseouts for Married Couples Filing Jointly				
	IRA Deduction Phaseout for You		IRA Deduction Phase-out for Your Spouse	
	2006	2007	2006	2007
You and your spouse are covered by retirement plans	$75,000 to $85,000	$80,000 to $100,000	$75,000 to $85,000	$80,000 to $100,000
You are covered by a retirement plan, but your spouse is not	$75,000 to $85,000	$80,000 to $100,000	$150,000 to $160,000	$150,000 to $160,000
You are not covered by a retirement plan, but your spouse is	$150,000 to $160,000	$150,000 to $160,000	$75,000 to $85,000	$80,000 to $100,000

Thus, for example, if you're married and filing jointly and you are covered by a retirement plan at work, but your spouse has no plan, your IRA deduction is phased out if your joint AGI is between $80,000 and $100,000. You get no deduction at all if your AGI is over $100,000. However, as a couple, you can fully deduct your spouse's IRA contribution as long as your AGI is below $150,000. But your spouse gets no deduction at all if your AGI is over $160,000.

If your income is in the phaseout range, you can use an online calculator at www.choosetosave.org/calculators to determine how much you may deduct.

By the way, if you're married and you and your spouse file separate tax returns, you get no IRA deduction if you or your spouse is covered by a retirement plan and your separate income is over $10,000. This is one reason why most married couples file joint tax returns.

You can still contribute to an IRA even if you can't take a deduction. This is called a nondeductible IRA. Your money will grow in the account tax free; and, when you make withdrawals, you'll only have to pay tax on your account earnings, not the amount of your contributions (which have already been taxed). However, figuring out how much is taxable and how much is tax free can be a big accounting headache.

You may not make any more contributions to a traditional IRA after you reach age 70½. Moreover, you'll have to start making distributions from the account after you reach that age (see "You must start withdrawing by 70½." below).

If your income is modest, you may qualify for a tax credit if you make an IRA contribution. The credit is in addition to any tax deduction you're entitled to (see Chapter 3).

Roth IRAs. Like traditional IRAs, Roth IRAs are tax deferred and allow your retirement savings to grow without any tax burden. Unlike traditional IRAs, however, your contributions to Roth IRAs are not tax deductible. In return for giving up an immediate tax deduction, you get to withdraw your money from the account tax free when you retire. Thus, you pay no taxes at all on your Roth IRA earnings.

> **EXAMPLE:** Felix opens a Roth IRA with a local bank and contributes $4,000 per year for ten years. He cannot deduct any of his contributions from his taxable income. By the time he's 60, Felix's Roth IRA has grown to $100,000. He pays absolutely no tax on his withdrawals from the account—he ends up getting his $60,000 in account earnings tax free.

You aren't required to ever withdraw any money from a Roth IRA (unlike traditional IRAs, see below). If you leave your money in your Roth IRA when you die, your heirs will inherit it tax free.

You can combine a Roth IRA with other retirement plans. But, once your income reaches a certain level, you won't be allowed to make any more contributions. If you are single and your modified adjusted gross income reaches $95,000, your ability to contribute to your Roth IRA will begin to phase out. Once your income reaches $110,000, you will no longer be able to make contributions. If you are married and file a joint return with your spouse, your ability to contribute to your account will start to phase out when your modified adjusted gross income reaches $150,000, and you will be prohibited from making any contributions at all when your income reaches $160,000. (But these limits do not apply to conversions of money from traditional IRAs to Roth IRAs; see "Roth IRA Conversions," below.) You can use the following calculator to determine how much you may contribute: www.moneychimp.com/articles/rothira/contribution_limits.htm.

Is the Roth IRA a good deal? If your tax rate when you retire is higher than your tax rate before retirement, you'll probably be better off with a Roth IRA than a traditional IRA because you won't have to pay tax on your withdrawals at the higher rates. The opposite is true if your taxes go down when you retire. The catch is that nobody can know for sure what their tax rate will be when they retire.

Establishing a Roth IRA and even transferring money into it from a traditional IRA (see "Roth IRA Conversions," below) can be a good way to hedge your bets about future tax rates and avoid deferring too much (as described at the start of this section). Roth IRAs make the most sense for younger people who have many years until retirement. The long timeframe means there is more time for the money in their Roth to grow enough to make up for the taxes they had to pay up front on their contributions.

You can find several online calculators that will help you compare your results with a Roth IRA versus traditional IRA at www.choosetosave.org/calculators.

Much more information on Roth IRAs can be found at www. rothira.com. Also, refer to IRS Publication 590, *Individual Retirement Arrangements.*

Retirement Plans for Employees

Employers aren't required to provide their employees with any retirement benefits, and many don't. Only about half of all private sector workers have pension plans. Larger companies usually provide some type of pension benefit, but small companies often don't.

401(k) plans. Today, the most commonly offered retirement plan for employees is the 401(k) plan. Employers are opting for 401(k) plans because they are much cheaper for them than traditional lifetime pensions (see "Traditional lifetime pensions," below).

With a 401(k) plan, each employee gets his or her own investment account. The employee may contribute a portion of his or her salary,

Roth IRA Conversions

If the Roth IRA sounds attractive to you and you have other tax-qualified retirement accounts, you may be able to convert them to a Roth IRA. In the past, you could only convert a traditional IRA to a Roth IRA. This meant that if you wanted to do a Roth IRA conversion, you would first have to place the funds in a traditional IRA and then convert to a Roth IRA. Starting in 2008, you'll be able to directly roll over funds from qualified retirement plans, such as 401(k)s, to a Roth IRA.

Until the year 2010, you may do such a conversion only if your modified AGI is under $100,000. Starting in 2010, anyone will be allowed convert to a Roth IRA, no matter what their income.

However, when you convert to a Roth from a traditional IRA or tax-qualified retirement plan, you'll have to pay income tax on the amount of the conversion. For example, if you convert $20,000 from your traditional IRA to a Roth IRA, you'll have to add $20,000 to your taxable income for the year. If you were in the 25% bracket, this would add $5,000 to your income taxes. (If you convert in 2010, you can pay the tax over two years instead of one.) One way to keep these taxes down is to convert only a portion of your traditional IRA or tax-qualified retirement plan into a Roth each year for several years instead of doing it all at once.

Whether a Roth conversion is a good idea or not depends on many factors including your age, your current tax rate, and your tax rate upon retirement. You can find an online calculator http://dinkytown.com/java/RothTransfer.html that allows you to compare the results when you convert to a Roth IRA.

up to an annual limit into the account. This is called a salary deferral or elective deferral (because it's voluntary). The money is deducted directly from your pay by your employer; you don't have to write a check. These contributions consist of pretax dollars—meaning money upon which you have paid no income tax.

In 2006, you could contribute up to $15,000 of your salary to your 401(k). Employees 50 years of age or over could elect to make an additional catch-up contribution of $5,000. These figures are adjusted for inflation each year. However, employers are permitted to place percentage caps on their employees' contributions, and many do. Employer's frequently limit contributions to 10% to 15% of employee salary.

Often, the employer will match all or part of the employee's contribution with its own money, although this is not required. Matching contributions vary from employer to employer. Some employers contribute 50 cents for every dollar their employees contribute; others contribute dollar for dollar or even more, up to a certain percentage of the employee's income—6% is a commonly used percentage. These matching contributions are not taxable income for the employee—they are a tax-free employee fringe benefit.

There is an outside limit on the total amount that can be contributed to an employee's 401(k) each year. For 2006, the maximum is the lesser of 100% of employee compensation or $44,000. (But catch-up contributions by employees over 50 are not counted toward the limit.)

Each employee owns and controls his or her own 401(k) account. It is not managed by the employer. The employee decides how much to contribute each year and chooses among the investments offered by the plan. Employees don't have to contribute any money to their 401(k) plan if they don't want to. About 20% of employees whose companies have 401(k)s contribute nothing.

A 401(k) is all about tax deferral. As described above, you pay no tax on the money you and your employer contribute to your 401(k) account each year. And the money in your account grows tax free. You don't pay any taxes on it until you withdraw it (there are restrictions on withdrawals, however, as described below in "Restrictions on Withdrawals From Retirement Accounts").

EXAMPLE: Mark, a 40-year-old single man employed by Acme, Inc., earns $100,000 per year. Acme permits its employees to contribute up to 15% of their annual salary to the Acme 401(k) plan and makes a matching dollar-for-dollar contribution of up to 6% of the employee's salary. Mark contributes the maximum to his 401k)— $15,000, and Acme makes a $6,000 matching contribution. Mark's $15,000 contribution is tax deferred—that is, he pays no tax on it until he withdraws money from his 401(k). Thus, this year he only has to pay income tax on $85,000 of his total $100,000 salary. He also has $21,000 more in his 401(k) account, which will grow tax free until he withdraws it.

Roth 401(k) plans. In 2006, a brand new type of 401(k) plan became available: the Roth 401(k). Roth 401(k)s are much the same as regular 401(k)s with one big difference: The money contributed to the plan is not tax deductible. In return, withdrawals made after age 59½ are tax free. This is the same type of tax treatment you get with a Roth IRA. Only the elective deferral portion of your annual 401(k) contribution receives the Roth treatment. This limits your 2006 contribution to $15,000 per year, or $20,000 if you're over 50 (see "401(k) plans", above). Not all companies with 401(k) plans offer Roth 401(k)s, but more and more are doing so.

The pros and cons for Roth 401(k)s are much the same as for Roth IRAs (see "Roth IRAs," above).

Other employer plans. Other retirement plans that employers may offer their employees include the SEP-IRAs, SIMPLE IRAs, and Keogh Plans described in "Retirement Accounts for Business Owners," below. If you work for an educational or religious institution, or a nonprofit organization, you may have a choice between a 401(k) and a 403(b) or 457 plan (see IRS Publication 571, *Tax-Sheltered Annuity Plans*).

Traditional lifetime pensions. Remember the lifetime employee pension? Well, these traditional pensions are going the way of the dodo bird. Fewer and fewer companies offer them and many that do are freezing their plans and switching to 401(k) plans. As a result, today, twice as many workers have 401(k)s as have lifetime pensions.

The traditional pension plan works like this: You work for the same company for several years and when you retire the company pays you a monthly pension for the rest of your life. The pension amount is based on your years of services and final salary. Long-term employees often receive 30% to 50% of their final salary, some even more.

Traditional pensions have nothing to do with tax deferral because they are paid for and managed by your employer, not you. All you have to do is collect your benefits when you retire. However, even if you have a traditional pension, you should think seriously about setting up an IRA and contributing your own money, which will defer taxes. The more sources of retirement income you have when you retire, the better off you'll be.

Why contribute your own money for retirement if you have a pension? Because your pension might not be there when you retire. More than 18,000 companies have underfunded their pension plans—in other words, their plans don't have the money to pay all the benefits their employees have been promised. The federal government insures private pensions; but if yours is underfunded, you may only get a portion of your promised benefits. Thus, it's unwise to rely on a traditional pension as your only source of retirement income other than Social Security.

Retirement Accounts for Business Owners

If you're self-employed or own a business, you don't have an employer to establish a retirement plan for you. You must do it yourself. There are several different retirement accounts for business owners that allow you to defer income tax on both your contributions and earnings. You can set up one or more of these plans, even if you only have a sideline or part-time business.

SEP-IRA. A SEP-IRA is very similar to an IRA—each participant has his or her own SEP-IRA account that he or she owns and controls. However, contributions to the account are made by your business, not by you personally. Far more money can be contributed each year to a SEP-IRA than to an individual IRA. If your business isn't incorporated, you may contribute 20% of your net profit from self-employment up to an annual limit ($44,000 in 2006). If your business is incorporated and you work as its employee, you may invest up to 25% of your compensation every year, up to the annual limit.

SEP-IRAs are easy and cheap to establish and administer, and the contribution limits are generous. However, if you have employees, establishing a SEP-IRA can be expensive because you must establish a SEP-IRA account for all employees who are at least 21 years old and have been employed by you for three of the last five years. Consult with a professional before setting up a SEP-IRA if you have employees.

SIMPLE IRA. Self-employed people and companies with fewer than 100 employees can set up SIMPLE IRAs. If you establish a SIMPLE IRA, you are not allowed to have any other retirement plans for your business (although you may still have an individual IRA). The money in a SIMPLE IRA can be invested like any other IRA.

You don't have to contribute to your SIMPLE IRA every year, and you can change the amount you contribute each year. Contributions to SIMPLE IRAs are divided into two parts: (1) a salary reduction contribution that is based on your net business income if you are a business owner, and on your employee salary if you are an employee of an incorporated business, and (2) an employer contribution. The salary reduction contribution can be up to $10,000 each year ($12,500 if you're over 50), as long as this amount is not more than 100% of your net earnings. The employer contribution can match the salary reduction contribution provided it doesn't exceed 3% of your net business income (or 3% of salary for employees).

The limits on contributions to SIMPLE IRAs might seem very low, but they could work to your advantage if you earn a small income from your business—for example, if you only work at it part-time. This is because you can contribute an amount equal to 100% of your earnings, up to the $10,000 or $12,500 limits. Thus, for example, if your net earnings are only $10,000, you could contribute the entire amount (plus a 3% employer contribution). You can't do this with any of the other plans because their percentage limits are much lower. For example, you may contribute only 20% of your net self-employment income to a SEP-IRA or Keogh, so you would be limited to a $2,000 contribution if you had a $10,000 profit.

As with SEP-IRAs, if you have employees, you'll have to include them in your SIMPLE IRA. SIMPLE IRAs must be offered to all employees who have earned income of at least $5,000 in any prior two years and are expected to earn at least $5,000 in the current year. You must match your employees' contributions dollar for dollar up to 3% of compensation or contribute 2% of each employee's salary.

Keogh plans. Keogh plans are qualified plans designed for business owners who are sole proprietors, partners in partnerships, or LLC members.

As with IRAs, you can set up a Keogh plan at most banks, brokerage houses, mutual funds, and other financial institutions, as well as with trade or professional organizations. You can also choose among a huge array of investments for your money. If you don't have employees, you can set up a Keogh plan yourself. If you have employees, consult a pension professional.

Most Keoghs are profit-sharing plans into which you can contribute up to 20% of your net self-employment income, up to a maximum of $44,000 per year (in 2006). Employees can contribute up to 25% of their salaries, in any amount up to the limit or they can decide not to contribute at all.

As is the case with SEP-IRAs and SIMPLE IRAs, Keogh plans can be expensive if you have employees. All employees over 21 must be allowed to participate if they have two years of service, or one year if the plan has a vesting schedule.

Solo 401(k) plans. Until recently, self-employed people and businesses without employees rarely used 401(k) plans, because they offered no benefit over other profit-sharing plans that are easier to set up and run. However, things have changed. Now, business owners can establish solo self-employed 401(k) plans (also called one-person or individual 401(k)s). Solo 401(k)plans are designed specifically for business owners without employees. They can also be used by professionals with one-person corporations.

Like all 401(k)s, solo 401(k) contributions consist of two separate elements:

- a profit-sharing contribution of up to 20% of your net profit from self-employment , plus
- a salary deferral contribution of up to $15,000 (in 2006).

The maximum total contribution per year is $44,000 (in 2006). However, business owners over 50 may make additional catch-up elective deferral contributions of up to $5,000 per year that are not counted towards the $44,000 limit. If your business is incorporated, you may contribute 25% of your employee compensation plus the elective deferral.

Solo 401(k)s permit you to contribute more money each year than any other plan if you have over $40,000 in net business income. Moreover, you can borrow money from a 401(k). However, you can't have any employees (other than your spouse), so it may not be a good fit if you are thinking of expanding your business in the near future.

However, if you already have a 401(k) plan with your employer, your contributions to a solo 401(k) will be limited. Your total salary deferral contributions to both plans cannot exceed the limit described above for a single plan—$15,000 in 2006. However, your profit-sharing contribution to your solo 401(k) is not limited because you have an employer 401(k).

Restrictions on Withdrawals From Retirement Accounts

The tax deferral benefits you receive by putting your money in a retirement account come at a price: You're not supposed to withdraw the money until you are 59½ years old and, after you turn 70½, you must withdraw a certain minimum amount each year and pay tax on it. Stiff penalties are imposed if you fail to follow these rules. So, if you aren't prepared to give up your right to use this money freely, you should think about a taxable account instead where there are no restrictions on your use of your money. You should also consider a Roth IRA or Roth 401(k)—you can withdraw your contributions to these accounts (but not earnings) at any time without penalty.

For detailed guidance on distributions from retirement accounts, refer to *IRAs, 401(k)s & Other Retirement Plans: Taking Your Money Out*, by Twila Slesnick and John C. Suttle (Nolo).

You must be at least 59½ years old to withdraw your money

The basic rule is that you are not allowed to distribute (withdraw) any money from an IRA, SEP-IRA, SIMPLE IRA, or tax-qualified retirement plan like a 401(k) or Keogh until you reach age 59½. Once you reach that age, you are free to withdraw as much or as little as you want from the account—at least until you reach age 70½. At age 70½, you are required to start making certain minimal withdrawals each year.

If you make a withdrawal before you are 59½, you must pay regular income tax on the amount you take out, plus a 10% federal tax penalty (unless an exception applies). Early distributions from SIMPLE IRAs are subject to a 25% tax penalty if the withdrawal is made within two years after the date you first contributed to your account.

There are some important exceptions to this early distribution penalty. Early distributions are permitted from all plans if you die or become disabled, or if you have to pay health expenses in excess of 7.5% of your adjusted gross income. In addition, employees 55 or older who leave their jobs may withdraw the funds from their former employer's retirement plan without penalty (this doesn't apply to IRAs). You may make penalty-free early distributions from a 401(k) for reasons of personal hardship (defined as an "immediate financial need" that can't be met any other way). Early distributions may also be made from retirement accounts no matter what your age if you take substantially equal periodic payments.

There are some additional exceptions for IRAs, SEP-IRAs, and SIMPLE IRAs. Penalty-free withdrawals are permitted within certain limits to pay for health insurance if you're unemployed, to buy your first home, or to pay for higher education expenses for yourself or a family member.

The rules differ for Roth IRAs and Roth 401(k)s. You can withdraw the money you contributed to these accounts penalty free anytime—you already paid tax on it so the government doesn't care. But the earnings on your investments in a Roth IRA or Roth 401(k) are a different matter. You can't withdraw these until after five years. Early withdrawals of your earnings are subject to income tax and early distribution penalties.

> **EXAMPLE:** Monica establishes a Roth IRA in 2005 and contributes $4,000. She contributes another $4,000 in 2006. By 2007, her account is worth $10,000—her $8,000 of contributions and $2,000

in interest the money in the account earned. Monica may withdraw her contributions at any time without penalty, so she may withdraw $8,000 in 2007 without paying any taxes. However, she must keep her earnings in the account for at least five years, which means she can't withdraw any of her $2,000 interest until 2010. If she withdraws any of the money early, she will have to pay income tax on it and a 10% penalty unless she has an acceptable excuse for the early withdrawal.

Borrowing Money From Your 401(k) or Other Employer Plan

If you need money and have a 401(k) or other qualified employer retirement plan, instead of taking a taxable distribution, you may be able to borrow from your account. You can borrow either $10,000 or up to 50% of your vested plan benefits, whichever is greater. But all of your loans cannot total more than $50,000 (you may be permitted to borrow more to purchase a home). You must pay a reasonable interest rate on the loan and pay it back within five years (the time can be longer for secured loans used to purchase a home). The borrowed funds are not income, because you must pay the money back. The interest you pay goes into your retirement account where it grows tax free. Not all employer plans permit loans; you should check to see if your does.

You must start withdrawing by age 70½

You may want to keep your money in your retirement account indefinitely since the longer you wait, the more tax deferral you get. However, just like the rules about early withdrawals before age 59½, there are rules about required withdrawals after age 70½. Once you are 70½ years old, you must begin to withdraw at least the IRS-specified minimum amount each year.

Most people use IRS tables to compute their minimum required distribution (MRD) each year. You can also use the following online calculator to determine your minimum distribution amount: www.

dinkytown.net/java/StretchIRA.html. The minimums go up each year as you get older. For example, if you're 71 and you have $100,000 in an IRA, you'd have to withdraw at least $3,775 that year. If you are 80, you'd have to withdraw $5,348 from a $100,000 account.

If you fail to distribute the minimum required amount for the year, you'll have to pay a 50% penalty on the shortfall. For example, if you are supposed to take a $10,000 distribution and you take only $5,000, you'll have to pay a 50% penalty tax on the $5,000 shortfall—a $2,500 penalty. This is one of the most onerous tax penalties there is.

Charitable Contributions From IRAs

Ordinarily, if you take money out of a traditional IRA and give it to charity, you must still include the amount of the IRA distribution as taxable income for the year. This means you must pay income tax on it. You can deduct your contribution if you itemize your deductions. If you take the standard deduction, you won't be able to deduct the contribution.

However, during 2006 and 2007, taxpayers over 70½ years old may make distributions from their traditional and Roth IRAs to charity without having to include the amount in income. Up to $100,000 may be contributed each year. The money must be transferred directly from the IRA to the charity. When this is done, you may not also take an itemized charitable deduction for the amount.

Why would you want to do this? One reason could be because you don't need to withdraw any money from your IRA for your personal needs, but you must still make a minimum required distribution. The distribution to charity can meet the minimum distribution requirement, but you won't have to pay tax on the amount.

EXAMPLE: Jean is 80 years old and has $100,000 in her IRA. She is required to withdraw at least $5,348 from her IRA in 2007 or incur a 50% penalty. She elects to withdraw $6,000 from the IRA and give it to her local United Way. She need not include the $6,000 IRA distribution in her income for the year and she has satisfied the minimum distribution requirement. She may not deduct the $6,000 as a charitable contribution.

Again, the rules differ for Roth IRAs and Roth 401(k)s: You are not required to make distributions from these accounts when you reach age 70½. Because Roth IRA and Roth 401(k) withdrawals are tax free, the IRS doesn't care if you leave your money in your account indefinitely.

Withdraw From Your Taxable Accounts First

Hopefully, when you retire you will have both taxable investment accounts and tax-deferred accounts such as IRAs and 401(k)s. As a general rule, when you start withdrawing money from these accounts you should take money from your taxable accounts first. Reason: The longer you leave your money in tax-deferred accounts, the more you'll benefit from tax-deferred compounding (see the chart at the beginning of this chapter). Roth IRAs and Roth 401(k)s should be the last accounts you withdraw money from because they benefit the most from tax-deferred compounding. Keep in mind, however, that the performance of your investments might call for you to break the general rule.

Paying income tax on your distributions

Whenever you take money out of one of the retirement accounts described above (except for Roth IRAs and Roth 401(k)s), you must pay income tax on your distribution at ordinary income rates. This is so even if all or part of your investment returns were from stocks or other capital assets. This is one of the biggest disadvantages of retirement accounts—you can't benefit from the lower capital gains rates when you sell capital assets held in these accounts.

EXAMPLE: Tommy, a self-employed consultant, establishes a solo 401(k) in 2006 and invests in stocks and mutual funds. By 2010, he has contributed a total of $100,000 to the account, which is worth $150,000 because of the appreciation of his investments. Tommy turns 59½ in 2010, and decides to withdraw $30,000 from his 401(k). He sells $30,000 worth of Acme, Inc., stock in his account and pockets the money. He must pay income tax on the $30,000 at ordinary income tax rates. With the addition of $30,000 to his income, Tommy's top tax rate jumps to 28%. Thus, he must pay $8,400 in federal income tax on the distribution. This is so even though he sold a capital asset—stock—to obtain the distribution. The 15% long-term capital gains rate does not apply to distributions from retirement accounts.

If your retirement account has noncash assets like stocks, bonds, and mutual funds, you don't have to take your distributions in cash. You may distribute noncash property to yourself instead. When you do this, you pay income tax at ordinary rates on the fair market value of the property.

EXAMPLE: Assume that Tommy from the above example distributes 1,000 shares of Acme, Inc., stock to himself, instead of selling it for cash. The shares were purchased for $20 each, but now have a fair market value of $30 per share. Tommy must pay income tax at ordinary rates on the stock's $30,000 fair market value. Tommy's tax basis in the stock is $30 per share. If he later sells the stock for $40 per share, he'll pay income tax only on his $10 per share profit. The tax will be paid at long-term capital gains rates if he keeps the stock for at least one year.

You may not claim any losses you incur on the investments in a retirement account. You simply pay income tax on your sadly diminished distributions.

EXAMPLE: Assume that Tommy's Acme, Inc., stock fell in value from $20 per share when purchased for his 401(k) to $10 in 2010. His 401(k) has lost $10,000 on the 1,000 shares. However, Tommy cannot deduct the loss. If he sells his 1,000 shares and distributes $10,000 to himself, he'll pay tax on the amount at ordinary income rates.

Hold on to Your Investments

Perhaps the simplest way to defer taxes is to purchase investments that produce little or no annual income and then hold on to them for as long as possible. You won't owe any tax on the investment itself until you sell it. Examples of such investments include stocks that issue few or no annual dividends, tax-managed mutual funds, index funds, and vacant land.

> **EXAMPLE:** Bugsy purchased a small vacant lot near the Las Vegas strip in 1980 for $1,000. Today, it's worth $100,000. As long as Bugsy doesn't sell the land, he doesn't have to pay any tax on his $99,000 profit. If he needs money, he can take out a loan using the land as collateral and still doesn't owe any tax.

If you hold on to the investment until you die, no tax will ever be due on the appreciation you earned while you were alive. This is because the basis of inherited property is ordinarily its fair market value on the date of the owner's death—often called stepped-up basis. This can result in enormous tax savings if the asset has appreciated in value since it was purchased.

> **EXAMPLE:** Bugsy is murdered by business rivals in 2007, and his vacant land is inherited by his daughter Annette. Annette's basis in the property automatically becomes equal to its fair market value when Bugsy died—$100,000. She quickly sells the property for $100,000. The sales price and her basis are the same so Annette doesn't owe any tax on the sale. The $99,000 increase in the property's value since Bugsy bought it goes untaxed.

This doesn't mean you should hang on to a losing investment just to defer taxes. Taxes are just one of the factors you should consider before deciding whether to keep an investment or get rid of it.

Changes in Tax Basis Rules Looming for 2010

Currently, there is no restriction on the amount of inherited property that can receive a stepped-up basis. However, this is scheduled to change in 2010. The heirs of anyone who dies in 2010 can only receive a stepped-up basis on inherited property worth a total of $1.3 million. (Surviving spouses receive a stepped-up basis of an additional $3 million worth of property.) All property above the limit will carry the same basis as it had for the deceased person. It is unclear whether this new rule will last beyond 2010, or if the old unrestricted stepped-up basis rule will return in 2011. Of course, this is something you need to worry about only if you have assets that have appreciated by more than $1.3 million since you bought them—a nice problem to have.

For a detailed discussion, refer to *Plan Your Estate*, by Denis Clifford and Cora Jordan (Nolo).

Happy New Year: Deferring Business Income to Next Year

If you're self-employed and are a cash method taxpayer (as most self-employed people are), you only have to pay tax on money you receive during the tax year—usually the calendar year. Thus, you can defer income by billing clients next year for work you've done this year. If this isn't practical, you could break down the payments due into installments and defer some of them until the following year. If clients or customers owe you money, don't press for payment until after the new year.

EXAMPLE: Bettina, a graphic designer, completes a project for Acme, Inc., in November 2006 for which she is owed $10,000. However, she doesn't bill Acme until the beginning of January 2007. This way, she won't have to report the $10,000 as income on her 2006 taxes. She's in the 25% federal income tax bracket, so this saves her $2,500 in federal income tax for 2006. She also saves another $1,340 in self-employment taxes, and $600 in state income tax. She will have to pay tax on the $10,000 in 2007, but in the meantime, she gets the use of the money.

There are rules that limit how you can defer business income. If you're a cash method taxpayer, payments are "constructively received" by you for tax purposes when an amount is credited to your account or otherwise made available to you without restriction. Constructive receipt is as good as actual receipt. If you authorize someone to be your agent and receive income for you, you are considered to have received it when your agent receives it.

EXAMPLE: Interest is credited to your business bank account in December 2006, but you do not withdraw it or enter it into your passbook until 2007. You must include the amount in gross business income for 2006, not 2007.

In addition, you cannot hold checks or other payments from one tax year to another to avoid paying tax on the income. You must report the income in the year the payment is received or made available to you without restriction.

EXAMPLE: On December 1, 2006, Helen receives a $5,000 check from a client. She holds the check and doesn't cash it until January 10, 2007. She must still report the $5,000 as income for 2006 because she constructively received it that year.

Whether you want to defer business income in any particular year depends upon your circumstances. If you expect your top bracket to be the same next year as this year, or lower, deferral is a good idea. But, if you expect your business income to go up substantially next year, you could be better off not deferring income to that year when you'll be in a higher tax bracket.

Deferring Employee Compensation: Benefits Served With a Little Risk

If you're an employee, deferring part of your salary or other compensation to a future year is another way to lower your taxes for the current year. For example, if you know you will be paid an annual bonus, you can ask your employer to defer paying it until January of the following year so you won't have to pay tax on it until that year. Many employers are willing to do this. If your company uses the accrual method of accounting, as most bigger companies do, it can probably deduct your bonus this year even if it doesn't actually pay it to you until the following year. You could also have your employer pay you your bonus over several years instead of one, and even pay interest on what it owes you.

For such income deferral to work, however, you must elect to have the income deferred *before the start of the calendar year in which it will be earned*—that is, by December 31 of the current year.

> **EXAMPLE:** Sid, a crack salesperson for Acme, Inc., gets a substantial bonus every year. He would like to have payment of his 2007 bonus deferred until 2008. He has until December 31, 2006, to ask Acme to defer the bonus. If he waits until 2007, he'll have to include the bonus in his 2007 income.

There is an important exception to the rule described above. An employee can elect to defer "performance-based compensation" as late as six months after the start of the year—in other words, June 30. Performance-based compensation can be a bonus or other compensation paid to an employee, but it must be tied to written preestablished criteria, such as meeting a certain sales goal over the next year. The services must be performed over at least 12 months.

There are many more sophisticated ways to defer employee compensation—for example:

- salary reduction arrangements in which your employer defers part of your salary to future years
- top-hat plans (also called supplemental executive retirement plans or SERPS) in which extra retirement benefits are provided to a select group of management or highly compensated employees, and

- excess benefit plans that provide benefits to selected employees beyond those allowed for tax-qualified plans.

Deferred compensation plans became subject to complex new tax rules in 2005. If you fail to follow these rules, you could owe tax on the deferred compensation plus a 20% penalty and interest. Your employer should be on top of these requirements and be able to explain them to you. If not, seek guidance from a tax professional.

⚠ **Deferring compensation can be risky.** If you end up in a higher tax bracket in the future when you receive the compensation, you will owe more taxes on the same amount of money than you would have if you took all your compensation sooner and paid taxes on it at a lower rate.

Also, if your company goes bankrupt, you could end up with little or nothing of what you're owed. Money held in a deferred compensation plan is usually a company asset subject to claims by the company's creditors in the event of bankruptcy. The way bankruptcy works, employees get paid after banks and secured creditors, so there may be nothing left to pay you.

Deferring an annual bonus can be a good move if you expect your top tax rate to be the same next year as this year. Deferring substantial amounts of compensation many years in the future through salary reduction arrangements or similar plans is ordinarily done only by highly paid employees and should be not be tried without the assistance of a professional advisor.

No Need to Ask: Automatic Interest Deferral on U.S. Savings Bonds

A simple way to defer income is to purchase U.S. savings bonds. You may defer payment of federal income taxes on the interest you earn on I Bonds or Series EE Savings Bonds until you redeem (cash) the bond or it stops earning interest 30 years from the issue year. This tax deferral feature is automatic—you don't have to do anything to get it. In addition, U.S. savings bond interest is not subject to state or local taxes. But you need to make sure you take the deduction on your state taxes. It's not automatic.

Moreover, you may not have to pay any federal income tax on your interest if you use the money from these bonds to pay for higher education expenses for yourself or someone else. (See Chapter 3.)

The main difference between I Bonds and Series EE bonds is how the interest is calculated. The interest I bonds pay is indexed for inflation, based on the Consumer Price Index. Thus, the interest rate will go up if inflation goes up. In contrast, Series EE bonds pay a fixed rate of interest based on ten-year Treasury note yields. Series EE bonds usually pay a lower interest rate than I bonds. You can buy up to $30,000 worth of each type each year.

For more information, see www.savingsbonds.gov and www.publicdebt.treas.gov.

Annuities: Complicated, But Sometimes Worth the Trouble

An annuity is a type of retirement plan, but it differs in many ways from the tax-qualified retirement plans discussed above. You establish an annuity by entering into a contract with a life insurance company. You give the insurer a single lump sum payment or a series of payments over time. In return, the insurance company promises to pay you (or your beneficiary or heirs) a benefit (money) on an agreed-upon retirement date in the future. The amount of the benefit is based on the plan's earnings. You receive your benefit either as a single lump sum payment, or a series of payments over time—usually for the rest of your life.

There are two basic types of annuities—fixed and variable. Fixed annuities pay a fixed interest rate on your investment and, like bank CDs, are conservative investments, except they are not insured by the federal government. With a variable annuity, you get to choose how your money is invested, typically in mutual funds. Variable annuities are similar to 401(k) plans in that your returns depend on the market performance of your annuity investments. There is no way of knowing how the stock market will perform in the future, so variable annuities are inherently riskier than fixed annuities invested in bank CDs and the like.

Tax-deferred annuities are not tax-qualified plans and thus don't offer most of the tax benefits of the retirement accounts discussed above.

Contributions to an annuity are not tax deductible, unlike most tax-qualified retirement accounts. Moreover, the money you receive from an annuity is taxed at ordinary income rates even if it's invested in capital assets like stocks. When you start receiving payments, you don't have to pay tax on the amount of your original investment, because you already paid tax on this money. However, your payments are all considered to be taxable income until you use up all of your earnings; only then will your payments be tax free.

Annuities have some good points: They are the only retirement investment that can give you a guaranteed income for the rest of your life. There are no limits on how much you can contribute to an annuity each year, and the money in your annuity account grows tax free until you withdraw it. Unlike with most retirement accounts, you don't have to make withdrawals by the time you are 70½. But, as with retirement accounts, you will pay a penalty if you make withdrawals before age 59½.

Tax-deferred annuities are not highly favored investments right now because the fees and costs charged by the insurance companies that sell them tend to be very high—more than you have to pay for IRAs, 401(k)s, and other retirement plans. However, annuities may be a good option for you if you have already contributed the maximum to your employer-sponsored retirement plans, but still want to set aside more on a tax-deferred basis. Consult your investment advisor for more information.

Swapping Real Estate: Deferring Taxes on Investment or Rental Property

When you sell property and have a profit, you usually pay tax on the profit at the time of the sale. In a like-kind exchange (also called a Section 1031 exchange), you can defer paying taxes upon the sale of property by swapping your property for similar property owned by someone else. The property you receive in a like-kind exchange is treated as if it were a continuation of the property you gave up. The result is that you postpone the recognition (taxation) of gain by shifting the basis of old property to the new property. So you defer paying taxes on any profit you would have received and own new property instead.

In this type of like-kind exchange, you can only exchange property held for investment or for business use. You can't exchange personal property, including the home you live in or a vacation house, unless you rent it out. And you can't exchange business inventory or stocks and bonds.

⚠ Like-kind exchanges are one of the most complex areas of taxation. They are subject to many rules that are strictly enforced by the IRS and should be done only with professional assistance.

> **EXAMPLE:** Eve exchanges a rental house with an adjusted basis of $250,000 for other real estate held for investment. The fair market value of both properties is $500,000. The basis of Eve's new property is the same as the basis of the old ($250,000). No gain is recognized on the transaction.

If you keep exchanging your property for property worth at least as much as yours, you'll never recognize any gain on which you must pay tax. However, sooner or later you'll probably want to sell the replacement property for cash, not exchange it for another property. When this occurs, the original deferred gain, plus any additional gain realized since the purchase of the replacement property, is subject to tax. For this reason, a like-kind exchange is tax deferred, not tax free.

> **EXAMPLE:** Assume that five years after the exchange described in the above example, Eve sells her rental house for $800,000 cash. Now she has to pay tax—and quite a lot at that—because she has a $550,000 long-term capital gain. Her gain is $550,000 because her basis in the property is only $250,000 (the basis of the property she exchanged for the building five years earlier). The $800,000 sales price minus $250,000 basis = $550,000 gain.

If you convert the last property you exchange into your personal residence, you can permanently exclude up to $500,000 of your gain from its sale. You must own the property for at least five years and live in it for at least two years to qualify for this exclusion. (See Chapter 2.)

EXAMPLE: Assume that Eve rents out her house for all of 2006 and 2007. On April 15, 2008, she moves into the house and uses it as her personal residence. She can sell the property any time after April 14, 2011, and pay no tax at all on up to $500,000 of her gain because she is a married taxpayer filing jointly (the exclusion is only $250,000 for single taxpayers).

In addition, you may only exchange property for other similar property, called "like-kind" property by the IRS. Like-kind properties have the same nature or character, even if they differ in grade or quality. Thus, a new car is like kind to a used car.

All real estate in the United States is considered to be like kind with all other real estate in the United States, no matter the type or location—for example, an apartment building in New York is like kind to an office building in California.

In practice, it's rarely the case that two people want to swap their properties with each other. Instead, one of the property owners usually wants cash for his or her property, not a swap. This transaction can still be structured as a like-kind exchange. This is often done with the help of a third party called a qualified intermediary, or QI, in the business of facilitating like-kind exchanges.

EXAMPLE: Abe owns vacant land he bought for $100,000 and that is now worth $200,000. He wants to exchange it for other property instead of selling it and having to pay tax on his $100,000 profit. He puts his property up for sale and in the meantime contacts Carl, a qualified intermediary. Carl locates a small commercial building for sale that Abe likes, but Bob, the owner, has no interest in exchanging it for other property. Carl and Abe enter into an exchange agreement. Carl purchases Bob's building for $200,000 cash that he borrows and then exchanges it for Abe's land. Carl receives a fee for facilitating the exchange and sells Abe's land to repay the funds he borrowed to buy Bob's property. With Carl's help, Abe has exchanged his vacant land for Bob's building, even though Bob didn't want to do an exchange.

There are strict time limits on such delayed exchanges, which can be more complicated than the above example, involving as many as four parties. You must identify the replacement property for your property within 45 days of its sale. And your replacement property purchase must be completed within 180 days of the initial sale. Because of these time limits, it's a good idea to have a replacement property lined up before you sell your property. Professional exchange companies (also called accommodators or facilitators) can help you find replacement property and handle the transaction for you. You can find listings for such companies through the website of the Federation of Exchange Accommodators at www.1031.org.

For more information on real property exchanges, see IRS Publication 544, *Sales and Other Dispositions of Assets*, and IRS Form 8824, *Instructions, Like-Kind Exchanges*. Also, refer to *The Real Estate Investor's Tax Guide*, by Vernon Hoven (Dearborn).

Exchanging Your Personal Residence

You can't do a like-kind exchange for your personal residence because exchanges are only allowed for business or investment property. But, you can exchange your residence if you convert it into a rental property before you sell it. To do this, you must move out of the home and rent it out for an appreciable amount of time. There is no time limit set by law, but most tax experts advise that you rent the house for at least one year before exchanging it.

Spreading Out the Profit (and Taxes) With Installment Sales

If you sell real estate or other property and are paid the entire purchase price at the close of sale, you'll have to pay tax that year on the entire profit you earned from the sale. But, if you want to defer some of the taxes you'll owe to another year, you can structure the sale as an installment sale instead. In an installment sale, you spread the payments out over more than one year. You include in your income each year only the part of the profit that you receive that year. This way, you'll pay tax on your profit over two or more years instead of just one, with the result that you'll defer part of the tax you owe from the sale.

Installment sales can be used for real estate and business or investment property only. However, you cannot use the installment method for sales of business inventory or stocks and securities traded on an established securities market. Also, the installment sale method may be used only where the property is sold at a gain (for a profit), not a loss

Each payment on an installment sale usually consists of the following three parts:

- interest income
- return of your adjusted basis (investment) in the property, and
- gain on the sale.

In each year that you receive a payment, you must include the interest part in your taxable income, as well as the part that is your gain on the sale. The interest is taxed at ordinary income rates, but the gain may be taxed at lower capital gains rates. You do not include in income the part that is the return of your basis in the property. Basis is the amount of your investment in the property for tax purposes.

EXAMPLE: In 2007, you receive $100,000 for land that you purchased for $40,000. Your gross profit on the sale is $60,000. You get a $20,000 down payment and the buyer's note for $80,000 that will be paid in four $20,000 annual installments, plus 6% interest, beginning in 2008. Thus, instead of getting $100,000 in 2007, you'll receive $20,000 a year for five years, plus 6% interest for four years. Only $12,000 of each $20,000 payment is counted as income, the other $8,000 is return of your $40,000 basis in the property.

Installment sales are most often used for sales of real estate and purchases of small business. For a detailed discussion of using the installment sale method to sell a business, refer to *The Complete Guide to Selling a Business*, by Fred Steingold (Nolo).

For more general information on this topic, see IRS Publication 537, *Installment Sales*.

Count Every Penny: Reducing Taxable Income With Deductions

Everybody knows that you can lower your income taxes by taking tax deductions. Unfortunately, not everybody takes all the deductions to which they are entitled. When the IRS processes your tax return, it won't be looking for deductions you might have missed. It's up to you, with or without the help of a tax professional, to figure out which deductions to claim each year. Each deduction you overlook costs you dearly—for example, if you're in the 25% top tax bracket, you'll pay $25 more in income tax for every $100 in deductions you fail to claim.

What Are Tax Deductions?

A tax deduction (also called a tax write-off) is an amount of money you are entitled to subtract from your income to determine your taxable income (the amount on which you must pay tax). The more deductions you have, the lower your taxable income will be and the less tax you will have to pay.

There are four basic types of tax deductions. Each is subject to its own special rules and limitations.

- **Standard Deduction.** A specified amount taxpayers may deduct each year instead of itemizing their deductions.
- **Itemized Deductions.** Certain types of expenses that may be deducted instead of taking the standard deduction. These include items such as home mortgage interest, state and local taxes, charitable contributions, and medical expenses above a threshold amount.
- **Adjustments to Income.** These are a group of expenses that you can deduct whether or not you itemize or take the standard deduction.
- **Business Deductions.** These are business-related expenses—for example, office space rent, supplies, and equipment. Most business expenses are deductible, but you'll only be able to take them if you own a business.

Don't ever spend money just to get a tax deduction. You should never, ever buy anything just to get a tax deduction. A deduction will never save you as much in tax as you had to pay to get the deduction in the first place so you'll end up out of pocket for something you don't want or need.

All deductions reduce your taxes, but not all deductions are created equal. Adjustments to income and business deductions are subtracted from your gross income—all the money you earn less certain exclusions. These deductions are often called "above the line deductions" because they go before the line listing your AGI on your tax form. The standard deduction or itemized deductions are subtracted from your adjusted gross income (AGI)—your income after adjustments to income and business deductions have been subtracted. These are called "below the line deductions" because they go after the AGI line. Above the line deductions are better because you get to deduct them whether or not you itemize your deductions. Itemized deductions are useless if you don't itemize. In addition, above the line deductions are not subject to the percentage of AGI limitations that apply to many itemized deductions. How all this works is discussed in detail in Chapter 1.

Deductions Sound Great, But What Are They Really Worth?

Most taxpayers don't fully appreciate just how much money they can—and can't—save with tax deductions. Only part of any deduction will end up back in your pocket as money saved. Because a deduction represents income on which you don't have to pay tax, the value of any deduction is the amount of tax you would have had to pay on that income had you not deducted it. So a deduction of $1,000 won't save you $1,000 — it will save you whatever you otherwise would have had to pay as tax on that $1,000 of income.

To determine how much income tax a deduction will save you, you must first figure out your marginal income tax bracket. The United States has a progressive income tax system for individual taxpayers with six different tax rates (often called tax brackets), ranging from 10% of taxable income to 35% (see the chart "2006 Federal Personal Income Tax Brackets," below). The higher your income, the higher your tax rate.

You move from one bracket to the next only when your taxable income exceeds the bracket amount. For example, if you are a single taxpayer, you pay 10% income tax on all your taxable income up to $7,550. If your taxable income exceeds $7,550, the next tax rate (15%) applies to all your income over $7,550—but the 10% rate still applies to the first $7,550. If your income exceeds the 15% bracket amount, the next tax rate (25%) applies to the excess amount, and so on until you reach the top bracket of 35%.

The tax bracket in which the last dollar you earn for the year falls is called your "marginal tax bracket." For example, if you have $70,000 in taxable income, your marginal tax bracket is 25%. The following table lists the 2006 federal income tax brackets for single and married individual taxpayers.

2006 Federal Personal Income Tax Brackets

Tax Bracket	Taxable Income If Single	Taxable Income If Married Filing Jointly
10%	Up to $7,550	Up to $15,100
15%	From $7,551 to $30,650	$15,101 to $61,300
25%	$30,651 to $74,200	$61,301 to $123,700
28%	$74,201 to $154,800	$123,701 to $188,450
33%	$154,801 to $336,550	$188,451 to $336,550
35%	All over $336,550	All over $336,550

To determine how much federal income tax a deduction will save you, multiply the amount of the deduction by your marginal tax bracket. For example, if your marginal tax bracket is 25%, you will save approximately 25¢ in federal income taxes for every dollar you are able to claim as a deductible business expense (25% x $1 = 25¢).

This calculation is only approximate because an additional deduction may move you from one tax bracket to another and thus lower your marginal tax rate. For example, if you're single and your taxable income is $75,000, an additional $1,000 deduction will lower your marginal tax rate from 28% to 25%. The first $800 of the deduction will save you $224 in tax (28% x $800 = $224); the remaining $200 will save you $50

(25% x $200 = $50). So your total tax saving is $274, instead of the $280 you would get if, say, your taxable income was $76,000.

Most federal income tax deductions can also be deducted from any state income tax you must pay. The average state income tax rate is about 6%, although seven states (Alaska, Florida, Nevada, South Dakota, Texas, Washington, and Wyoming) don't have an income tax. You can find a list of all state income tax rates at www.taxadmin.org/FTA/rate/ind_inc.html.

Business deductions can also reduce your taxable income for purposes of the 15.4% Social Security and Medicare tax, which makes them especially valuable.

The Standard Deduction: Definitely the Easiest Route and Sometimes the Best One

Believe it or not, Congress doesn't want to tax you into the poorhouse. To help avoid this, all individual taxpayers are allowed to deduct certain personal expenses. Personal expenses are those that are not incurred to run a business—for example, medical expenses, home mortgage interest and property taxes, and charitable contributions.

There are two ways to deduct these expenses—by taking the standard deduction or itemizing your deductions. The easiest way—both for you and the IRS—is to claim the standard deduction. The standard deduction is a specified dollar amount you are allowed to deduct instead of deducting your actual personal expenses. The amount you are allowed to take depends on your filing status and is adjusted for inflation each year. The standard deduction amounts for 2006 are shown in the following chart.

2006 Standard Deductions	
Filing Status	**Standard Deduction**
Single or Married filing separately	$5,150
Married filing jointly	$10,300
Head of household	$7,550

The standard deduction is increased for people who are 65 or older or who are blind. These people get an additional $1,000 if they are single, or $1,250 if they are married. Dependents who don't work get $850; those who work can get as much as adults, depending on how much they earn. (See Chapter 2.)

Whether to take the standard deduction or itemize your deductions is a choice you must make each year. However, if you choose the standard deduction, you can't take any itemized deductions. But you can still deduct adjustments to income and business expenses—your above the line deductions.

You will have to decide which makes sense for you. The standard deduction will be to your advantage if it exceeds the value of your itemized deductions. In fact, if you have few itemized deductions, you'll save much more in taxes by taking the standard deduction. You'll also have a much simpler tax return to fill out and greatly reduced record keeping.

Approximately two-thirds of all taxpayers take the standard deduction instead of itemizing. It's usually better for people with modest incomes, particularly those who are not homeowners and, thus, have no deductible expenses for mortgage interest or property taxes. As the following chart shows, at income levels below $50,000, more people took the standard deduction than itemized their deductions in 2003. On the other hand, few taxpayers with AGIs over $100,000 took the standard deduction.

Taxpayers Claiming Standard Versus Itemized Deductions (2003)				
Adjusted Gross Income	Standard Deduction		Itemized Deductions	
$20,000–$30,000	8,211,219	(84%)	1,617,007	(16%)
$30,000–$40,000	9,504,261	(68%)	4,449,065	(32%)
$40,000–$50,000	5,950,870	(57%)	4,501,574	(43%)
$50,000–$75,000	7,050,508	(41%)	10,321,837	(59%)
$75,000–$100,000	2,067,496	(22%)	7,475,102	(78%)
$100,000 –$200,000	862,219	(10%)	8,016,424	(90%)
$200,000–$500,000	122,413	(6%)	1,876,601	(94%)

> ## People Who Can't Take the Standard Deduction
>
> You can't take the standard deduction and must itemize your deductions if:
>
> - you are married, filing a separate return, and your spouse itemizes deductions, or
> - you are a nonresident or dual-status alien during the year. You are considered a dual-status alien if you were both a nonresident and resident alien during the year. If you are a nonresident alien who is married to a U.S. citizen or resident at the end of the year, you can choose to be treated as a U.S. resident. If you make this choice, you can take the standard deduction.

Don't Miss Out on Itemized Deductions

Itemizing your deductions means you deduct the actual amounts of certain expenses item by item instead of taking the standard deduction. You must list all the deductions on IRS Schedule A and include this schedule with your tax return. This is a lot more work than taking the standard deduction. You have to know what expenses are deductible and keep track of them. You also need to keep records of your expenses. Cancelled checks or credit card statements are not enough—you need to keep receipts and other bills showing what you spent the money on.

Itemized deductions are usually personal in nature, and don't include business expenses (although they do include job expenses). Some of the more common ones are:

- medical and dental expenses
- state and local income taxes or sales tax
- real estate and personal property taxes
- home mortgage and investment interest
- charitable contributions
- casualty and theft losses
- job expenses, and

- miscellaneous deductions for such things as investment expenses, hobby expenses, gambling losses, and tax preparation fees.

The largest of these deductions are those for home mortgage interest, property taxes, and state income tax. For this reason, homeowners usually itemize, while renters often do not.

However, most of these expenses cannot be deducted in full. Instead, they are subject to special limitations—for example, medical expenses can be deducted only to the extent that they exceed 7.5% of your adjusted gross income (AGI), and job expenses to the extent they exceed 2% of AGI. In addition, for high-income taxpayers, many of their itemized deductions are partly phased out because of overall income level restrictions. Consequently, you may find that few or none of your personal expenses are deductible.

Choosing Whether to Itemize

You must choose whether to itemize or take the standard deduction each year. The IRS won't tell you what's in your best interest—it doesn't care if you make the wrong choice and overpay your taxes. You (or your tax preparer) must decide. Obviously, you should itemize if it will give you a larger total deduction than the standard deduction. For example, for 2006, if you're a single taxpayer, you should itemize if your itemized deductions are worth more than $5,150. If you're married and file jointly, you should itemize if your itemized deductions are more than $10,300.

> **EXAMPLE:** Linda and Larry are a married couple who file jointly. Thus, they can choose the $10,300 standard deduction or itemize their deductions. When they add up all their itemized deductions, they come up with $12,000. They should itemize because it will allow them to deduct $1,700 more than if they took the standard deduction.

Unfortunately, many people get it wrong. Failing to itemize personal deductions is the single biggest mistake people make when they do their taxes. According to a recent Government Accountability Office report, as many as 2.2 million taxpayers overpay their taxes by an average of $610 per year because they fail to itemize their deductions.

If you itemized last year, you should probably do it this year, too, unless there has been a major reduction in your deductible expenses. If you took the standard deduction last year, you may be better off itemizing this year if you:

- had large uninsured medical and dental expenses during the year
- paid interest and taxes on your home
- had large unreimbursed job expenses or other miscellaneous deductions
- had significant uninsured casualty or theft losses, or
- made large charitable contributions.

The only way to know for sure if you'd be better off itemizing is to keep track of your deductible expenses each year. To do this, you have to know what is and isn't deductible. There's no point in keeping track of things that are not deductible.

Through careful planning, you can often increase your deductible expenses so that it pays to itemize.

Medical and Dental Expenses

Taxpayers who itemize are entitled to a tax deduction for medical and dental expenses for themselves, their spouses, and their dependents. Eligible expenses include both health insurance premiums and out-of-pocket expenses not covered by insurance. But your total deductible medical expenses for the year must be reduced by any health insurance reimbursements paid directly to you or to the doctor or hospital.

Unfortunately, there is a significant limitation on the deduction, which can make it useless for many taxpayers: You can deduct only the amount of your medical and dental expenses that is more than 7.5% of your adjusted gross income (AGI). (Your AGI is your total taxable income, minus deductions for retirement contributions and one-half of your self-employment taxes (if any), plus a few other items (as shown at the bottom of your Form 1040).) So, unless your medical expenses are substantial and/or your income is low, the 7.5% limitation often eats up most or all of the deduction. The more money you make, the less you can deduct.

> **EXAMPLE:** Al is a self-employed accountant whose adjusted gross income for 2006 is $100,000. He pays $450 per month for health insurance for himself and his wife. He spends another $2,200 in out-of-pocket medical and dental expenses for the year. Al may deduct his medical expenses only to the extent they exceed 7.5% of his AGI, which is $7,500 (7.5% x $100,000 = $7,500). Because he only paid a total of $7,600 in medical expenses for the year, his itemized deduction is limited to just $100. The other $7,500 in medical expenses cannot be deducted.

Many people assume they'll never be able to deduct their medical expenses so they don't bother to keep track of them. This is a risky assumption. Your deductible medical expenses may be larger than you think, so you may be giving up a valuable deduction without even knowing it.

First of all, remember that you may deduct medical expenses for yourself, your spouse, your dependent children, and any other dependents you claim on your tax return. For example, if an elderly parent qualifies as your dependent, you may deduct your out-of-pocket expenses for his or her medical care. These costs can be substantial.

Moreover, lots of things you might not regard as medical expenses are deductible. The IRS broadly defines deductible medical expenses to include any payment for "the diagnosis, cure, mitigation, treatment, or prevention of disease, or treatment affecting any structure or function of the body." That covers a lot of territory.

It includes, of course, money you spend on doctors and dentists, as well as nursing care, hospitalization, lab fees, and long-term care. But medical expenses include much more—for example, you may deduct fees you pay to chiropractors, psychiatrists, optometrists, psychologists, osteopaths, acupuncturists, podiatrists, and even Christian Science practitioners. You can also deduct things like transportation costs for health treatment and the cost of remodeling your home to accommodate a handicap (adding wheelchair ramps, for example).

The following chart lists the types of medical expenses you may deduct. You should keep track of all of these expenses during the year.

Deductible Medical Expenses

abdominal supports

abortion

acupuncture

air conditioner (when necessary for relief from an allergy or for difficulty in breathing)

alcoholism treatment

ambulance

arch supports

artificial limbs

birth control pills (by prescription)

blood tests

blood transfusions

braces

breast reconstruction surgery

cardiographs

chiropractor

Christian Science practitioner

contact lenses

contraceptive devices (by prescription)

convalescent home (for medical treatment only)

crutches

dental treatment

dentures

dermatologist

diagnostic fees

diathermy

drug addiction therapy

elastic hosiery (prescription)

eyeglasses

fees paid to health institute prescribed by a doctor

fertility treatment

fluoridation unit

guide dog

healing services

hearing aids and batteries

hospital bills

hydrotherapy

insulin treatments

lab tests

laser eye surgery

lead paint removal

legal fees to authorize treatment for mental illness

lodging while away from home for outpatient care

medical conference expenses (only if the conference concerns the chronic illness of yourself, your spouse, or a dependent)

metabolism tests

neurologist

nursing (including board and meals)

nursing home

obstetrician

operating room costs

ophthalmologist

optician

optometrist

Deductible Medical Expenses (continued)

oral surgery

organ transplant (including donor's expenses)

orthopedic shoes

orthopedist

osteopath

oxygen and oxygen equipment

pediatrician

physician

physiotherapist

podiatrist

postnatal treatments

practical nurse for medical services

prenatal care

prescription medicines

psychiatrist

psychoanalyst

psychologist

radial keratotomy to correct vision

radium therapy

sex therapy

special education costs for the handicapped

splints

sterilization

stop-smoking programs (not including nonprescription drugs)

surgeon

telephone or TV equipment to assist the hard-of-hearing

therapy equipment

transportation expenses to obtain health care (fares for taxis, buses, trains, or ambulances; and car expenses, including tolls and parking fees)

ultraviolet ray treatment

vaccines

vitamins (if prescribed)

weight loss program (only if it is a treatment for a specific disease diagnosed by a doctor—for example, obesity; cost of reduced-calorie foods is not deductible)

wheelchair

x-rays

There are some health-related expenses that are not deductible. For example, you may not deduct nonprescription drugs or the cost of cosmetic surgery (but reconstructive surgery is deductible). Nor can you deduct veterinary fees (too bad for Fido). The following chart lists these nondeductible expenses.

Health Expenses You Can't Deduct

You may not deduct the following health-related expenses:

advance payment for services to be rendered next year

athletic club membership

bottled water

child care for a healthy child

commuting expenses of a disabled person

cosmetic surgery and procedures

cosmetics, hygiene products, and similar items

diaper service

domestic help

funeral, cremation, or burial expenses

health programs offered by resort hotels, health clubs, and gyms

illegal operations and treatments

illegally procured drugs

maternity clothes

nutritional supplements (unless recommended by a medical practitioner to treat a specific illness diagnosed by a doctor)

nonprescription medications

premiums for life insurance, income protection, disability, loss of limbs, sight, or similar benefits

Scientology counseling

social activities

specially designed car for the handicapped other than an autoette or special equipment

swimming pool or swimming lessons

travel for general health improvement

tuition and travel expenses to send a child to a particular school

veterinary fees

Finally, there are certain medical expenses that you can deduct even if you don't itemize your deductions. These are adjustments to income you deduct from your gross income to arrive at your AGI. These include:

- contributions to health savings accounts (but payments for health insurance paired with HSAs must be itemized), and
- health insurance premiums paid by self-employed people (deductible up to the amount of profit from the business).

Interest

Certain types of interest are deductible, including mortgage interest, investment interest, and interest paid on home equity loans. If you own a home and are paying off a mortgage, you should probably be itemizing because mortgage interest payments are usually large enough to get most people over the standard deduction amount.

Home mortgage loans. Home mortgage interest is any interest you pay on a loan secured by your main home and/or a second home. The loan may be a mortgage to buy your home, a second mortgage, a line of credit, or a home equity loan. Home mortgage interest for a loan or loans totaling up to $1 million is deductible. If you borrow more than $1 million, the interest on the overage is not deductible.

If you are lucky enough to have more than one vacation home, you must select the one to be treated as the second home for purposes of the mortgage interest deduction. This selection is made anew each year, so you can select one vacation home as your second home one year, and another the next year.

Home mortgage loans can be complicated and include all sorts of charges not labeled interest. The largest of these is usually points. A point is equal to 1% of the loan amount—for example, one point on a $100,000 loan is $1,000. These charges are also called loan origination fees, maximum loan charges, or premium charges. If any of these charges (points) are solely for the use of money and not for a specific service such as appraisal services, they are prepaid interest for tax purposes. As a general rule, you must deduct points a little at a time over the life of your loan. However, there is a special exception for points to obtain a mortgage to buy or build your main home. These points can all be deducted in the year paid. Points paid for refinancing generally can only be deducted over the life of the new mortgage. However, you may deduct the points in a single year if you use the money to improve your main home—for example, add a new bathroom.

Most other expenses you pay to obtain a mortgage cannot be deducted as interest. Instead, they are added to your basis in the property and increase its value for tax purposes. These costs include:

- abstract fees
- charges for installing utility services
- legal fees

- appraisal fees
- mortgage commissions
- recording fees
- surveys
- transfer taxes
- title insurance, and
- any amounts the seller owes that you agree to pay, such as back taxes or interest, recording or mortgage fees, charges for improvements or repairs, and sales commissions.

It's easy to keep track of how much interest you pay each year on a home mortgage loan. If you paid $600 or more of mortgage interest (including certain points) during the year on any one mortgage, you will receive an IRS Form 1098 from the lender. This form lists how much interest you paid during the year.

Home equity loans. A home equity loan is a loan for which you use your main home or second home as collateral. Interest on home equity loans of less than $100,000 is deductible as an itemized personal deduction. This is so regardless of how the money is spent.

Investment interest. You may take an itemized deduction for investment interest, but you may not deduct more than your net annual income from your investments. Any amount that you can't deduct in the current year can be carried over to the next year and deducted then.

> **EXAMPLE:** Donald borrows $10,000 on his credit card to invest in the stock market. The interest he pays on the debt is deductible as an itemized personal deduction on his Schedule A, Form 1040. But he can't deduct more than he earned during the year from his investments.

Personal interest. Personal interest is not deductible. This is interest you pay to buy something for your personal use (except for interest paid for a mortgage for a personal residence or second home, and some interest on student loans). Thus, you may not deduct interest you pay on credit cards, car loans, or other loans where the proceeds are used for personal purposes. For example, if you buy a new dishwasher for your residence with a credit card, you may not deduct the interest you pay to the credit card company on the amount. Likewise, you can't deduct any part of the interest you pay on a car loan unless you use your car for a business or investment activity.

Because personal interest is not deductible, but home equity loan interest is, you should consider borrowing against your home to make consumer purchases instead of charging them on your credit card or taking out a consumer loan. For example, if you need a $20,000 loan to buy a car for personal use, all the interest will be deductible if you obtain the money through a home equity loan. Of course, you must have a home and have equity to obtain such a loan.

Taxes

Several types of taxes can be deducted.

State income taxes. All but seven states impose their own income taxes. If you itemize, these taxes are deductible in full. This is one of the largest itemized deductions.

Property taxes. State and local property taxes on your home and other nonbusiness property can be deducted as an itemized deduction. There is no dollar limit on the deduction, and you can claim as many vacation homes as you want to each year. However, you may not deduct charges for improvements that increase the value of the property—for example, a special assessment for new sidewalks or sewers.

State sales taxes. Alaska, Florida, Nevada, South Dakota, Texas, Washington, and Wyoming don't have any state income taxes. If you live in one of these states, you may be able to deduct your state and local sales taxes as an itemized deduction.

The state sales tax deduction expired at the end of 2005. As this book went to press, Congress was expected to extend it to 2006 and perhaps beyond. Be sure to check whether the deduction has been extended to the current tax year.

If you live in one of the 43 states that has income taxes, you may be able to choose to deduct your sales taxes instead of your state income taxes. But you may not deduct both. You could get a larger deduction from sales taxes if, for example, you purchased expensive items during the year that required you to pay substantial sales tax—for example, a car. Or, your state income taxes could end up being quite small this year because you took state income tax credits—for example, a state credit for installing solar power in your home.

There are two ways to figure out how much sales tax you can deduct: the easy way and the hard way.

The easy way involves using IRS tables to figure your deduction. If you use this method, you don't need to keep receipts or keep track of what you actually spent on sales tax. Instead, you use your income level and number of exemptions to find the sales tax amount listed in the tables for your state. This number is an IRS estimate of the average sales tax a person with your income and exemptions would pay. You may add to this any sales taxes you paid during the year for a car, aircraft, boat, home (including mobile or prefabricated), or home building materials.

The hard way means you figure out how much you actually spent on sales taxes and you deduct that amount. You must save all your sales receipts and then add them up—which is often a lot of work. You might get a bigger deduction this way, but you need to consider whether it's worth it?

Personal property taxes. State and local taxes on personal property are deductible if they are based on the property's value (an "ad valorem" tax) and charged on a yearly basis. How often the taxes are collected doesn't matter. Personal property taxes vary from state to state. Some states don't have any. However, more and more states are charging personal property taxes on things like cars, motorcycles, boats, mobile homes, trailers, and aircraft. Your state's annual automobile registration fee is wholly or partly deductible if it is based on your car's value. Check your state taxing agency's website for more information on state property taxes. Links to these websites can be found at www. bankrate.com/brm/itax/state/state_tax_home.asp.

Foreign income taxes. You can take either a deduction or a credit for income taxes imposed on you by a foreign country or a U.S. possession. Generally, you're better off using the credit. (See Chapter 3.) However, you cannot take a deduction or credit for foreign income taxes paid on income that is exempt from U.S. tax under the foreign earned income exclusion or the foreign housing exclusion.

Charitable Contributions

Charitable contributions can be a big itemized deduction. In 2005, Vice President Dick Cheney took over $6.8 million in charitable deductions.

You're probably not in Dick Cheney's league, but you can still reap valuable tax benefits by doing good.

However, don't get the idea that making charitable contributions will end up saving you money, because they won't (unless you cheat by overvaluing property donations). Dick Cheney is a good case in point: He saved over $2.4 million in 2005 income taxes because of his contributions, but he contributed $6.8 million to charity to get those tax savings. In other words, his contributions left him $4.4 million poorer than he otherwise would have been.

But, if you want to make a charitable contribution, it will lower your taxes if you itemize your deductions, which in turn can enable you to make a larger contribution with the money you save.

Unlike most of the other itemized deductions, charitable contributions are completely voluntary and can be planned far in advance. The best time to make such donations is at the end of the year. You get the same deduction no matter what time of the year you donate; but donating late in the year permits you to keep your money longer and earn interest or other income from it prior to making the donation.

What contributions are deductible? Subject to overall limits, you may take an itemized deduction for contributions of money or property to charity. However, not just anything qualifies as a charity. Only contributions to "qualified organizations" are deductible. These include:

- churches, temples, synagogues, mosques, and other religious organizations
- most nonprofit charitable organizations, such as the Red Cross and United Way
- most nonprofit educational organizations, including the Boy and Girl Scouts of America, colleges, museums, and day care centers for working parents, and
- nonprofit hospitals and medical research organizations.

Not all people or organizations asking for donations are legitimate charities—what the IRS calls qualified organizations. To become a qualified organization, most organizations, other than churches and governments, must apply to the IRS. You can ask any organization whether it is a qualified organization, and most will be able to tell you. They should have an IRS letter saying so—you can ask for a copy. You can also call the IRS at 877-829-5500 to find out if a charity is qualified; or check IRS Publication 78, which lists most qualified organizations. Not all qualified organizations are listed in Publication 78 though—for example, churches, synagogues, temples, and mosques are not required to apply for IRS recognition to be qualified charities and are frequently not listed. You can check the website www.guidestar.org which lists 1.5 million qualified charities and contains in-depth financial information about them as well.

Not every gift you make is a deductible charitable contribution. Even if they seem charitable to you, you may not deduct contributions:

- to individuals—for example, you can't get a charitable deduction for giving money to your brother Fred (even if he's broke), to the local panhandler, or to an individual priest, reverend, or rabbi
- for raffle, bingo, or lottery tickets
- for political candidates or groups
- to for-profit schools and hospitals, or
- to civic leagues, social and sports clubs, labor unions, or chambers of commerce.

In addition, most people don't realize that they can't deduct gifts to foreign charities or governments (except certain Canadian, Israeli, and Mexican charities). If you want to help people in a foreign country, you should donate to a qualified U.S. charity providing aid in that country. That way, you can deduct your donation.

How much can you deduct? There are overall limits on how much you can deduct each year as a charitable deduction. However, you don't have to worry about them unless your charitable deductions are quite substantial. Specific limits vary according to whether you give cash or property, but the overall limit is that your charitable contributions cannot exceed 50% of your AGI for the year. Any contributions you make over this amount may be carried forward to the following year and deducted then. You can keep carrying forward any remaining amount for up to five years.

> **EXAMPLE:** Jerry, a waiter, had a $30,000 AGI this year. He inherits a good deal of money from an uncle and decides to give $50,000 to his favorite charity. Jerry may only deduct $15,000 of his contribution this year, since this amount is equal to 50% of his AGI. He may carry forward the remaining $35,000 and deduct it over the next five years. If his AGI is $30,000 the following year, he'll be able to

deduct another $15,000, and carry forward the remaining $20,000 to the next year, and so on.

Contributions of money. It's easiest to give cash, which is usually most welcome by charities. Cash includes currency, checks, and credit card contributions.

Ordinarily, cash contributions can be deducted until they reach the 50% of AGI limit. However, a few types of cash contributions may only be deducted up to 30% of your AGI. These are contributions to veteran's organizations, fraternal societies, nonprofit cemeteries, and certain private foundations that fail to timely distribute all the donations they receive.

Buying Tickets for Charity

If you buy a ticket for a charitable event such as a ball, banquet, show, dinner, or sporting event, you'd naturally think you may deduct what you spend for the ticket. Not so. When you give money to a charity and get a benefit in return—such as the right to attend a banquet—you can only deduct the amount that is more than the value of the benefit you receive.

> **EXAMPLE:** You pay $250 to a qualified charity for a ticket to attend a football game. The ticket is worth $50, so that portion of the ticket price is not deductible because it benefited you—you get to go to the game. The remaining $200 is deductible.

If the ticket shows the price of admission to the event and the amount of the contribution, you can deduct the contribution amount. If not, the charity hosting the event will usually be able to tell you the exact value of the benefit for an event. Indeed, charities are required to give donors written confirmation of the value of any benefit they receive that is worth more than $75.

Whether you actually use the tickets has no effect on the amount you can deduct. However, if you return the ticket to the charity for resale, you can deduct the entire amount you paid for the ticket. So, if you want to maximize your deduction and don't want to attend the event, be sure to return your ticket (and don't ask for a refund).

Contributions of property. You don't have to contribute cash to a charity to get a deduction. You may also contribute property. Property contributions include items such as old clothes, furniture, household goods, cars, and jewelry. They also include intangible property such as stocks, bonds, and mutual funds. (In its poetic way, the IRS calls contributions of property "noncash" contributions.)

Contributing property to charity is very popular—you can get rid of old stuff you no longer need and get a tax deduction too. However, it's more complicated than contributing hard cash.

You can ordinarily deduct property contributions in full up to 30% of your adjusted gross income; however, the limit is lowered to 20% for property donated to veteran's organizations, fraternal societies, nonprofit cemeteries, and certain private foundations that fail to timely distribute all the donations they receive.

Let's say you clean out your closets and give your old clothes to charity. How much do you get to deduct? Unfortunately, a charity is not allowed to set the value of a donation—you, the donor, must do so. This is where the charitable contribution deduction can cause problems because (1) most people have no idea what their donations are worth, and (2) there is a strong temptation to overvalue charitable contributions of property for tax purposes. The IRS is well aware that some people wildly inflate the value of their property contributions and is now cracking down on abuses. There are also special record keeping and valuation rules for large property donations.

You may deduct no more than the property's "fair market value" when you make the deduction. The IRS says that fair market value means the amount that a "willing buyer would pay and a willing seller would accept for the property, when neither party is compelled to buy or sell, and both parties have reasonable knowledge of the relevant facts." In other words, it's a fair price—not too high or too low.

The IRS gives very little guidance on how to determine fair market value other than to say that you shouldn't use a fixed formula. Rather, all relevant factors should be considered, including:

- the item's cost or selling price
- sales of comparable items
- replacement cost, and
- opinions of experts (ordinarily used only for big-ticket items).

You'll need to obtain an appraisal from a qualified appraiser if the property is worth more than $5,000. But a formal appraisal is not required for less expensive property. (Appraisal expenses are not deductible as a charitable contribution, but can be deducted as a miscellaneous itemized deduction subject to the 2% of AGI floor; see "Miscellaneous Itemized Deductions," below.)

So how much are items like your old clothes worth? Obviously, you can't use the price you paid for an item as its fair market value because used clothing (and most other used property) is worth far less than new. Fortunately, several well-known charities have created price guides for frequently donated items such as clothing, household goods, and furniture. It's hard to imagine that the IRS would complain if you used one of these guides. These guides can be found at the following websites (the Salvation Army guide is the most detailed):

- Salvation Army Donation Value Guide: www.salvationarmysouth. org/valueguide.htm
- Goodwill Industries: www.goodwillpromo.org
- Children's Home Thrift Shop Guide to Valuing Donated Goods: www.childrens-home.org/valuationguide.htm

Online auction sites, such as eBay, can also provide a good idea of what used items are worth. Simply check to see what similar items have sold for. You could use the average price of a few recent sales.

> **EXAMPLE:** Barry wants to buy a new computer and get rid of his old one. He decides to donate the old computer to a local charity and try to figure out is value by looking at sales data for similar computers on eBay. Three computers identical to his recently sold for $950, $1,150, and $900—for an average price of $1,000. Thus, Barry determines that his used computer's fair market value is $1,000. Barry should keep a copy of the eBay sales data with his tax records.

There are also two specialized software programs you can use to determine the fair market value of used property. These are *It'sDeductible* from Intuit (www.itsdeductible.com), and *DonationPro* from H & R Block (www.hrblock.com). You describe the item you're donating and the program gives you an estimate of its value based on surveys of thrift store sales and online auctions. You may be able to download

DonationPro from the H & R Block website for free. A comparison of the results obtained using these programs and the price guides created by charities found that the software usually gives higher valuations.

⚠ No deduction for clothing and household items in poor condition. In 2003, American taxpayers claimed over $9 billion in charitable deductions for contributions of clothing and household items. To put it mildly, it's highly doubtful these items were really worth that much. So, Congress has decided to crack down. Starting in August 2006, donations of used clothing and household items are deductible only if the item is in good used condition or better. Thus, for example, old clothing in poor condition won't be deductible.

In addition, Congress has given the IRS the power to enact regulations denying any deduction at all for low-value items such as socks and underwear. This has not happened yet, but it could.

Household items include furniture, electronics, appliances, linens, and similar items. Food, paintings, antiques, and other objects of art, jewelry and gems, and collections are not included.

The law does not define what "good used condition" is. You may wish to photograph clothing and household items you donate so you can prove they were in good condition if the IRS later questions you. You should also obtain a statement from the charity that the item was in good condition.

There is one important exception to the rule: You may take a deduction for an item in poor condition if it is worth more than $500 and you obtain an appraisal of its value that you include with your tax return.

Donating used cars and other vehicles. If you have an old car you want to get rid of, donating it to charity can seem like a great idea—it's easy to do and you'll get a tax deduction. Charities often like getting donations of used cars because they can, and usually do, quickly sell them for cash.

Unfortunately, hundreds of thousands of taxpayers already had this idea and many of them abused the charitable deduction rules by grossly inflating the value of their used cars to get larger tax deductions. In one case, a taxpayer claimed a $2,915 deduction for a 1980 Mercury station wagon that was ultimately sold by the charity for $30. A study by the

Government Accountability Office concluded that the IRS was losing hundreds of millions of dollars every year because of similar abuses.

As a result, the rules for deducting donated used cars were significantly tightened starting in 2005. Today, if you donate a car or other vehicle to charity and claim a deduction greater than $500, your charitable deduction is limited to the amount the charity receives when it sells the car. Thus, the owner of the Mercury station wagon described above would only get a $30 deduction today. The charity must provide you with IRS form, 1098-C, *Contributions of Motor Vehicles, Boats, and Airplanes*, documenting the sale price. You must file a copy with your tax return and also file IRS Form 8283, *Noncash Charitable Contributions*.

As a result of the new rules, vehicle donations to charities have plummeted because the amount a charity sells a used car for is usually much less than a private party can get. Unless your car is a real clunker, you'd be better off selling it yourself and giving the money you get to charity.

These rules apply to cars, trucks, motorcycles, and any motor vehicle manufactured primarily for use on public roads; boats; and airplanes.

There are a few situations where you can claim your car's fair market value as your deduction amount, such as:

- when your claimed deduction is $500 or less
- when the charity keeps the vehicle for its own use, or
- when the charity gives or sells the vehicle to a needy person at a price significantly below fair market value.

You'll need a written acknowledgement from the charity if you use any of these exceptions and in no event can the fair market value you claim exceed the private party sales price listed in a used vehicle pricing guide, such as the *Kelly Blue Book*. For more information, see IRS Publication 4303, *A Donor's Guide to Vehicle Donations*.

Donating stock and other capital gain assets. If you want to donate money to charity and you own property—such as stocks, bonds, or mutual funds—that has gone up in value since you bought it, a great tax strategy is to donate the property directly to the charity. When you do this, you may deduct the fair market value of the property on the date of the donation and you don't have to pay any capital gains taxes on the property's increase in value since you purchased it. The charity can then sell the property and pay no tax at all on the proceeds.

EXAMPLE: Dick owns 1,000 shares of Acme Gun Co. stock. He paid $1,000 for the shares back in 1995 and they are worth $10,000 today. He gives the stock to his favorite charity, the Red Cross, and deducts its $10,000 fair market value as a charitable contribution. Dick need not pay the 15% capital gains tax on the $9,000 gain in the value of his stock. The Red Cross sells the stocks and pays no taxes on the $10,000 it receives. Had Dick sold the stock he would have had to pay a $1,350 long-term capital gains tax on his $9,000 profit (15% x $9,000 = $1,350). This would have left him only $8,650 from the stock sale to donate to charity.

You may only take charitable deductions for capital assets like stocks up to 30% of your adjusted gross income for the year. If your deduction is more than 30% of your AGI, you can spread it out over up to five years.

Don't contribute stocks you've held in a tax-free retirement account such as an IRA or 401(k). If you do, you'll have to pay tax on the earnings. Only contribute property held in taxable accounts.

This strategy only works for capital assets you've owned for one year or more. Also, you should never do this for stocks or other capital assets that have gone down in value because you won't be able to deduct your loss. In this event, you should sell the asset, deduct the loss, and give the sales proceeds to charity.

EXAMPLE: Assume that Dick's Acme Gun Co. stock is worth only $100. He has lost $900 on his investment. He sells the stock and gives the $100 proceeds to charity. He then deducts his $900 loss as a capital loss for the year. He's in the 28% tax bracket, so this saves him $252 in income tax. Had Dick given the stock to charity instead of selling it, he would have had no capital loss deduction.

For a detailed discussion of capital gains taxes, see Chapter 6.

Contributions of services. Many people volunteer their services to a charity. Volunteering for a charity is a great thing to do, but it won't help you much with your taxes. You get no deduction for the value of your time or services. However, you can take an itemized deduction for your out-of-pocket expenses such as travel expenses. To be deductible, the expenses must be:

- unreimbursed
- directly connected with your charitable services
- expenses you had only because of the services you gave, and
- not personal, living, or family expenses.

For example, you can deduct unreimbursed out-of-pocket expenses, such as the cost of gas and oil, that are directly related to the use of your car in giving services to a charitable organization. If you do not want to bother keeping track of your actual expenses, you can use a standard mileage rate of 14 cents a mile to figure your contribution (the rate is 32 cents per mile for 2006 if you help Hurricane Katrina victims). Given the cost of gasoline today, the 14 cent per mile limit is absurdly low, so you'd be better off keeping track of your actual driving expenses.

> **EXAMPLE:** Dr. Smith, a radiologist, volunteers 10 hours of his time every week to a nonprofit hospital in his community. He may deduct the cost of his gas and parking, but not the value of his time or medical services.

Out-of-pocket expenses incurred while performing services for a charity are deducted in the same way as cash contributions. You must have adequate records to prove the amount of your expenses, and get an acknowledgement from the charity containing:

- a description of the services you provided
- a statement whether the charity provided you any goods or services to reimburse you for your work
- a description and a good faith estimate of the value of any goods or services (other than intangible religious benefits) provided to reimburse you, and
- a statement of any intangible religious benefits provided to you.

Record-keeping requirements. As shown in the following chart, record-keeping requirements vary according to what you donate. You don't have to file any of these records with your tax return. However, if you make a contribution of property worth more than $500, you'll need to file IRS Form 8283, Noncash Charitable Contributions, with your tax return, containing the information in your records.

Recordkeeping for Cash Donations		
Donation Amount	**Record of value of donation**	**Receipt or written acknowledgement from charity**
All Cash Donations Total Less than $250	Must be shown by cancelled check, account statement, or other reliable records, unless you have a receipt	Not required, but if you obtain receipt, then cancelled check, account statement, or other record is not needed
Single Cash Donation Less than $250 (2006 and Earlier)	Must be shown by cancelled check, account statement, or other reliable records, unless you have a receipt	Not required if you obtain receipt, then cancelled check, account statement, or other record is not needed.
Single Cash Donation Less than $250 (2007 and Later)	Must be shown by cancelled check or bank statement. (Credit or debt card contributions may be shown by bank statement.) Not required if you have receipt.	Not required if you you have a cancelled check or bank record. Receipt must contain: • name of charity • date of contribution, and • amount of contribution
Single Cash Donation Over $250 (2006 and Earlier)		Receipt required and must contain: • amount you contributed • statement whether you received goods or services for donation, and • estimated value of such goods or services. Receipt may be email, postcard, letter, or form.
Single Cash Donation Over $250 (2007 and Later)	Must be shown by cancelled check or bank statement. (Credit or debt card contributions may be shown by bank statement.)	Receipt required and must contain: • name of charity • date of contribution • amount of contribution • statement whether you received goods or services for donation and • estimated value of such goods or services. Receipt may be email, postcard, letter, or form.

Recordkeeping for Property Donations			
Donation amount	**Record of value of donation**	**Description of donated property**	**Receipt or written acknowledgement from charity**
Single Property Donation Less than $250	Must describe how you figured value.	Description need only be reasonable under the circumstances.	Receipt required unless it's impractical to get one—for example, furniture left at charity drop site. Receipt must contain: • name of charity • date and location of contribution, and • description of the property.
Single Property Donation of $250-$500	Must describe how you figured value.	Description need only be reasonable under the circumstances.	Receipt required and must contain: • name of charity • date and location of contribution • description of the property • statement whether you received goods or services for donation, and • estimated value of such goods or services.
Single Property Donation of $500-$5,000	Must describe how you figured value.	Must describe how and when you obtained property and its cost.	Receipt required and must contain: • name of charity • date and location of contribution • description of the property • statement whether you received goods or services for donation, and • estimated value of such goods or services.
Single Property Donation Over $5,000	Written appraisal from qualified appraiser required. For detailed information, refer to IRS Publication 561, *Determining the Value of Donated Property*.	Must describe how and when you obtained property and its cost.	Receipt required and must contain: • name of charity • date and location of contribution • description of the property • statement whether you received goods or services for donation, and • estimated value of such goods or services.

Keep this information with your tax records in case you're audited. The IRS record-keeping requirements are summarized in the following chart. For detailed information, refer to IRS Publication 526, *Charitable Contributions.*

! **Cancelled check or receipt required for all cash contributions after 2006.** Starting in 2007, you'll need to keep a cancelled check, bank record, or receipt for all your cash contributions, however small. This is a significant change from the law in effect during 2006 and earlier, which required a receipt only for donations over $250. As a result, you may wish to make all your monetary contributions by check or credit card, rather than by cash. If you do give cash, be absolutely sure to get a receipt.

Here's an easy way to keep track of all your donations during the year: Get a file folder, label it "donations," and use it for all your cancelled checks to charities, receipts for cash contributions, credit card bills and electronic transfer notices for contributions, and acknowledgements of donations for property contributions.

Casualty and Theft Losses

Casualty losses are damage to property caused by fire, theft, vandalism, earthquake, storm, floods, terrorism, or some other sudden, unexpected, or unusual event. There must be some external force involved for a loss to be a casualty loss. Thus, you get no deduction if you simply lose or misplace property, or it breaks or wears out over time.

You may take a deduction for casualty losses only to the extent that the loss is not covered by insurance. Thus, if the loss is fully covered, you'll get no deduction.

The personal deduction for casualty losses to personal property is severely limited: You can deduct only the amount of the loss that exceeds 10% of your adjusted gross income for the year. This greatly limits or eliminates many casualty loss deductions. To add insult to injury, you must also subtract $100 from each casualty or theft you suffered during the year.

EXAMPLE: Ken's suffers $5,000 in losses to his personal property when a fire strikes his home. His adjusted gross income for the year is $75,000. He can deduct only that portion of his loss that exceeds $7,500 (10% x $75,000 = $7,500). He lost $5,000, so he gets no deduction.

💡 **These limits don't apply to casualty losses caused by Hurricanes Katrina, Rita, or Wilma.** For more information, refer to IRS Publication 4492, *Information for Taxpayers Affected by Hurricanes Katrina, Rita, and Wilma.*

How much you may deduct depends on whether the property involved was stolen, completely destroyed, or only partially destroyed. You must always reduce your casualty losses by the amount of any insurance proceeds you actually receive or reasonably expect to receive. If more than one item was stolen or wholly or partly destroyed, you must figure your deduction separately for each item and then add them all together.

If the property is stolen or completely destroyed, your deduction is figured as follows: Adjusted Basis – Salvage Value – Insurance Proceeds = Casualty Loss. (Your adjusted basis is the property's original cost, plus the value of any improvements.) Obviously, if an item is stolen, there will be no salvage value.

> **EXAMPLE:** Sean's computer is stolen from his apartment by a burglar. The computer cost $2,000. Sean has taken no tax deductions for it because he purchased it only two months ago, so his adjusted basis is $2,000. Sean is a renter and has no insurance covering the loss. Sean's casualty loss is $2,000. ($2,000 adjusted basis – $0 salvage value – $0 insurance proceeds = $2,000 loss.)

If the property is only partly destroyed, your casualty loss deduction is the lesser of the decrease in the property's fair market value or its adjusted basis (your basis is reduced by any insurance you receive or expect to receive).

> **EXAMPLE:** Assume that Sean's computer (from the example above) is partly destroyed due to a small fire in his home. Its fair market value in its partly damaged state is $500. Because he spent $2,000 for it, the decrease in its fair market value is $1,500. Sean didn't

receive any insurance proceeds so the computer's adjusted basis is $2,000. Thus, his casualty loss is $1,500.

Unreimbursed Job Expenses

If you work as an employee, you may have various job-related expenses you end up paying out of your own pocket, such as:

- work-related travel, transportation, meal, and entertainment expenses
- business liability insurance premiums
- depreciation on a computer or cellular telephone your employer requires you to use in your work
- dues to a chamber of commerce if membership helps you do your job
- dues to professional societies
- education that is work related
- home office expenses for part of your home used regularly and exclusively in your work
- expenses of looking for a new job in your present occupation
- legal fees related to your job
- malpractice insurance premiums
- a passport for a business trip
- research expenses of a college professor
- subscriptions to professional journals and trade magazines related to your work
- tools and supplies used in your work
- union dues and expenses, and
- work clothes and uniforms (if required and not suitable for everyday use).

What to do about job expenses? *Don't pay them!* The best thing to do with expenses you incur while on the job is *not* to pay them yourself. Have your employer pay them. Use a company credit card or have your employer billed directly for the expense. If you must pay for something out of your own pocket, have your employer reimburse you. Provided they are for work-related expenses and are properly documented, these reimbursements are not taxable income to you and should not be included in the W-2 form your employer files with the IRS showing how much you were paid for the year. Your employer meanwhile gets to deduct these expenses as a business expense.

You're much better off being reimbursed than paying for something yourself and deducting it because (1) your deduction for job expenses is limited (as described in "If you have to pay job expenses yourself," below), and (2) any deduction you get will only recoup part of the expense. For example, if you spend $1,000 for a business trip and deduct it as an unreimbursed job expense, you'll get at most a $1,000 deduction. If you're in the 28% tax bracket, you'll save $280 on your taxes. Thus, your trip ends up costing you $720. If, on the other hand, your employer reimburses you for the $1,000, the trip will cost you nothing because the $1,000 is not taxable income.

Make sure you know what your employer's reimbursement policy is. If the policy is to reimburse the expense, be sure to claim it. If an employee has a right to reimbursement, but fails to claim it, a personal deduction for the employee's expenses is not allowed because the employee's expenditures are not "necessary."

It may be worth your while to take a salary reduction in order to get your employer to reimburse you for some expenses. Note, however, that your employer may be required by law to reimburse you for work-related expenses. For example, this is required in California (see Cal. Labor Code Sec. 2280).

Any reimbursement from your employer should be made under an "accountable plan." An accountable plan is a set of procedures that ensures that employees don't get reimbursed for personal expenses. In brief, you must:

- make an "adequate accounting" of the expense—that is, follow all the applicable record-keeping and other substantiation rules for the expense; for example, you must keep receipts (except for travel, meal, and entertainment expenses below $75; or travel and meal expenses paid on a per diem basis)
- timely submit your expense report and receipts to your employer, and
- timely return any payments that exceed what you actually spent.

If you fail to follow the rules, any reimbursements you receive must be treated as employee income subject to tax. Thus, the corporation must include them on your W-2. You'll then have to deduct the expense on your personal tax return.

Reimbursements for Personal Expenses Are Taxable Income

An expense reimbursement from your employer is tax free only if the expense was workrelated. If your employer reimburses you for a personal expense, the amount is considered income you must pay tax on. You can't, for example, have your employer reimburse you for your vacation and avoid tax on the payment.

What if you buy something for both work and personal use? The fair market value of any personal use of the item must be included in your compensation and you must pay tax on it.

EXAMPLE: Lloyd is an employee of a small engineering firm. His employer tells him to purchase a cell phone so he can keep in touch with his office and clients when he's in the field. The company reimburses him for the expense. If Lloyd uses the cell phone 100% for his work, the reimbursement is tax free to him. But if he uses it only 50% of the time for work and 50% of the time for personal purposes, he'll have to pay income tax on 50% of its fair market value.

If you have to pay job expenses yourself. If your employer does not reimburse you for your out-of-pocket work-related expenses, you can deduct them as a personal itemized deduction. Unreimbursed employee expenses are deductible to the extent they would be deductible by a self-employed person. They are subject to the same rules and limitations as business expenses (with a few variations). Thus, they are deductible only if they are ordinary, necessary, and reasonable in amount. Special rules also apply to many deductions—for example, education expenses may only be deducted to maintain or improve skills required in your current job, or to maintain your professional or work status. (These rules are covered below.)

However, an employee's deduction for unreimbursed job expenses is subject to an important limitation inapplicable to regular business expenses: Employee expenses fall under the category of miscellaneous itemized deductions, and as such are deductible only if, and to the extent that, they (along with your other miscellaneous deductions) exceed 2% of your adjusted gross income.

> **EXAMPLE:** Carolyn, an employee salesperson, spends $1,500 for a sales trip that her company does not reimburse her for. She has no other miscellaneous itemized deductions and her AGI is $50,000. She may deduct the expense only to the extent it exceeds 2% of her AGI. Since 2% of $50,000 is $1,000, she may only deduct $500 of her $1,500 travel expense.

Because of this limitation, the higher your AGI, the fewer expenses you'll be able to deduct. It doesn't seem fair, does it?

Home Office and Education Expenses

Two common expenses many employees have that are often not reimbursed by their employers are those for education and home offices. These items can be deductible, but there are significant restrictions.

Home offices. Qualifying for the home office deduction is hard to do for an employee. First of all, you must satisfy the ordinary requirements for the home office deduction, which means that (1) you must use a part of your home regularly and exclusively for work, and (2) your home office must be your principal workplace or you must regularly perform administrative or management tasks there. In addition, employees may only take the home office deduction if they maintain the home office for the convenience of their employer. An employee's home office is deemed to be for an employer's convenience only if it is:

- a condition of employment
- necessary for the employer's business to properly function, or
- needed to allow the employee to properly perform his or her duties.

The convenience of employer test is not met if using a home office is for your convenience or because you can get more work done at home. For example, you won't pass the test if you have an outside office provided by your employer but like to take work home with you. But you would pass the test if your employer doesn't provide you with an office, or if there is some valid business reason why you must work at home. In one case, for example, an employee was entitled to the home office deduction because her employer required her to perform work during off-hours when her regular office was closed.

If you don't qualify for the home office deduction, but regularly use your office for work, try to get your employer to reimburse you for your home office expenses. The reimbursement would not be taxable income so long as you properly account for your expenses.

Education expenses. Unreimbursed expenses for business-related education are deductible only if the education:

- maintains or improves skills required in your profession, or
- is required by law or regulation to maintain your professional status.

This includes the cost of attending a continuing professional education course or seminar, convention, or professional meeting. Deductible education expenses include tuition, fees, books, and other learning materials. They also include transportation and travel.

> **EXAMPLE:** Sue is an attorney. Every year, she is required by law to attend 12 hours of continuing education to keep her status as an active member of the state bar. The legal seminars she attends to satisfy this requirement are deductible education expenses.

However, you cannot currently deduct education expenses you incur to qualify for a *new* line of work or profession. For example, courts have held that IRS agents could not deduct the cost of going to law school, because a law degree would qualify them for a new profession—being a lawyer (*Jeffrey L. Weiler*, 54 T.C. 398 (1970)).

Likewise nondeductible are the costs required to meet the minimum or basic level educational requirements for a job or profession. Thus, for example, you can't deduct the expense of going to law school, medical school, or dental school.

Investment Expenses

You can earn money by engaging in personal investing—for example, by having personal bank accounts that pay interest or investing in stocks that pay dividends and appreciate in value over time (hopefully). The IRS calls activities like these—that are pursued primarily for profit but aren't businesses—income-producing activities.

You are entitled to deduct the ordinary and necessary expenses you incur to produce income, or to manage property held for the production of income. Such expenses include:

- appraisal fees for a casualty loss or charitable contribution
- clerical help and office rent in caring for investments
- depreciation on home computers used for investments
- fees to collect interest and dividends
- investment fees and expenses
- investment interest (see the section "Interest", above)
- legal fees for producing or collecting taxable income
- losses on traditional IRAs or Roth IRAs, when all amounts have been distributed to you
- losses on deposits in an insolvent or bankrupt financial institution
- safe deposit box rental fees
- service charges on dividend reinvestment plans
- tax advice fees, and
- trustees' fees for your IRA, if separately billed and paid.

These expenses fall within the category of miscellaneous itemized deductions. As such, they are deductible only if and to the extent they, along with your other miscellaneous deductions, exceed 2% of your adjusted gross income.

For detailed guidance on tax deductions for investments, refer to IRS Publication 550, *Investment Income and Expenses.*

Miscellaneous Itemized Deductions

There is a large group of deductions lumped together in a category called "miscellaneous itemized deductions." The most important of these—unreimbursed job expenses and investment expenses—have already been discussed in the preceding two sections. Miscellaneous itemized deductions also include the items listed below.

Except where otherwise noted, miscellaneous itemized deductions are subject to a 2% limit—that is, they are deductible only to the extent they exceed 2% of a taxpayer's adjusted gross income. Ordinarily, you apply the 2% limit after you apply any other deduction limit. For example, you apply the 50% limit on charitable deductions before the 2% limit.

EXAMPLE: Betty, a single taxpayer, has an adjusted gross income of $50,000. She may deduct her miscellaneous itemized deductions only to the extent that they exceed 2% of $50,000 or $1,000. This year she had $500 in charitable contributions, $100 in tax preparation fees, and $600 in unreimbursed employee expenses. Her total miscellaneous itemized deductions are $1,200, but because of the 2% of AGI limit, she may only deduct $200 of this amount—the amount that exceeds $1,000.

By far, the most important miscellaneous itemized deductions are charitable contributions and unreimbursed job expenses (which have already been discussed above). But they also include the following:

Tax preparation fees. These fees include the cost of tax preparation software programs and tax publications. They also include any fee you pay for electronic filing of your return. However, if you pay your taxes by credit card, you cannot deduct any convenience fee you are charged. If you own a business, you can deduct the cost of preparing the tax forms for your business as a business expense. You'll be deducting these fees for the prior year, not the current year—for example, in 2007 you may deduct the tax preparation fees you paid in 2006 to prepare your 2005 tax returns. If you have a tax pro prepare both your personal and business taxes, have him or her give you a separate bill for preparing your business return. Reason: This amount will be fully deductible as a business expense whether or not you itemize your deductions, but the costs of preparing your personal return are deductible only as a miscellaneous itemized deduction and subject to the 2% of AGI threshold.

Fees to fight the IRS. You may deduct attorney fees, accounting fees, and other fees you incur to determine, contest, pay, or claim a refund of any tax.

Gambling losses. These are deductible but only up to the amount of your gambling winnings for the year. You cannot reduce your gambling winnings by your gambling losses and report the difference. You must report the full amount of your winnings as income and claim your losses (up to the amount of winnings) as an itemized deduction. Therefore, your records should show your winnings separately from your losses. These losses are not subject to the 2% limit on miscellaneous itemized deductions.

Hobby expenses. A hobby is an activity you engage in primarily for a reason other than to earn a profit—for example, to have fun. Expenses from a hobby are deductible only if you have income from the hobby and only up to the amount of hobby income earned during the year. (See "Hobby Expenses," below.)

For more information, see IRS Publication 529, *Miscellaneous Deductions.*

Limit on itemized deductions for high-income taxpayers. High-income taxpayers lose the benefit of some of their itemized deductions because there are income thresholds that affect how much you can deduct. If you exceed the thresholds, you must reduce your deductions by a certain percentage, which depends on your AGI. This percentage is scheduled to go down over the next several years so it won't make as much difference as it has in the past. In 2010, there will be no limit at all (unless Congress changes the law again).

This rule is a bit complicated. Here's how it works:

- First of all, the limit applies only if your AGI is above a threshold amount. In 2006, the threshold was $150,500 (this figure is adjusted each year for inflation).
- If your AGI exceeds the threshold amount, total up the amount of all your itemized deductions subject to the limit. Do not include your deductions for medical expenses, investment interest, casualty and theft losses, and some gambling losses, because they are not subject to the limit.
- Apply the applicable limits to these deductions—the 2% of AGI limit on miscellaneous itemized deduction and the limits on charitable deductions.
- Take this total and reduce it by the smaller of 3% of the amount of your AGI that exceeds the threshold, or 80%. This means that in no event can your affected itemized deductions be reduced by more than 80%.

EXAMPLE: Jessica is an executive employed by a hightech company. Her 2006 AGI was $250,500. She had $50,000 in itemized deductions, including $20,000 in unreimbursed employee expenses. Her employee expenses are first reduced by 2% of her AGI (2% x $250,500= $5,010). Her total itemized deductions are now $44,090. Her AGI is $100,000 above the $150,500 threshold for the 3% reduction. Thus, her itemized deductions must be reduced by the lesser of 3% of the amount her AGI exceeds the limit or 80%. Three percent of her AGI is $3,000 (3% x $100,000 = $3,000), subtracting this amount leaves her with $41,090 in itemized deductions. Eighty percent of her affected itemized deductions is $35,272 (80% x 44,090). Because $3,000 is less than $35,272, Jessica's itemized deductions are reduced by $3,000.

Confused yet? What we've shown up to now is how the limit is ordinarily applied. However, the limit will be phased out over the next several years and then eliminated entirely for at least for one year. It was cut by one-third for tax years 2006 and 2007, by two-thirds for 2008 and 2009, and will be eliminated entirely in 2010. It will be reinstated in its original form starting in 2011, unless Congress acts to eliminate it permanently—something President Bush has requested. These scheduled changes are shown in the following chart.

Year	Reduction in Itemized Deduction Limit
2006–2007	33.33%
2008–2009	66.67%
2010	100%
2011 and later	0

Thus, up until 2010, you must reduce your itemized deduction limitation by one-third or two-thirds, depending on the year.

EXAMPLE: Jessica from the above example reduces her $3,000 reduction amount for 2006 by 33.33%, leaving her with $2,000. Thus, she only reduced her affected itemized deductions by $2,000. So Jessica ends up deducting $42,090 in itemized deductions instead of the $44,090 she could have deducted if the reduction didn't apply.

If your AGI is in the reduction range, but not too far above it, you can try to reduce it by increasing your adjustments to income or business deductions. For example, increase your contributions to your retirement accounts such as a 401(k) or IRA—these contributions reduce your AGI. If you own losing stocks, you can sell them and deduct up to $3,000 of your losses from your AGI.

Adjustments to Income: Like a Deduction, But With a Different Name

There are some expenses you can deduct whether you itemize your deductions or take the standard deduction. Technically speaking, these are not deductions at all, but adjustments to income (also called above the line deductions). But, just like a deduction, they reduce your taxable income. To paraphrase Shakespeare, a deduction by any other name would be as sweet.

You deduct them directly from your gross income, not from your adjusted gross income as you do with itemized deductions. (See Chapter 1 for a detailed explanation of gross income and adjusted gross income.) They are not subject to any of the limits that apply to itemized deductions, which makes them particularly valuable.

! **The adjustments to income for educator expenses and college tuition and fees expired at the end of 2005.** As this book went to press, Congress was expected to extend them to 2006 and perhaps beyond. Be sure to check whether these adjustments have been extended to the current tax year.

The only problem with adjustments to income is that there aren't very many of them. The most significant are health insurance expenses and retirement contributions by self-employed people. If you're not self-employed, you can still deduct IRA contributions and contributions to health savings accounts. However, many taxpayers have no adjustments to income at all.

You deduct nonitemized expenses on the first page of your IRS Form 1040. Don't list them on Schedule A, the form you file to claim itemized deductions. These deductions include:

Educator expenses. Because of inadequate school funding, teachers sometimes pay for needed supplies and other teaching items out of their own pockets. A special tax deduction is designed to help them out. Kindergarten through grade 12 teachers may deduct up to $250 that they pay for books, supplies, equipment, (including computer equipment, software, and services), and other materials used in the classroom. These expenses are not deductible if the teacher is reimbursed for them. This deduction began in 2005 and is extended by Congress on a year-to-year basis, so be sure it's in effect during the current year.

Employee moving expenses. If you moved because of a change in your job location or because you started a new job, you may be able to deduct your moving expenses as a nonitemized deduction. To qualify for the deduction, you must meet both a distance and time test (unless you are a member of the armed forces and your move was due to a permanent change of station).

Your move meets the distance test if your new main job location is at least 50 miles farther from your former home than your old main job location was. Use the shortest distance of the most commonly traveled routes between these points. To determine this, first figure the distance between your former residence and your new job and then subtract the distance between your former residence and your old job. If the result is 50 miles or more, you have met the distance test. For example, if the distance from your former residence to your new job is 70 miles and the distance from your former residence to your old job is five miles, you will meet the distance test.

The second test concerns time. If you are an employee, you must work full-time for at least 39 weeks during the 12 months right after you move. If you are self-employed, you must work full time for at least 39 weeks during the first 12 months and for a total of at least 78 weeks during the first 24 months after you move. There are exceptions to the time test in case of death, disability, and involuntary separation.

If you meet the requirements, you can deduct the reasonable expenses of moving your household goods and personal effects to your new home. You can also deduct the expenses of traveling to your new home, including your lodging expenses. You cannot, however, deduct meals.

For more information, refer to IRS Publication 521, *Moving Expenses.*

Health savings account contributions. See Chapter 2.

Retirement plan contributions by self-employed taxpayers. See Chapter 4.

Self-employed health insurance. See "Medical and Dental Expenses," above.

50% of self-employment taxes. This is a 12.4% Social Security tax on net self-employment income up to an annual ceiling and a 2.9% Medicare tax on all net self-employment income.

Penalty on early savings withdrawals. Penalties you have to pay to banks and other financial institutions because you withdraw your savings early from certificates of deposit accounts or similar accounts.

Alimony. Alimony is a court-ordered payment to a separated spouse or divorced ex-spouse. It does not include child support payments. For more details, see IRS Publication 504, *Divorced or Separated Individuals.*

IRA contributions. See Chapter 4.

Student loan interest. A certain amount of student loan interest is deductible from your gross income each year provided that your adjusted gross income—before subtracting any deduction for student loan interest—is below a ceiling amount. For 2006, a student loan interest deduction starts to be phased out if your AGI is over $50,000 ($105,000 for joint filers) and is eliminated if your AGI exceeds $65,000 ($135,00 if filing jointly). Up to $2,500 in interest can be deducted each year.

College tuition and fees. You can deduct up to $4,000 of the tuition and fees you pay so that you, your spouse, or child or other dependent can attend any accredited college, university, or other postsecondary school such as a vocational school. The deduction can be claimed whether you pay the tuition and fees with your own money or take out school loans to pay it. But you can't deduct tuition you pay with tax-free scholarship money or tax-free interest from U.S. savings bonds. Also, you can't take the deduction at all if you or anyone else claims a Hope or Lifetime Learning credit for that same student in the same year. (See Chapter 3 for a discussion of education credits.)

Do You Have a Business? Don't Forget to Deduct Your Expenses

The tax law recognizes that people in business must spend money to make money. Virtually every business, however small, incurs some expenses. Even someone with a low overhead business (such as a freelance writer) must buy paper, computer equipment, and office supplies. Some businesses incur substantial expenses, even exceeding their income.

You are not legally required to pay tax on every dollar your business takes in (your gross income). Instead, you owe tax only on the amount left over after your business's deductible expenses are subtracted from your gross income (this remaining amount is called your "net profit"). The more deductions you take, the lower your net profit will be, and the less tax you will have to pay.

> **EXAMPLE:** Karen, a sole proprietor, earned $50,000 this year from her consulting business. Fortunately, she doesn't have to pay income tax on the entire $50,000—her gross income. Instead, she can deduct from her gross income various business expenses, including a $5,000 home office deduction and a $5,000 deduction for equipment expenses. She deducts these expenses from her $50,000 gross income to arrive at her net profit: $40,000. She pays income tax only on this net profit amount.

If, like a majority of small business owners, you're a sole proprietor, you deduct your business expenses on IRS Schedule C, Profit or Loss From Business. Your net profit (or loss) is then transferred to the first page of your Form 1040. Business deductions are above the line deductions that are deducted from your gross income, just like adjustments to income. However, business expenses are even more valuable than itemized deductions or adjustments to income because they reduce self-employment tax (Social Security and Medicare tax) as well as income taxes. Reason: The amount of self-employment tax you have to pay is based on your net self-employment income—business deductions reduce this income and thus lower your self-employment taxes. The self-employment tax is a combined 15.3% Social Security and Medicare tax up to an annual income ceiling.

If the money you spend on your business exceeds your business income for the year, your business incurs a loss. This isn't as bad as it sounds because you can use a business loss to offset other income you may have—for example, interest income or your spouse's income if you file jointly. You can even accumulate your losses and apply them to reduce your income taxes in future or past years.

You must keep track of your expenses. You can deduct only those expenses that you actually incur. You need to keep records of these expenses to (1) know for sure how much you actually spent, and (2) prove to the IRS that you really spent the money you deducted, in case you are audited.

This section provides only an overview of a complex subject, but one well worth careful study by any business owner. For a detailed discussion of business deductions, refer to one or more of the following:
- *Deduct It! Lower Your Small Business Taxes*, by Stephen Fishman (Nolo)
- *Home Business Tax Deductions: Keep What You Earn*, by Stephen Fishman (Nolo), and
- *Tax Deductions for Professionals*, by Stephen Fishman (Nolo).

Virtually any business expense is deductible as long as it is:
- ordinary and necessary—that is, common, accepted, helpful, and appropriate for your business or profession
- directly related to your business—that is, not a personal expense, and
- for a reasonable amount.

Business owners can deduct four broad categories of business expenses.

Start-Up Expenses

The first money you will have to shell out will be for your business's start-up expenses. These include most of the costs of getting your business up and running, like license fees, advertising costs, attorney and accounting fees, travel expenses, market research, and office supplies expenses. You may deduct up to $5,000 in start-up costs the first year a new business is in operation. You may deduct amounts over $5,000 over the next 15 years.

EXAMPLE: Cary, a star hairdresser at a popular salon, decides to open his own hairdressing business. Before Cary's new salon opens for business, he has to rent space, hire and train employees, and pay for an expensive preopening advertising campaign. These start-up expenses cost Cary $20,000. Cary may deduct $5,000 of his $20,000 in operating expenses the first year he's in business. He may deduct the remaining $15,000 in equal amounts over the next 15 years.

Operating Expenses

Operating expenses are the ongoing day-to-day costs a business incurs to stay in business. They include such things as:

- advertising costs—for example, the cost of a Yellow Pages advertisement, brochure, or business website
- attorney and accounting fees for your business
- bank fees for your business bank account
- car and truck expenses
- costs of renting or leasing office space, vehicles, machinery, equipment, and other property used in your business
- education expenses—for example, the cost of attending professional seminars or classes required to keep up a professional license
- expenses for the business use of your home
- fees you pay to self-employed workers you hire to help your business—for example, the cost of paying a marketing consultant to advise you on how to get more clients
- health insurance for yourself and your family
- insurance for your business—for example, liability, workers' compensation, and business property insurance
- interest on business loans and debts—for example, interest you pay for a bank loan you use to expand your business
- license fees
- office expenses, such as office supplies
- office utilities
- postage
- professional association dues
- professional or business books you need for your business

- repairs and maintenance for business equipment, such as a photocopier or fax machine
- retirement plan contributions (see Chapter 4)
- software you buy for your business
- subscriptions for professional or business publications
- business travel, meals, and entertainment, and
- wages and benefits you provide your employees.

These expenses (unlike start-up expenses) are currently deductible—that is, you can deduct them all in the year in which you pay them.

> **EXAMPLE:** After Cary's salon opens, he begins paying $5,000 a month for rent and utilities. This is an operating expense that is currently deductible. When Cary does his taxes, he can deduct from his income the entire $60,000 that he paid for rent and utilities for the year.

Capital Expenses

Capital assets are things you buy for your business that have a useful life of more than one year, such as land, buildings, equipment, vehicles, books, furniture, machinery, and patents you buy from others. These costs, called capital expenses, are considered to be part of your investment in your business, not day-to-day operating expenses.

Large businesses—those that buy at least several hundred thousand dollars of capital assets in a year—must deduct these costs by using depreciation. To depreciate an item, you deduct a portion of the cost in each year of the item's useful life. Depending on the asset, this could be anywhere from three to 39 years (the IRS decides the asset's useful life). Small businesses can also use depreciation, but they have another option available for deducting many capital expenses: They can currently deduct up to $108,000 in capital expenses per year under a provision of the tax code called Section 179.

> **EXAMPLE:** Cary spent $5,000 on fancy barber chairs for his salon. Because the chairs have a useful life of more than one year, they are capital assets that he will either have to depreciate over several years or deduct in one year under Section 179.

Certain capital assets, such as land and corporate stock, never wear out. Capital expenses related to these costs are not deductible; the owner must wait until the asset is sold to recover the cost.

Inventory

Inventory includes almost anything you make or buy to resell to customers. It doesn't matter whether you manufacture the goods yourself or buy finished goods from someone else and resell the items to customers. Inventory doesn't include tools, equipment, or other items that you use in your business; it refers only to items that you buy or make to sell.

You must deduct inventory costs separately from all other business expenses—you deduct inventory costs as you sell the inventory. Inventory that remains unsold at the end of the year is a business asset, not a deductible expense.

> **EXAMPLE:** In addition to providing hair styling services, Cary sells various hair care products in his salon that he buys from cosmetics companies. In 2006, Cary spends $15,000 on his inventory of hair care product, but sells only $10,000 worth of the product. He can only deduct $10,000 of the inventory costs in 2006.

You must be in business to claim business deductions. Only businesses can claim business tax deductions. This probably seems like a simple concept, but it can get tricky. Even though you might believe you are running a business, the IRS may beg to differ. If your business doesn't turn a profit for several years in a row, the IRS might decide that you are engaged in a hobby rather than a business. This may not sound like a big deal, but it could have disastrous tax consequences: People engaged in hobbies are entitled to very limited tax deductions, while businesses can deduct all kinds of expenses. Fortunately, this unhappy outcome can be avoided by careful taxpayers.

Business Versus Hobby Distinction

A venture is a business if you engage in it to make a profit. It's not necessary that you earn a profit every year. All that is required is that your main reason for doing what you do is to make a profit. A hobby is any activity you engage in mainly for a reason other than making a profit—for example, to incur deductible expenses or just to have fun.

The IRS can't read your mind to determine whether you want to earn a profit. And it certainly isn't going to take your word for it. Instead, it looks to see whether you do actually earn a profit or behave as if you want to earn a profit.

Profit test. If your venture earns a profit in three out of five consecutive years, the IRS must presume that you have a profit motive. The IRS and courts look at your tax returns for each year you claim to be in business to see whether you turned a profit. Any legitimate profit—no matter how small—qualifies; you don't have to earn a particular amount or percentage. Careful year-end planning can help your business show a profit for the year. If clients owe you money, for example, you can press for payment before the end of the year. You can also put off paying expenses or buying new equipment until the next tax year.

Even if you meet the three-of-five-years test, the IRS can still claim that your activity is a hobby, but it will have to prove that you don't have a profit motive. In practice, the IRS usually doesn't attack ventures that pass the profit test unless the numbers have clearly been manipulated just to meet the standard.

The presumption that you are in business applies to your third profitable year and extends to all later years within the five-year period beginning with your first profitable year.

> **EXAMPLE:** Tom began to work at home as a self-employed graphic designer in 2002. Due to economic conditions and the difficulty of establishing a new business, his income varied dramatically from year to year. However, as the chart below shows, he managed to earn a profit in three of the first five years that he was in business.
>
> | Year | Losses | Profits |
> |------|--------|---------|
> | 2002 | $ 10,000 | |
> | 2003 | | $ 5,500 |
> | 2004 | | $ 9,000 |
> | 2005 | $ 6,000 | |
> | 2006 | | $ 8,000 |
> | 2007 | | $ 30,000 |

If the IRS audits Tom's taxes for 2006, it must presume that he was in business during that year. Tom earned a profit during three of the five consecutive years ending with 2006, so the presumption that Tom is in business extends to 2008, five years after his first profitable year.

Behavior test. If you keep incurring losses and can't satisfy the profit test, you by no means have to throw in the towel and treat your venture as a hobby. You can continue to treat it as a business and fully deduct your losses. However, you must take steps that will convince the IRS that your business is not a hobby in case you're audited.

You must be able to convince the IRS that earning a profit—not having fun or accumulating tax deductions—is the primary motive for what you do. This can be particularly difficult if you're engaged in an activity that could objectively be considered fun—for example, creating artwork, photography, or writing—but it can still be done. People who have incurred losses for seven, eight, or nine years in a row have convinced the IRS that they were running a business.

You must show the IRS that your behavior is consistent with that of a person who really wants to make money. There are many ways to accomplish this.

First and foremost, you must show that you carry on your enterprise in a businesslike manner—for example, you:

- maintain a separate checking account for your business
- keep good business records
- make some effort to market your services—for example, have business cards and, if appropriate, a Yellow Pages or similar advertisement
- have business stationery and cards printed
- obtain a federal employer identification number
- secure all necessary business licenses and permits
- have a separate phone line for your business if you work at home
- join professional organizations and associations, and
- develop expertise in your field by attending educational seminars and similar activities.

You should also draw up a business plan with forecasts of revenue and expenses. This will also be helpful if you try to borrow money for your business.

For detailed guidance on how to create a business plan, see *How to Write a Business Plan,* by Mike McKeever (Nolo).

The more time and effort you put into the activity, the more it will look like you want to make money. So try to devote as much time as possible to your business and keep a log showing the time you spend on it.

It's also helpful to consult with experts in your field and follow their advice about how to modify your operations to increase sales and cut costs. Be sure to document your efforts.

EXAMPLE: Otto, a professional artist, has incurred losses from his business for the past three years. He consults with Cindy, a prominent art gallery owner, about how he can sell more of his work. He writes down her recommendations and then documents his efforts to follow them—for example, he visits art shows around the country and talks with a number of gallery owners about representing his work.

You'll have an easier time convincing the IRS that your venture is a business if you earn a profit in at least some years. It's also very helpful if you've earned profits from similar businesses in the past.

Rental Property Deductions

If you own residential rental property such as a rental house or apartment building, your activity may constitute a business for tax purposes or be an investment activity. Either way, you deduct your rental expenses from your rental income and add what's left over to your other taxable income for the year on the first page of your Form 1040. Thus, you only pay income tax on your net rental income. Most landlords file IRS Schedule E, *Supplemental Income and Loss*, to report their income and expenses. Rental deductions are above the line deductions that are deducted from your gross income, just like adjustments to income.

Most expenses a landlord incurs to operate a rental property are deductible. They include such things as mortgage interest, utilities, salaries, supplies, travel expenses, car expenses, and repairs and maintenance. Rental property itself is depreciated over 27.5 years. Capital assets other than real estate are depreciated over a much shorter period—for example, vehicles and furniture are depreciated over five years. The cost of land is not deductible, the owner must wait until land is sold to recover the cost.

If your rental expenses exceed your rental income, you'll have a rental loss. Rental losses can be deductible from nonrental income, but there are significant restrictions.

 For a detailed discussion of tax deductions for landlords, refer to *Every Landlord's Tax Deduction Guide*, **by Stephen Fishman (Nolo).**

Make the Most of Your Deductions: Plan Ahead for the Greatest Tax Savings

As a general rule, you want to deduct as much as possible as fast as possible. That way you'll pay the least tax possible. Some smart planning can help.

Bunch Your Itemized Deductions

Every year you have the right to choose whether to take the standard deduction or itemize your deductions. You should take the standard deduction only if it exceeds your itemized deductions for the year. If you don't have enough itemized deductions to itemize every year, you should consider bunching your itemized deductions. This means that you pile on your itemized deductions every other year, giving yourself the maximum itemized deduction for that year. You then take the standard deduction the following year, when you have fewer itemized deductions.

During the year you plan to itemize, you should do everything you can to ensure that your itemized deductions exceed your standard deduction by as much as possible. Pay every bill that will result in an itemized deduction this year. If you don't have the cash to do so, you can pay by credit card or borrow the money.

You particularly want to bunch expenses for those itemized deductions that are subject to a deduction floor—medical expenses and most miscellaneous itemized deductions. This way, you don't have to struggle every year to satisfy the 2% of AGI threshold for miscellaneous itemized deductions and 7.5% of AGI for medical expenses.

> **EXAMPLE:** Frank and Flora are a married couple who file jointly. In 2005, their itemized deductions were only $8,000, so they took the standard deduction. They want to itemize their deductions in 2006, when their standard deduction is $10,300. To do this, they spend as much as possible on itemized deductions in 2006 using the techniques described below. As a result, they end up with $12,000 in itemized deductions for 2006, and can therefore itemize. They plan to take the standard deduction in 2007, so they will keep their itemized deductions as low as possible that year, and then load up on their itemized deduction for 2008.

Charitable Contributions

Increase your cash or property contributions for the year—you may even want to contribute double what you ordinarily do and donate nothing the following year.

Property Taxes

If you own a home, pay the next year's property taxes before the end of the current year.

State Income Taxes

If you pay your state income taxes by paying estimated tax four times per year, you ordinarily make your fourth payment for the current year in January of the following year. Make this payment in December instead of January so you can deduct it this year.

State Sales Taxes

If your state doesn't have income taxes or the state income taxes you pay are small, you could take the state sales tax deduction. You can maximize this deduction by buying any big-ticket items you want this year—for example, if you're thinking about buying a new car, buy it by the end of the year so you can deduct the sales tax this year.

Medical Expenses

There is no shortage of ways to load up on medical expenses. For example, if you or a family member need to have elective surgery or an expensive dental procedure like orthodontia, have it this year. Stock up on prescription medications. Get new eyeglasses. If your doctor has advised you to make improvements to your home to safeguard your health—for example, installing an air filtration system to protect from allergies—make them this year.

Employee Expenses

Maximize any employee expenses that are not reimbursed by your employer—for example, subscriptions to work-related publications, professional or union dues, or education expenses.

Investment Expenses

If you need to buy things for your investment activities, do it this year. For example, renew your subscriptions to investment publications.

Hobby Expenses

If you have a hobby from which you earn money, you can increase your itemized deductions for the year by spending money on the hobby. Hobby expenses are deductible as a miscellaneous itemized deduction, but only up to the amount of hobby income. Any expenses that exceed hobby income are not deductible at all. Thus, ideally, in any year you wish to itemize your deductions, your annual hobby expenses should match your hobby income. For example, a hobby artist who sells two paintings during the year for $1,000, and wants to itemize his deductions for the year, should have $1,000 in art expenses he can deduct. If you don't itemize, no hobby expenses are deductible, so try to spend as little as possible in any year you take the standard deduction.

Take a Gambling Vacation

If you're a gambler and you've won more than you've lost during the year, take a gambling vacation. If you lose no more than your total winnings for the year, your losses will be made up by your tax savings since they are deductible against your gambling winnings. If you don't lose, you won't save on taxes, but you'll have even more winnings. Either way, you're ahead.

When Is an Expense Paid?

An expense is paid when you pay it by check, credit card, or electronic funds transfer, as well as by cash. If you pay by check, the amount is deemed paid during the year in which the check is drawn and mailed—for example, a check dated December 31, 2006 is considered paid during 2006 only if it has a December 31, 2006 postmark. If you're using a check to pay a substantial expense, you may wish to mail it by certified mail so you'll have proof of when it was mailed. If you pay by credit card, the amount is deemed paid on the date you use the card, not the date when you actually pay the amount you owe to the credit card company.

Reduce Your AGI With Adjustments to Income

You can deduct adjustments to income whether or not you take the standard deduction, so you don't have to worry about meeting a threshold amount as you do with itemized deductions. This might make it seem like there is no reason to bunch itemized deductions. But there is. If you bunch your itemized deductions, you should also maximize your adjustments to income for that year so you can keep your AGI as low as possible.

Having a lower AGI helps you deduct more of your itemized deductions because most of them can be deducted only to the extent they exceed a certain percentage of your AGI—7.5% for medical expenses, and 2% for most miscellaneous itemized deductions.

For example, if your AGI is $100,000, you'll only be able to deduct those medical expenses that exceed $7,500 (7.5% x your AGI). But if your AGI is $75,000, you'll be able to deduct medical expenses that exceed $5,625 (7.5% x $80,000 = $5,625)—likewise for miscellaneous itemized deductions subject to the 2% of AGI floor.

To keep your AGI as low as possible, you can:
- make an IRA contribution
- if you're self-employed, contribute to your retirement accounts
- if you have a health savings account, make the maximum annual contribution
- move by year end so you can take the moving expense deduction (but only if the move is job-related)
- if you're a teacher, take the teacher's deduction (if available, see above)
- prepay college tuition and fees (if this deduction is still available) (the rules for this deduction allow you to deduct these expenses even if they aren't due until the following year)
- prepay student loans if you qualify for the student loan interest deduction (you can prepay this expense just like tuition and fees), or
- if you pay alimony to an ex-spouse, pay part of next year's payments this year.

Of course, you can also reduce your AGI by deferring income until a later year. (See Chapter 4.)

Accelerate Your Business Deductions

As a general rule, business owners want to get their tax deductions as soon as possible. To do this, you should incur as many deductible business expenses as you can by the end of the year (assuming you're a cash basis taxpayer, like most small business owners). Don't buy anything you don't need, but go ahead and buy or prepay for items you will need. For example:

- make any needed equipment purchases before the end of the year (be sure to place the equipment in service by the end of the year or you'll get no deduction)
- deduct the cost of business assets in one year under Section 179 rather than depreciating them over several years
- pay any business-related fees this year—for example, attorney fees or accounting fees, and
- if you plan to borrow money for your business, do so before the end of the year so you can deduct your interest payments this year.

Deferring Deductions to Avoid AMT

If you could be subject to the AMT, it may be advisable to defer to later years certain deductions that are not allowed for the AMT. These expenses include taxes, employee business expenses, and investment expenses. (See Chapter 1.)

Don't Prepay Expenses More Than One Year in Advance

If, like most small business owners, you're a cash basis taxpayer, the general rule is that you can't prepay business expenses and deduct them from the current year's taxes. An expense you pay in advance can be deducted only in the year to which it applies.

However, there is an important exception called the 12-month rule. Under this rule, you may deduct a prepaid expense in the current year if the expense is for a right or benefit that extends no longer than the earlier of:

- 12 months, or
- until the end of the tax year after the tax year in which you made the payment.

EXAMPLE 1: You are a calendar year taxpayer and you pay $10,000 on July 1, 2006 for a malpractice insurance policy that is effective for one year beginning July 1, 2006. The 12-month rule applies because the benefit you've paid for—a business insurance policy—extends only 12 months into the future. Therefore, the full $10,000 is deductible in 2006.

EXAMPLE 2: You are a calendar year taxpayer and you pay $3,000 in 2006 for a business insurance policy that is effective for three years, beginning July 1, 2006. This payment does not qualify for the 12-month rule because the benefit extends more than 12 months. Therefore, you must use the general rule: $500 is deductible in 2006, $1,000 is deductible in 2007, $1,000 is deductible in 2008, and $500 is deductible in 2009.

To use the 12-month rule, you must apply it when you first start your business. You must get IRS approval if you haven't been using the rule and want to start doing so. Such IRS approval is granted automatically. You must file IRS Form 3115, *Application for Change in Accounting Method* with your tax return for the year you want to make the change.

CHAPTER 6

Join the Low-Tax Rate Club: Reduce Your Tax Rate Through Investing

T ax rates make a big difference. If you have to pay a 35% tax on $1,000, you're out $350. But if you pay a 15% tax instead, you lose only $150. If you're going to pay taxes on your income, you might as well do it at the lowest tax rate possible.

Tax rates vary depending on the type of income being taxed. The lowest rates are reserved for income from investments—things like stocks, bonds, mutual funds, and real estate. The profits you earn from these investments are taxed at capital gains rates. Right now, these rates are lower than they have been at any time since 1933—as low as 5%. In fact, starting in 2008, there will be a 0% tax on capital gains earned by some investors. In contrast, the average working stiff must pay income tax on his salary or business income at ordinary income rates, which can be as high as 35%. So, it's the perfect time to start saving and investing your hard-earned money—that way you can join the club of people who make money from money.

⚠ **Investments held in retirement accounts are taxed differently.** The information in this chapter about the lower tax rates for capital gains and dividends is not applicable to mutual funds, stocks, and other investments held in retirement accounts such as a traditional IRA, 401(k), or SEP-IRA. These types of retirement accounts are tax deferred—that is, you don't pay any tax on your contributions or the income they earn as long as it stays in the account. However, when the money in the account is withdrawn upon retirement (or earlier in some cases), it is taxed at ordinary income rates. This is true even though the money in the account comes from capital assets like stocks and bonds or dividends. The only exception is a Roth IRA or Roth 401(k); withdrawals from these accounts are all tax free, but contributions are not tax deferred. See Chapter 4 for a detailed discussion of retirement accounts.

Capital Gains—The Best Rate in Town

There are two separate sets of tax rates that apply to income. One is for ordinary income; the other is for capital gains. Ordinary income is what most people think of as income—your salary from a job, interest on savings accounts or bonds, rental income, income you earn from owning a business, and income from retirement accounts and pensions. Ordinary income is taxed at ordinary income rates with tax brackets ranging from 10% to 35%—something we're all familiar with.

Another way you can receive income is to sell something you own— a house, mutual fund shares, stocks, bonds, or collectibles like coins and stamps. These are all capital assets and any profit you receive from selling a capital asset is taxable income. However, this profit is classified as a capital gain, not ordinary income, and you pay tax on the income at capital gains tax rates. These rates can be significantly lower than those for ordinary income—in some cases, as low as 5% or (in limited circumstances) even 0%. There are things you can do to make sure you pay the lowest capital gains tax rate. But first you must understand how capital gains are taxed.

This chapter only scratches the surface of a complex subject. For more information on capital gains and losses, refer to the following IRS publications:

- Publication 550, *Investment Income and Expenses*
- Publication 551, *Basis of Assets*, and
- Publication 564, *Mutual Fund Distributions*.

The book *Capital Gains, Minimal Taxes*, by Kaye A. Thomas (Fairmark Press), also provides excellent in-depth coverage of tax issues for investors in mutual funds and stocks.

What Are Capital Assets?

Almost everything you own for any purpose, other than business, is a capital asset. This includes both tangible property like your home and intangible property like stocks and mutual funds. There are two main types of capital assets: personal use property and investment property. Personal use property consists of things you use in your daily life such as:

- your main home
- a vacation home or boat
- household furnishings
- a coin or stamp collection
- clothing
- jewelry, and
- any vehicle used for pleasure or commuting.

Investment property consists of things like:

- corporate stocks and bonds (including stock in a small company that is not publicly traded).
- mutual funds
- government bonds
- vacant land, and
- partnership and limited liability company ownership interests.

The one significant type of property that is not a capital asset is business property. This includes:

- inventory or merchandise held mainly for sale to customers (or property that will become part of merchandise)
- equipment and other personal property used by a business—for example, office furniture and computers
- real property used for business or as rental property, and
- the copyright in a literary, musical, or artistic work you create yourself, pay someone to create, or purchase from someone else.

Because business property is not considered a capital asset, different tax rules apply to how income or loss from the sale of this property is treated. For example, the profit a business earns from selling inventory is taxed at ordinary income rates, as is money earned from copyrights. However, the sale of depreciable business property is taxed at the same rates as capital gains—and there are certain tax advantages unique to selling of business property that you don't get with capital assets. (See "Business Property Sales," below.)

Figuring Out Your Basis

Whenever you sell a capital asset, you must determine whether you've earned a profit, incurred a loss, or broken even. This will tell you whether you've had a capital gain or loss for IRS reporting purposes. To figure this out, you need to know your basis in the property. Once you have this information, you can determine whether you owe any taxes on the sale.

The basis of a capital asset is its cost (the purchase price), plus any other costs incurred by the buyer at the time of the purchase, such as sales fees and commissions, shipping expenses, sales tax, and installation costs. To determine whether you have a capital gain or loss, you subtract what you paid for the asset (its cost or basis) from what you are selling it for (its selling price): Selling Price – Cost (Basis) = Capital Gain or Loss. If you sell a capital asset and the selling price is higher than your cost or basis, you have a capital gain.

> **EXAMPLE:** Sue buys ten shares of BigTech stock for $1,000 ($100 per share). She pays a $20 sales commission to an online broker. She later sells all of her shares for $1,520. She paid another $20 brokerage fee to close the sale. Her basis in the ten shares is $1,000 + $20 + $20 = $1,040. Her capital gain on the sale is $460 ($1,500 – $1,040).

Unfortunately, capital assets aren't always sold for a profit. If you incur a loss when you sell a capital asset, you have a capital loss. These losses are treated very differently for tax purposes than other types of losses (see "Deducting Capital Losses," below).

> **EXAMPLE:** Assume that Sue from the above example sold her ten shares of stock for $900. She has a capital loss of $140 ($900 – $1,040).

What if you didn't buy the asset you are selling? For example, you received the item as a gift or inherited it. With gifted property, your basis in the property is the same as the giftor's if the value of the property has gone up since the time you received it (which is usually the case). This is called a "carryover basis."

> **EXAMPLE:** Assume that Sue receive her BigTech shares as a gift from her father. Her father paid $500 for the shares plus $50 in broker fees. Sue's basis is $550. Sue sells the shares for $1,500. Her capital gain is $950.

If someone has the nerve to give you property that has gone down in value since it was purchased, your basis is the lower of its fair market value at the time of the gift, or the giftor's basis.

In contrast, the basis of inherited property is its fair market value on the date of the owner's death—often referred to as stepped-up basis. This can result in enormous tax savings if the asset has appreciated in value because no tax is ever owed on the gain in value from the time of the asset's purchase to the owner's death.

> **EXAMPLE:** Assume that Sue inherited her BigTech stock from her late Uncle Ralph. He had purchased his ten shares for $1,000. On the date he died, the stock was worth $1,500. Sue sells the shares for $1,500 and has no capital gain—the sale is tax free. No tax is ever paid on the $500 increase in value of the stock.

If property is transferred to you from your spouse (or former spouse, if the transfer is part of your divorce), your basis is the same as your spouse's or former spouse's basis at the time of the transfer.

Holding Periods—Long-Term and Short-Term

How long you own a capital asset (the holding period) is a critical factor in determining what tax rate will apply when you sell the property. There are two holding periods for capital assets: long-term and short-term. If you own the property for more than one year, any profit or loss you receive from its sale is a long-term capital gain or loss. If you hold a capital asset for one year or less, any gain or loss is a short-term capital gain or loss. Different tax rates apply depending on whether you have a long-term or short-term gain or loss.

The holding period begins the day after you acquire the asset and ends on the day you sell it. The day you sell the asset is part of your holding period.

> **EXAMPLE:** Harry buys a summer vacation home on February 5, 2004 for $200,000 and sells it on February 5, 2005, for $250,000. His holding period is not more than one year so he has a short-term capital gain of $50,000. If he had sold it one day later, his holding period would have been more than one year and he would have had a long-term capital gain instead.

When you purchase stocks, bonds, mutual fund shares, and other securities traded on an established securities market, your holding period begins the day after the trade date when you buy the securities, and ends on the trade date when you sell them. Be careful not to confuse the trade date with the settlement date. The trade date is the day you enter into the transaction. The settlement date, which usually comes a few days later, is the date ownership of the shares is delivered to you and you pay for them.

The holding period for gifted assets is the giftor's holding period, plus the time the person receiving the gift holds the property. In contrast, all inherited property is deemed to be a long-term capital asset, no matter how long it is actually held by the deceased person and his or her heir.

Capital Gains Tax Rates

You don't have to pay any tax on the appreciation of a capital asset while you own it—you can earn millions of dollars on paper and never have to pay the IRS a cent. But, once you sell a capital asset, you have to pay taxes on any profits you receive from the sale—your capital gains. Selling a capital asset for a profit is called realizing a gain.

Capital gains are taxed at capital gains rates, which vary depending on the type of asset involved, how long you owned it (your holding period), and your top income tax bracket. The IRS knows about your capital gains because the proceeds of any stock, bond, or other securities sold during the year are reported on IRS Form 1099-B by the brokerage or financial institution that carried out the sale.

Long-term capital gains. To encourage people to make long-term investments, long-term capital gains receive the most favorable tax treatment with the lowest tax rates. The following chart shows the long-term capital gains rates in effect from May 7, 2003, through December 31, 2010. As you can see, your long-term capital gain tax rate depends on your top income tax bracket.

Long-Term Capital Gain Rates 5/7/2003 through 12/31/2010		
If your taxable income is (2006 tax rates):	Then your top income tax bracket is:	And your capital gains tax rate is:
Up to $61,300 if married filing jointly, or up to $30,650 if single	10% or 15%	5% through 12/31/07 0% from 1/1/08 through 12/31/10
$61,301 and over if married filing jointly, or $30,651 and over if single	25% to 35%	15%

EXAMPLE: Harry, a dentist whose taxable income is $100,000, buys 100 shares of stock for $1,000 on February 1, 2007. He sells the stock for $1,200 on March 1, 2008. He owned the stock for more than one year so the long-term capital gains tax rates apply. His income puts him in the 25% to 35% tax bracket, so his long-term capital gains tax rate for the stock sale is 15%. He pays 15% tax on his $200 profit, resulting in a $30 tax.

If your total taxable income for the year, including any capital gains, is within the income ceiling for the 15% tax bracket, you'll pay an incredibly low 5% tax rate on your capital gains. As the chart above shows, the income ceiling for the 15% tax bracket in 2006 is $61,300 for a married couple and $30,650 for singles. Any capital gains you have that push you over the 15% income tax ceiling would be taxed at the higher 15% long-term capital gains rates.

EXAMPLE: Carl and Charlotte, a married couple filing jointly, have $50,000 in ordinary income in 2006, and $20,000 in long-term capital gains. The $50,000 ordinary income plus $11,300 of the $20,000 capital gain is within the $61,300 income ceiling for the 15% income tax bracket. So they pay 5% capital gains tax on $11,300 of their $20,000 capital gain. They pay the 15% rate on the remainder of their capital gain ($8,700) because this amount is over the $61,300 income ceiling.

For taxpayers in the 10% and 15% tax brackets, they will owe *no tax at all* on long-term capital gains from January 1, 2008 through December 31, 2010. But, remember—the zero percent rate applies only to those capital gains that fall between the taxpayer's ordinary income and the income limit for the 15% federal tax bracket in 2008-2010. Any capital gains that push you into the 15% income tax ceiling would be taxed at the higher 15% capital gains rate.

> **EXAMPLE:** Assume that Carl and Charlotte from the above example sell their capital assets in 2008. Let's also assume the top of the 15% bracket in 2008 is $63,000. They pay zero taxes on $13,000 of their $20,000 in long-term capital gains. Reason: Their $50,000 ordinary income plus $13,000 in capital gains equals the $63,000 income limit for the 15% bracket. They must pay a 15% long-term capital gains tax on the remaining $7,000 in capital gains, because this amount puts them over the 15% tax bracket.

The capital gains rate is scheduled to increase in 2011. The 0%, 5%, and 15% long-term capital gains tax rates are scheduled to expire at the end of 2010. Starting in 2011, the rates will go back to what they were before May 7, 2003, unless Congress acts to change them. These rates were 10% for taxpayers in the 10% and 15% income tax brackets, and 20% for all other taxpayers. In addition, 8% and 18% rates applied to capital gains for assets held at least five years. No one (not even Congress at this point) knows whether these rates will go into effect in 2011, whether they will extend the 5% and 15% rates, or whether they will enact other rates.

Short-term capital gains. If you hold a capital asset for less than a year before you sell it, your gain will be a short-term capital gain. Short-term capital gains are all taxed at ordinary income tax rates. The tax you'll pay will be at your highest income tax rate (also called your marginal tax rate), which can be determined from the chart below.

2006 Federal Income Tax Brackets

Tax Bracket	Income If Single	Income If Married Filing Jointly
10%	Up to $7,550	Up to $15,100
15%	$7,551 to $30,650	From $15,101 to $61,300
25%	$30,651 to $74,200	$61,301 to $123,700
28%	$74,201 to $154,800	$123,701 to $188,450
33%	$154,801 to $336,550	$188,451 to $336,550
35%	All over $336,550	All over $336,550

EXAMPLE: Bill bought stock on March 15, 2006 and sold it for a $1,000 profit on December 30, 2006. He owned the stock for less than 12 months so the short-term capital gains rates apply. This means his $1,000 profit will be taxed at his top personal income tax rate. Bill's taxable income for the year is $125,000, so his top rate is 28%. He must pay a 28% capital gains tax on his $1,000 gain, for a $280 tax. Had he waited at least one year and one day to sell the stock, his profit would have been taxed at the 15% long-term capital gains rate instead.

Obviously, this creates a strong incentive to hold a capital asset for at least one year before you sell it.

Real estate. Your personal residence is a capital asset, and any profit you make when you sell it is taxed at the long- or short-term capital gains rates described above. However, there is a special exclusion from tax for profits from home sales—up to $250,000 if you're single and $500,000 if you're married filing jointly. This exclusion—the home sale tax exclusion—is discussed in detail in Chapter 2. Real estate that is not your principal home, but is used for personal purposes—a vacation home, for example—is taxed like any other capital asset.

Rental real estate gets different tax treatment. When you sell rental property at a profit, you must pay a 25% tax on the total amount of depreciation you deducted for the property in prior years. Any profit left over is taxed at the normal capital gains rates.

Collectibles. Collectibles include such things as stamps, coins (there are exceptions for certain coins minted by the U.S. Treasury), artwork, baseball cards, antiques, rugs, gems, alcoholic beverages like rare wines, and metals like gold and silver (there are exceptions for certain kinds of bullion). Although these are capital assets, they are taxed differently from other capital assets. All gains from selling collectibles are taxed at a single 28% rate, no matter how long you own the asset. Thus, it makes no difference how long you hold a collectible before you sell it.

> **EXAMPLE:** Lucy sells her extensive stamp collection for a $10,000 profit. She must pay a 28% tax on this amount, even though she owned the collection for many years.

Before buying coins or artwork as an investment keep in mind that you'll have to pay a much higher tax on any profits you earn when you sell than on investments like stocks.

Small business stock. The stock in certain types of small corporations receives special capital gains treatment. If you hold stock at least five years, 50% of any capital gain you realize from its sale is exempt from tax. The remaining 50% is taxed at a single 28% rate. In effect, this means a 14% capital gains tax is paid on the total gain.

There are many restrictions on who can qualify for this tax break. Among other things:

- The corporation must be a regular C corporation, not an S corporation.
- You must own the stock for at least five years.
- The corporation can't be one that provides personal services—for example, a professional corporation formed by a doctor, dentist, or lawyer.
- The corporation can't have more than $50 million in assets.
- You must purchase the stock directly during its initial issuance.

For a complete discussion of all the restrictions on this tax, see IRS Publication 550, *Investment Income and Expenses.*

Deducting Capital Losses

Any losses you incur when you sell personal use property, like your principal home or collectibles, are not deductible at all.

EXAMPLE: Virginia bought a drawing she thought was by Picasso for $10,000. It turned out the drawing was a fake. She sold it to an art dealer for $100. Her $9,900 loss is not deductible.

You can deduct a loss on personal use property only if it results from a casualty loss or theft—for example, your house is destroyed in a hurricane.

Losses on investment property, like stocks and real estate, are deductible, but they cannot be deducted directly from your ordinary income like a business loss or casualty loss. Instead, all your capital losses from investment property must be subtracted from your investment property capital gains. You have to do the following:

- Tally up all your long-term and short-term gains and losses for the year.
- Subtract the short-term losses from the short-term gains.
- Subtract the long-term losses from the long-term gains.
- If you have a loss in one category and a gain in another, subtract the loss from the gain—the result you obtain is considered to be in the same category as the larger of the two numbers.

You'll end up with either a short-term gain, short-term loss, long-term gain, or long-term loss. Or, if gains and losses are equal, you'll have zero gains and losses.

EXAMPLE: Ken bought and sold stock during the year as follows:

Asset	Cost	Holding Period	Gain on Sale	Loss on Sale
100 shares XYZ stock	$25,000	6 months		$5,500
50 shares ABC stock	$5,000	3 months	$500	
Vacation home	$100,000	2 years	$10,000	
Mutual fund	$50,000	1 year, 1 day		$9,000

Ken subtracts his short-term capital losses ($5,500 on XYZ stock) from his short-term capital gains ($500 on ABC stock), resulting in a net $5,000 short-term loss for the year. Ken then subtracts his long-term capital loss ($9,000 from mutual fund) from his long-term capital gain ($10,000 from vacation home), resulting in a $1,000 net long-term capital gain for the year. He subtracts the loss from the gain. Thus, he subtracts his $5,000 short-term loss from his $1,000 long-term gain. The result is a net $4,000 short-term capital loss for the year.

If you have a capital loss for the year, whether long-term or short-term, you may deduct up to $3,000 of the loss from your ordinary income. Any losses left over may be carried over to future years to be deducted then. Thus, Ken from the above example may deduct $3,000 of his $4,000 capital loss for the year from his ordinary income, such as salary income from his job. The remaining $1,000 loss is carried forward to the next year. Ken is in the 28% income tax bracket so the $3,000 deduction saves him $840 in tax for the year (28% x $3,000 = $840).

Dividends: Timing Is Everything When It Comes to Low Rates

A dividend is money a corporation distributes to its shareholders from its earnings and profits. Thus, you can only receive dividends if you own stock in a corporation. This includes mutual funds, which are a type of corporation. Income from bonds and government obligations (such as Treasury bills and notes) is interest, not dividends. Thus, the tax rules for dividends do not apply to these investments.

Dividends are usually paid in cash, but can also consist of additional shares in the company, which are given to shareholders instead of cash. Dividends are reported to the IRS by the company that distributes them on IRS Form 1099-DIV.

Dividends are taxable income. Until recently, dividend income was taxed at ordinary income rates—anywhere from 10% to 35% depending on your income tax bracket. However, starting in 2003, the tax rate for many dividends was changed to the same rate as for long-term capital gains. As described above, this is a 15% tax for most taxpayers and 10% for taxpayers in the lowest two income brackets. These reduced dividend rates (which do not apply to income from bonds) are scheduled to expire at the end of 2010. Starting in 2011, dividends will again be taxed at ordinary income rates, unless Congress acts to extend the lower rates.

To benefit from the lower rates, your dividends must be "qualified dividends." Your dividends will be qualified if:

- your stock is in a U.S. corporation, or a foreign corporation traded on a U.S. stock exchange, or from a country with which the U.S. has signed a tax treaty (this includes most major countries—see IRS Publication 550 for a list), and
- you satisfy the holding period described below.

Holding Period for Low Dividend Tax Rates

To benefit from the low dividend tax rates, you must hold the stock for at least 60 days—but not just any 60 days. To understand how the holding period rule works, you need to know how corporations issue dividends. A corporation's board of directors decides whether to issue a dividend each year—if so, they "declare" a dividend, which is usually paid four times per year, but can be paid less often. To receive a dividend, you must own shares in the company on the record date—the date the corporation's books are closed. After the record date, the corporation's stock is "ex-dividend," Latin for without a dividend. The day after the record date is the ex-dividend date—the first date following the declaration of a dividend on which the buyer of the stock will not receive the next dividend payment.

To qualify for the low dividend tax rates, you must own the stock for at least 60 days during the 121-day period that begins 60 days before the ex-dividend date. In other words, there is a 121 day window that begins 60 days before the ex-dividend date and ends 61 days after that date. You must own the stock during any 60-day period falling within this window. When counting the number of days you held the stock, include the day you disposed of the stock, but not the day you acquired it.

> **EXAMPLE:** Mary buys 5,000 shares of XYZ Corp. stock on June 30, 2006. XYZ Corp. pays a cash dividend of 10 cents per share. The ex-dividend date is July 8, 2006. Mary sells the shares on August 3, 2006. She held her shares of XYZ Corp. for only 34 days during the 121 day window—from July 1, 2006, through August 3, 2006. The 121-day period began on May 9, 2006 (60 days before the ex-dividend date), and ended on September 6, 2006 (61 days after

the ex-dividend date). Mary has no qualified dividends from XYZ Corp. because she held the XYZ stock for less than the required holding period. This means she must pay income tax on her XYZ dividends at ordinary income tax rates.

Put simply—what all this means is that you can't purchase a stock just before it issues a dividend, collect the dividend, and then immediately sell the stock. You must hold on to the stock for at least 61 days to qualify for the lower tax rates.

Dividends Used to Buy More Stock

Investors often use their dividends to buy more stock in the company, instead of taking them in cash. Many companies have dividend reinvestment plans that allow shareholders to do this automatically. It may not seem fair, but you must still report the dividends as income, even though you use the money to buy more stock instead of receiving cash. If you are allowed to buy more stock at a discount, you must report as dividend income the fair market value of the additional stock on the dividend payment date.

Dividends From Stocks in Retirement Accounts

If you own stock or mutual fund shares in a tax-deferred retirement account, such as an IRA, you do not have to pay any income tax on the dividends you receive and leave in the account. However, you'll have to pay income tax at ordinary rates on all the money you withdraw from the account when you retire, including those from dividends. The only exception is for Roth IRAs and Roth 401(k)s. Withdrawals from these accounts are tax free. (See Chapter 4.)

Tricky Tax Consequences of Buying Mutual Funds

Mutual funds are some of the most popular investments around. However, they can present devilish tax complications. Many investors don't really understand how their mutual funds are taxed. You don't want to be one of these investors.

What Is a Mutual Fund?

A mutual fund is a company in the business of making money from investments. It pools money from its investors (who can number in the millions) to build an investment portfolio. Mutual funds come in many varieties. For example, stock funds specialize in the common shares of publicly traded corporations. Bond funds specialize in the longer-term debt of governments and corporations. Money market funds invest in debt instruments, too, but focus on those with short terms and low risk of default. Within each of those broader categories, many funds have a narrower focus, such as Asian stocks or long-term, tax-exempt municipal bonds. Hybrid funds invest in a mixture of bonds and stocks.

When you purchase a mutual fund, you are buying shares in such an investment company. These shares give you part ownership of the fund's investment portfolio. Thus, although it may not seem like it, when you buy into a mutual fund, you are purchasing shares (stock) in a corporation.

Mutual funds earn income by receiving interest payments and dividends on the securities they hold. They also realize capital gains and losses from selling securities. Mutual funds' net income is the amount that remains from interest, dividends, and capital gains after subtracting capital losses and operating expenses.

The value of your shares is based on the fund's net asset value (NAV), which is the value of the fund's total assets minus its liabilities. The value of each mutual fund share is calculated by dividing the fund's NAV by the number of outstanding shares. For example, if a mutual fund has a NAV of $100 million, and investors own 10,000,000 of the fund's shares, the fund's per share NAV will be $10. Because per share NAV is based on fund NAV—which changes daily—and on the number of shares held by investors—which also changes daily—per share NAV also will change daily. Most mutual funds publish their per share NAVs online and in the daily newspapers.

You can make money from a mutual fund in two ways:

First, you'll earn money if you sell your mutual fund shares at a profit. Mutual fund shares are "redeemable." This means that when mutual fund investors want to sell their fund shares, they sell them back to the fund (or to a broker acting for the fund) at their approximate net asset value, minus any fees the fund imposes. If the fund's NAV has gone up since the shares were purchased, the investor will earn a profit on the sale. Any profit you earn from the sale will be either a short-term or long-term capital gain, depending on whether you owned the shares for over one year. The gain is taxed like any other capital gain (as described above in "Capital Gains Tax Rates").

You can also earn money from your share of the profits, dividends, and interest that a mutual fund earns from its investments each year and distributes to you. It is these mutual fund distributions that can make mutual fund taxation complex.

Mutual Funds Don't Pay Taxes, But You Do

Ordinarily, a corporation must pay tax on any income it earns from investments, such as stocks and bonds. However, a mutual fund is a special type of corporation called a "regulated investment company." It doesn't pay any tax on the earnings from its investments as long as it distributes to its shareholders 98% of all the income and capital gains it realizes each year (which most do). Unfortunately, the shareholders do have to pay tax on these distributions just as they would if they held the underlying assets themselves.

Taxing Mutual Fund Distributions

Some mutual fund distributions are taxed at ordinary income rates, others at the lower long-term capital gains rates. It all depends on the type of income earned by the mutual fund. Mutual funds may distribute five types of income, based on their investments.

You must pay taxes, even if you reinvest your distributions. Mutual fund shareholders choose whether to receive their distributions in cash or have them reinvested in the fund through the purchase of new shares. It's important to understand that the distributions you receive from a mutual fund are still subject to income tax if you reinvest them in the mutual fund to buy more shares. The only exception is if your mutual fund shares are held in a tax-deferred account like an IRA or 401(k). Obviously, if you reinvest your distributions, you're going to have to come up with the cash to pay the taxes due from some source other than your mutual fund income.

Long-term capital gains. One way a mutual fund can earn income is to sell at a profit stock, bonds, or other securities it owns. Income earned from selling securities owned by a mutual fund for more than one year is a long-term capital gain. When this income is passed on to you by the fund, you pay income tax on it at long-term capital gains rates—the 0%, 5%, or 15% rates described above in "Capital Gains Tax Rates".

Short-term capital gains. If a mutual fund sells for a profit securities it held for less than one year, the profit is a short-term capital gain. You must pay tax on any short-term capital gains you receive from a mutual fund at ordinary income rates.

Qualified dividends. Instead of selling a stock to make money, a mutual fund can hold on to the stock and collect dividends. If the mutual fund holds the stock long enough, the dividend will ordinarily be a qualified dividend. Distributions of qualified dividends are taxed at long-term capital gains rates.

Interest and nonqualified dividends. Interest a mutual fund earns from its investments and then distributes to you is taxed at your ordinary income tax rates. Dividends that don't meet the requirements to be qualified, are also taxed at ordinary income rates.

Tax-exempt dividends. Some mutual funds have investments in state and local bonds that are exempt from state and federal taxes. Any interest and dividends they distribute from these investments is tax free.

Mutual funds group interest, qualified or nonqualified dividends, and short-term capital gains together under the term income distributions, or sometimes just dividends. Long-term capital gains are identified separately as capital gains distributions.

How do you know what type of income your mutual fund distributes to you? It will tell you. Each year, the funds you own are required to give you a copy of IRS Form 1099-DIV, which will show the various types of income you received during the year. Many funds also issue their own tax reports that contain this information and more. Many funds also provide extensive information about taxes on their websites and in their literature—they can be a great resource.

Business Property Sales: A Mixed Bag Taxwise

Even though business property is not a capital asset, income from certain business property sales are taxed at long-term capital gains rates. The type of business property that qualifies for long-term capital gains rates is depreciable business property, also known as Section 1231 property (based on the provision of the tax code governing taxation of its sale). It includes:

- business real estate
- business equipment, automobiles, trucks, and furniture, and
- intangible personal property like patents and copyrights.

If a business sells Section 1231 property at a profit, part of the money can be taxed at the long-term capital gains rates. However, you don't get capital gains rates for all the proceeds. Any depreciation you deducted for the property while you owned it is recaptured—meaning it is taxed at ordinary income rates, or a flat 25% rate for business real estate.

> **EXAMPLE:** Phil, an optometrist, owns a small office building. He bought it for $200,000 several years ago, and has taken a total of $100,000 in depreciation deductions for the property. He sells the property this year for $300,000. His profit—$100,000—is taxed at long-term capital gains rates (15% because Phil is in the 28% tax bracket). However, he must pay a flat 25% income tax on the $100,000 of depreciation he previously deducted.

If business property is sold at a loss, as it often is (unless the property is real estate), the losses are ordinary losses, not capital losses. This means you can directly deduct them from your gross income. In contrast, if you sell a capital asset at a loss, you must deduct it from your capital gains and only $3,000 of capital losses can be deducted from your gross income each year. This is an important tax advantage depreciable business property has over capital assets.

> **EXAMPLE:** Phil sells a computer he purchased six months ago for his business at a $1,000 loss. He may deduct the $1,000 from all of his income.

Remember, however, that the depreciation deductions you take on business property each year reduce your basis in the property, and therefore increase your taxable profit or decrease your deductible loss when you sell the property.

> **EXAMPLE:** Assume that Phil purchased his computer for $1,000 three years ago and has depreciated 52% of its cost. His basis in the computer has gone down from $1,000 to $480 (52% x $1,000 = $520). He sells the computer for $400. He has only an $80 loss he can deduct.

For detailed guidance on the tax and other legal issues involved in selling business property, refer to *The Complete Guide to Selling a Business*, **by Fred S. Steingold (Nolo).**

What You Can Control: Tips on Lowering Your Tax Rate

You have little or no control over how well an investment like a mutual fund does. But you do have a large measure of control over how much tax you pay on the profits from your investments. By taking advantage of the low tax rates for long-term capital gains and dividends, you can significantly reduce your taxes. This can make an enormous difference in the total returns you get from your investments.

Here are some tips on how to accomplish this.

Hold on to capital assets for at least one year. As explained above, tax rates on long-term capital gains are much lower than those for short-term gains. You must hold the investment for over one year to benefit from the long-term capital gains rates. Always consider the effect of the extra tax you'll have to pay before you sell a capital asset after less than one year. This doesn't mean you should hang on to a losing investment just to pay a lower capital gains rate. Taxes are just one of the factors you should consider before selling any investment.

You can find a capital gains calculator at www.moneychimp.com that will compare the taxes for short-term versus long-term and show the advantage of waiting at least one year before selling.

Take advantage of low capital gains rates before 2011. Since the inception of the income tax in the early 20th century, long-term capital gains have usually, but not always, been taxed at lower rates than ordinary income. Currently, long-term capital gains tax rates are the lowest they have been since 1933. And, never in U.S. history has there been a zero tax on capital gains as there will be for lower income taxpayers during 2008 through 2010.

These low rates are scheduled to end after 2010 and return to their pre-2003 levels. However, no one really knows what long-term capital rates will be after 2010. If you have long-term capital assets that have appreciated in value, you should consider selling them by the end of 2010 to take advantage of the low capital gains rates.

Harvest your capital losses each year. Capital losses may be deducted from capital gains, except for losses from personal property like collectibles and your main home. This makes it possible to engage in tax-loss harvesting: selling securities or other investment property to realize a capital loss, and then using the loss to offset your capital gains. If you have enough losses you can offset all your gains for the year.

> **EXAMPLE:** Dave purchased 100 shares of XYZ Corp. a few years ago. Unfortunately, the stock has steadily gone down in value. However, Dave has also picked some winners: He has shares in the ABC Mutual Fund and Acme Mutual Fund that are worth far more than Dave paid for them. Dave sells his XYZ shares for a $10,000 loss and realizes a long-term capital loss, since he owned the shares for more than one year. He also sells the Acme and XYZ shares for $7,000 and $3,000 gains, respectively. These are short-term capital gains. Come tax time, Dave has a $10,000 long-term capital gain for the year and a $10,000 short-term capital loss. The $10,000 capital loss offsets the $10,000 capital gain, so Dave pays no taxes on his $10,000 profit. Had Dave not realized the losses, he would have had to pay income tax on his short-term capital gains at ordinary income tax rates. His top tax bracket is 28%, so he would have had to pay $2,800 in taxes on his short-term gains (28% x $10,000 = $2,800).

But wait, it gets even better. If your total capital losses exceed all your capital gains for the year, you may deduct each year up to $3,000 of such extra losses from your ordinary income, such as salary income, interest, and dividends.

> **EXAMPLE:** Assume that Dave sells some additional mutual fund shares for a $3,000 loss. He may deduct the $3,000 from his salary income for the year. Dave is in the 33% income tax bracket, so this saves him $990 in taxes.

Make sure you know your basis. The amount of your basis will determine if you have a gain or a loss when you sell an investment or any other capital asset. As discussed above, your initial basis is the cost of the capital asset plus sales expenses like sales commissions. The basis of individual stocks or mutual fund shares you acquire by reinvesting your dividends or distributions is the amount of the dividends or distributions used to purchase each share. Some mutual funds and brokers will calculate your basis for you, but not all do, and the calculation may not always be accurate.

Also, keep in mind that an asset's basis can change over its life, resulting in an "adjusted basis." For example, if you receive more stock from nontaxable stock dividends or stock splits, you must reduce the basis of your original stock.

> **EXAMPLE:** You own one share of XYZ, Inc., common stock that you bought for $45. The corporation distributes two new shares of common stock for each share held. You have three shares of common stock. Your basis in each share is $15 ($45 ÷ 3).

The basis of real property can also change over time. Your basis is increased by the cost of any capital improvements you make—for example, adding a new room to your home or replacing the roof. For this reason, it's important to keep good records of all improvements you make to your real property. The basis of real property used in business is decreased by any depreciation you take.

You can keep track of your basis in your assets by using computer software such as *Quicken* and *Microsoft Money*. There are also specialized programs for this purpose—*Gainskeeper*, for example. Brokerages and fund companies like Fidelity Investments and Vanguard also have online tools to help you keep track of the basis in your investments.

If you haven't kept good records, it is usually possible to reconstruct your basis in an asset by figuring out what you paid for it and using your cost as your basis. In the case of stocks, bonds, and mutual fund shares, you should check with your brokerage or fund company. Also, if you know when you bought a stock, you can find out the price on the website www.bigcharts.com. It has a free database of historical stock prices, adjusted for stock splits, back to 1985.

Records You Should Keep

Be sure to keep copies of all the statements and reports you receive from your mutual fund or broker. The 1099 forms you receive each year are particularly important. When you buy or sell shares (including those purchased by reinvesting your dividends or fund distributions), keep the confirmation statements you receive. The statements show the price you paid for the shares when you bought them and the price you received for the shares when you disposed of them. The information from the confirmation statement when you purchased the shares will help you figure your basis in the shares. Keep track of any adjustments to the basis of the shares as they occur.

Don't buy mutual funds just before year-end distributions. Mutual funds need to distribute 98% their profits to their shareholders by the end of each year. For this reason, they often make large distributions of capital gains to their shareholders in December. If you invest in a mutual fund near the end of the year, you'll have to pay tax on the distributions, even though you really don't benefit from them because the fund's share price drops by the amount of the distribution. Most mutual funds have websites that can tell you when capital gain distributions are scheduled.

EXAMPLE: You want to invest $1,000 in the Acme Mutual Fund. Its shares currently cost $5. Acme has announced that it will distribute a $1 dividend to its shareholders on December 15. If you buy

200 Acme shares on December 14, you'll have to pay tax on the $200 dividend you receive. Moreover, on December 16, the price of the shares will drop to $4 per share to reflect the $1 dividend distribution. So you end up with 200 shares worth $800 and a $200 dividend you must pay tax on. Had you waited until December 16 or later to buy Acme shares, you could have purchased 250 shares for $1,000 and not had to pay tax on a distribution.

Sell highest-cost shares first. Investors often purchase shares in the same mutual fund or company in separate lots over time. Each lot will typically have a different selling price, and therefore a different basis.

If you want to sell only part of your holdings of a mutual fund, stock, or other security, how do you decide which ones to sell? You'll always pay the lowest taxes possible on your profit by selling your highest-cost shares first. These shares will have the highest basis and therefore their sale will result in the smallest taxable profit (your profit is the selling price minus your basis).

To accomplish this, you must use the "specific identification method" to identify which of your shares you want to sell. You identify the shares by specifying their cost and purchase dates. You're also supposed to receive a written confirmation of your instructions from the broker. Many discount and online brokers won't do this. In this event, keep a record of your oral instructions and put this in your tax file for safekeeping.

EXAMPLE: Caroline owns 200 shares of the Acme Mutual Fund. She purchased 100 of the shares five years ago for $1,000 and the other 100 shares two years ago for $5,000. Acme shares are currently worth $75 per share. Caroline decides to sell half of her shares. She instructs her broker to sell the shares she purchased two years ago for $5,000 ($50 per share). She earns $2,500 on the sale, leaving her with a $2,500 long-term capital gain she must pay income tax on.

Using the specific identification method requires careful record keeping. You can use easier methods, but these will often result in higher taxes. In the case of mutual funds, you can use the first-in, first-out method, or one of two averaging methods. The averaging methods may not be used when you sell individual stocks—that is, shares in companies other than mutual funds. Think carefully about which method you want to use because you'll have to stick with your choice for as long as you own the mutual fund or stock.

With the first-in, first-out (FIFO) method, the shares you buy first are considered sold first. The shares you buy first probably have the lowest basis, thus you'll have the largest taxable gain if the FIFO method is used. The IRS assumes that you use the FIFO method unless you choose another method.

> **EXAMPLE:** Assume that Caroline from the example uses the FIFO method to value her shares. This means that the shares she purchased first are the shares that are deemed sold by the IRS. These shares cost $1,000 ($10 per share), so Caroline would have a $6,500 taxable capital gain ($7,500 − $1,000 = $6,500). That's $5,500 more taxable gain than Caroline has using the specific identification method.

With the single-category method, you figure the average cost of all of your shares and use this average as your basis. You simply add up the purchase price of all your shares and then divide that number by the total number of shares. This is the most commonly used method, and most funds will calculate and provide this figure to you.

> **EXAMPLE:** Caroline from the above examples bought 100 shares of the Acme Mutual Fund for $1,000 and 100 shares for $5,000. The average cost of her shares is $30 ($6,000 ÷ 200 = $30), so she uses $30 as her basis. In fact, 100 of the shares cost $10 per share and the other 100 shares cost $50 per share.

The multiple-category method is a refinement of the single-category method in which long-term and short-term holdings are averaged separately. This can result in a lower basis than using the single-category method.

Avoid the wash sale rule. Because capital losses are deductible from capital gains, investors might be tempted to buy and sell a stock or other security, sell it at a loss, and then buy back the same investment. They'll have a deductible loss and still own the shares. The "wash sale rule" was created to prevent this.

A wash sale occurs when you sell or trade stock or securities at a loss and within 30 days before or after the sale you buy substantially identical stock or securities. You cannot deduct losses from sales or trades of stock or securities in a wash sale. However, you do get to add the loss to the basis of the stock.

> **EXAMPLE:** You buy 100 shares of the Acme Mutual Fund for $1,000. You sell these shares for $750 and within 30 days of the sale, you buy 100 shares of the same stock for $800. Because you bought substantially identical shares, you cannot deduct your loss of $250 on the sale. However, you add the disallowed loss of $250 to the cost of the new stock—$800—to obtain your basis in the new shares, which is $1,050.

There are ways around the wash sale rule. For example, you could sell a stock you owned personally and then buy it back within 30 days in a tax-deferred account such as an IRA. Now, the IRA owns it instead of you personally. Deferred accounts like IRAs are considered separate taxpayers, so the wash sale rule is not violated.

Borrow against your equity in capital assets. Do you need some cash right now but don't want to add to your tax liability for the year? Instead of selling capital assets like real estate, stocks, bonds, and mutual fund shares to raise cash, borrow against them. A loan is not taxable income because you must pay it back. Moreover, if you use the money for a business purpose, the interest is deductible as a business expense.

If you have equity in a house or other real estate, you'll have no problem getting a loan or establishing a line of credit. You can also get a stock loan using stocks or other securities as collateral. You can also establish a margin account at a brokerage that permits you to borrow against stock and other securities; this is similar to a line of credit.

Charitable contributions of capital assets can save taxes. You can save on taxes by giving to charity stocks, bonds, other securities, and real estate that has gone up in value. This is because you won't have to pay any tax on your gain, and will be allowed to deduct the fair market value of the asset, which should be more than you paid for it.

EXAMPLE: Jake owns 100 shares of the Acme Mutual Fund he purchased for $1,000 ten years ago. The shares are now worth $11,000. If he sold the shares, he'd have to pay a 15% capital gains tax on his $10,000 profit, for $1,500 tax. Instead of selling the shares, he donates them to his favorite charity. He pays no taxes on the gain in value of the shares. He also gets to deduct as a charitable deduction the full $11,000 value of the shares which, because he's in the 28% income tax bracket, saves him $3,080 in income taxes.

Of course, giving to charity only makes sense if you really want to help a charity. If not, you'd be better off not making the gift, since your tax savings will always be less than the value of the gift.

There are limitations on how much you can deduct each year as a charitable contribution. See Chapter 5 for a detailed discussion of charitable gifts.

Give capital assets to family members. If you don't want to give appreciated assets to charity, consider giving them to your children or grandchildren, or other family members who are in the 10% or 15% income tax bracket.

The basis of such gifted assets is not increased to its fair market value, as are charitable contributions. But, if the recipient of the gift is in the 10% or 15% tax bracket, he or she will owe only a 5% capital gains tax on all or part of the profit from the asset's sale. Moreover, during 2008–2010 all or part of the profit will be taxed at 0%. This assumes the asset is held for over one year and its sale therefore qualifies as a long-term capital gain. Fortunately, the giver's holding period is added to the holding period of the recipient for this purpose.

EXAMPLE: Assume that Jake (from the example above) gave his Acme shares to his 16-year-old daughter, Maria, who is in the 10% income tax bracket. Jake's ten year holding period for the shares is added to Maria's holding period. Maria sells the stock for a $10,000 profit and pays only a 5% long-term capital gains tax on the profit, for a $500 tax.

If a child is under 18 years of age, he or she will be subject to the kiddie tax. This requires the child to pay income tax at the parents' top tax rate on all unearned income over $1,700 from capital gains, interest, and dividends. So, there will be a tax benefit only if the all the child's unearned income, including income from selling gifted capital assets, is less than $1,700.

Invest in tax-efficient mutual funds. When you purchase a mutual fund (or ETF), you have no control over how much money the fund distributes to its shareholders each year. The fund's managers control this. But you do have control over which mutual funds to buy. Some funds are more tax efficient than others—that is, they keep taxable distributions to a minimum. By investing in a tax-efficient mutual fund, you defer paying most of your taxes until you sell your shares.

This doesn't mean you shouldn't invest in mutual funds that are not tax efficient. Such funds—for example, those that invest in growth stocks—can be highly profitable. However, it's best to place these funds in tax-deferred accounts such as IRAs, 401(k)s, and traditional IRAs. That way, you won't have to pay any tax on the distributions the fund makes each year (so long as you leave them in your account). Of course, you must pay income tax at ordinary rates when you withdraw your earnings upon retirement.

So how do you know if a mutual fund is tax efficient? Some mutual funds, such as index funds, are inherently tax efficient because they are not actively managed; rather, their holdings simply mirror a stock index or some other criteria such as investing in specific industries or countries. The securities in these funds ordinarily don't have to be traded very often.

Other funds are managed so as to keep distributions to a minimum. These funds sell shares as infrequently as possible and use other techniques to avoid having to distribute capital gains to their shareholders. Such funds often bill themselves as "tax managed."

Since 2002, the Securities and Exchange Commission has required mutual funds to show their after-tax investment returns in their prospectuses. For example, the 2006 prospectus for the Vanguard Explorer Fund, a fund that invests in growth stocks, shows that in 2005 the fund earned 9.28% before taxes, but only 7.59% after taxes on distributions to its shareholders. In stark contrast, the Vanguard 500

Index Fund, a tax-efficient fund that invests in all the stocks on the Standard and Poor 500 Index, had a 10.74% return in 2006 before taxes, and a 10.44% return after taxes on distributions.

A mutual fund that claims to be tax efficient or tax managed must also show after-tax returns in its marketing literature. Mutual fund prospectuses and literature can be easily obtained from mutual fund websites and broker websites. You can find a useful online calculator at http://calculators.aol.com/tools/aol/fund10/tool.fcs that can help you compare the before- and after-tax returns from mutual funds.

Exchange Traded Funds (ETFs)

Exchange traded funds (ETFs for short) are a new type of investment that combine many of the attributes of individual stocks and mutual funds. They are traded on stock exchanges, just like regular stocks, which makes them easier to buy than mutual funds. You can also buy just one share (a boon for small investors). Like mutual funds, most ETFs are registered investment companies that offer investors a share of a portfolio of stocks or other investments. Almost all ETFs are index funds, and, as such, are highly tax efficient. Moreover, they often have the lowest operating expenses around—lower than comparable mutual funds—which saves you money. You can find good information on ETFs at the Vanguard Group website at http://flagship2.vanguard.com/VGApp/hnw/FundsVIPER.

All in the Family:
Shifting Income in Your Household
to Lower the Tax Burden

The United States has a progressive income tax system with tax rates ranging from a low of 10% to a high of 35%. That's a 25% difference. Obviously, if you're in one of the higher brackets you could save a lot of taxes if you could somehow shift your income to someone in a lower tax bracket—for example, your children. This process is called income shifting or income splitting. Recent changes in the tax laws have made income shifting more difficult than it has been in the past, but it remains a tried and true tax reduction strategy for the more affluent.

Income shifting is a tax strategy primarily for well-off people in high tax brackets. It can be especially useful for those with assets like stocks that have greatly appreciated in value. It can also work well for people who own their own business. But, if you're an average working stiff, this game is probably not for you. Instead, think about socking away as much money as possible in retirement accounts like IRAs and 401(k)s (see Chapter 4). If you want to save for your children's education, Coverdell ESAs and/or 529 savings plans are a good option (see Chapter 2).

The Family That Pays Taxes Together Stays Together: How Income Shifting Works

Income shifting works because the IRS views a family as a collection of separate individual taxpayers. Except for husbands and wives who can (and usually do) file a joint return, each family member pays taxes on his or her income at his or her own tax rate. Family members with lower incomes pay taxes at a lower rate than those with higher incomes.

> **EXAMPLE:** Matt and Martha Smith are a married couple with an 18-year-old child, Tom. Their total taxable family income from work and investments for 2006 is $200,000. If all the family income belongs to Matt and Martha and they file a joint return, the chart below shows that their top tax bracket will be 33%. Tom will pay zero taxes because he has no income. The family's total income tax would be $45,982. If, instead, only $175,000 of taxable income belongs to Matt and Martha and $25,000 belongs to Tom, the couple's top tax rate will be 28%. Tom will have to pay taxes

because he has income, but his top rate is only 15%. Matt and Martha will pay $38,404 in income tax on their joint return and Tom will pay $3,373 on his separate return—for a total of $41,777.

2006 Federal Income Tax Brackets		
Tax Bracket	Income If Single	Income If Married Filing Jointly
10%	Up to $7,550	Up to $15,100
15%	$7,551 to $30,650	From $15,101 to $61,300
25%	$30,651 to $74,200	$61,301 to $123,700
28%	$74,201 to $154,800	$123,701 to $188,450
33%	$154,801 to $336,550	$188,451 to $336,550
35%	All over $336,550	All over $336,550

To the IRS, it's a big deal who reports what income on which return. But in the real world, it may not be such a big deal to you. What benefits your children, benefits you as well because you view your family as a single economic unit. Thus, it makes little or no difference to you who receives the income in your family for tax purposes—it directly or indirectly benefits every family member.

Thus, income shifting works because you're mainly concerned about the total income tax your entire family pays, not what each family member pays. In the example above, the total tax for the Smith family was $45,982 when the Smith parents had $200,000 in taxable income and Tom had no income, but only $41,777 when part of the family income was shifted to Tom. As far as the entire family is concerned, they save $4,205 if they split the family income between themselves and their child.

The key question is how do you arrange it so that a family member in a lower income tax bracket legally ends up with part of the family's income?

You can't simply allocate or assign part of your income to your children or others and have them pay tax on it instead of you—for example, give part of your salary to your child. The IRS says that the person who earns money for doing work is the one who must pay tax on that money. Nor can you avoid paying income tax on investment income by giving a child or other person the income you earn from investments, such as savings accounts or stocks. The person who owns investment property is the one who must pay tax on the income from the property.

Because of these rules, income shifting requires some careful thought and planning. There are two main ways to achieve income shifting:

- transfer ownership of income-producing property to your children, grandchildren, or others in a lower income tax bracket, or
- hire your children or other family members to work in your business and pay them a salary and/or other compensation.

Other Tax Advantages of Income Shifting

Income shifting can not only lower the tax rates that have to be paid on income, it can have other beneficial effects as well:

Lower AGI. Income shifting reduces your adjusted gross income (AGI) for the year. This can be very beneficial because many deductions and exemptions are phased out as your AGI goes up. Also, many personal deductions are deductible only to the extent they exceed a specified percentage of your AGI. For example, medical expenses are deductible only to the extent they exceed 7.5% of your AGI. The lower the AGI, the more you can deduct. (See Chapter 5.)

Smaller estate. Gifting assets to your children or others will also reduce the size of your estate when you die, reducing the chance that any estate taxes will have to be paid. For detailed information on estate taxes, see *Plan Your Estate*, by Denis Clifford and Cora Jordan (Nolo).

The more money a child has in his or her name, the less college financial aid will be available. So giving your children money or property will likely make it more difficult for them to qualify for financial aid when they go to college. When doling out aid, colleges and universities figure students should spend at least 35% of all assets in their name on their college expenses. In contrast, only 5.6% of parents' assets are factored into determining how much the family is expected to contribute for their child's education. This is one important reason income shifting to children is used mainly by well-off families—their children won't qualify for financial aid anyway, or will only be able to obtain loans. Coverdell ESAs and 529 savings plans are a good option if you want to save for your children's college and don't want to ruin their chances of getting aid (see "Education accounts," below). For more information on college financial aid, see the Department of Education's website at http://studentaid.ed.gov.

Thanks Mom: Giving Your Children Income-Producing Property

The simplest way to shift income is to give income-producing property to your lower-tax-bracket children (or other relatives or nonrelatives with whom you want to share your income). A gift is not taxable income to the recipient, so your child need not pay any tax on its value. Since the child now owns the property, he or she will pay tax on any income it generates at the child's own (lower) tax rates.

Gifts to People Other Than Your Children

Income-shifting gifts are most commonly made to children or grandchildren, but this doesn't have to be the case. You could, for example, give money or investment property to your parents or other relatives to shift your income to a lower- income taxpayer (assuming they are in a lower income tax bracket). However, gifts to your spouse will have no income-shifting effect if you and your spouse file a joint return because your income is combined. What about spouses filing separate returns? Generally, there is little or no advantage to be gained because the tax brackets have been adjusted to largely eliminate the marriage penalty. (See Chapter 6.)

Income-producing property (or investment property) is property that generates investment income—interest, dividends, and profits from asset sales. Such investment income is also called unearned income because it is obtained without working at a job or business. Investment property includes:

- cash
- stocks
- bonds
- mutual funds, and
- real estate.

EXAMPLE: Ed and Edna have $20,000 in a savings account that generates $1,000 in interest each year that they must pay tax on at their top 28% income tax rate. They give the money to their daughter, Edwina. She now reports the interest income on her own tax return and pays tax on it at her own tax rate—15%. This saves $130 in tax and Edwina can use the money to pay for her college education.

However, a new tax rule enacted in 2006 limits the tax savings you can achieve by shifting income by giving assets to children under 18 years of age (at the end of the tax year).

Kiddie tax for children under 18. The IRS isn't exactly thrilled about the income-shifting concept, and a special kiddie tax was adopted in the 1980s to limit its usefulness. Until 2006, the kiddie tax only applied to children under 14. However, in 2006 the age was increased to children under 18—a major change in the tax law that makes income shifting to your children more difficult than it used to be. These rules establish three stages of taxes on investment income for children aged 17 and younger:

- **Investment income $0 to $850.** Children under 18 do not have to pay any tax on the first $850 of their unearned income for the year. The income is tax free because the minimum standard deduction for children and other dependents is $850 (in 2006). The income need not be reported to the IRS.
- **Investment income $851 to $1,700.** Investment income from $851 to $1,700 is taxed at the child's tax rate—usually the lowest income tax rate which is currently 10%.
- **Investment income over $1,700.** Any investment income over $1,700 is added to the parent's taxable income and taxed at the parent's top income tax rate, which can be as high as 35%.

EXAMPLE: Sue and Stan have a 12-year-old daughter, Sarah. They give Sarah a $50,000 savings account that generates $3,000 in income in 2006. The first $850 of this income is tax free. Sarah must pay a 10% income tax on the next $850 in income. The remaining $1,300 is taxed at Sarah's parents' highest income tax rate, 35%.

(By the way, the kiddie tax doesn't apply to a child under 18 who is married and files a joint return with his or her spouse. Who knew Congress was in favor of teenage marriage?)

Obviously, you don't want your child under 18 to have more than $1,700 in unearned income during the year. But that is not a negligible amount. For example, a child whose investments earn 8% per year could have a total of $21,250 in cash or property and be within the $1,700 limit each year. Moreover, the child would only pay $85 in income tax on the $1,700 in income—no tax is due on the first $850 because of the standard deduction and only a 10% tax is paid on the remaining $850. In contrast, if you kept that $21,250, you would have to pay taxes on the $1,700 profit at your own income tax rates. If, for example, your top rate was 28%, this would come to $476—a $391 difference.

There is another way to stay within the $1,700 limit—give your child investments that appreciate in value over time but generate little or no taxable income until they are sold. If they are sold after the child turns 18, there is no kiddie tax. Such investments include:

- **U.S. savings bonds.** You can purchase U.S. savings bonds for your child and defer the payment of interest until the child reaches age 18. All the interest will then be taxed at the child's tax rate. In addition, if the bonds are used to pay for college, the interest is tax free provided the parents' adjusted gross income is under an annual ceiling. The bonds must be registered in the parents' name, not the child's. For more information, see IRS Publication 970, *Tax Benefits for Education.*

- **Municipal bonds.** Interest earned on municipal bonds is exempt from federal income tax. If a muni bond is ultimately sold at a profit, it is taxed as a capital gain.

- **Growth stocks or growth mutual funds.** These are stocks, or funds made up of stocks, from companies that reinvest their profits for future growth rather than paying them to shareholders as taxable dividends. The stocks or funds can be sold after the child reaches 18 with the profit taxed at the child's capital gains rate (see "Giving Assets to Children 18 and Older—A Potential Tax Bonanza," below).

- **Index funds.** Funds whose investments mirror a stock index or some other criteria and usually generate minimal taxable annual income.
- **Tax-managed mutual funds.** These are specifically designed to generate little taxable income. Again, they can be sold after the child reaches age 18 and the profits are taxed at the child's capital gains rate. (See Chapter 4 for more information these funds.)
- **Treasury bills.** If your child is close to age 18, buy a Treasury bill for him or her that won't mature until he or she reaches 18. The interest won't be earned by the child until he or she is 18, so there is no kiddie tax problem.

Children 18 and over. There is no kiddie tax for children 18 and over (by the end of the year), even if they are their parents' dependents. These children are taxed like adults—all their income is taxed at their own income tax rates, not their parents' rates. If such a child doesn't work, he or she will have an $850 standard deduction (just like children under 18) and won't have to pay any tax on that amount of income. Any income over $850 will be taxed at his or her own tax rates, which are usually lower than the parents.

> **EXAMPLE:** Victor, an 18-year-old, earned $2,000 in investment income in 2006 and did not work. He pays no tax on the first $850 of his income and is taxed on the remainder at his own tax rate, which is 10%, instead of his parents' 28% rate.

Because there is no kiddie tax for children 18 and over, you want them to have unearned income that they will be taxed on at their lower rates. You don't have to worry about keeping their total unearned income below $1,700. Thus, the amount of investment property you give the child can be substantial.

> **EXAMPLE:** Victor's parents take $100,000 out of their own savings and use it to establish a savings account in Victor's name. The account earns $5,000 in interest per year. Victor pays income tax on this amount at his 10% income tax rate.

Giving Assets to Children 18 and Older—
A Potential Tax Bonanza

It's fine to give children 18 and over cash, but the really big tax savings come from giving them assets you own that have appreciated (gone up) in value since you bought them—for example, stocks, mutual funds, and real estate. If you're fortunate enough to have such assets, read this section carefully because you have a great tax-planning opportunity.

Investment properties like stocks, bonds, mutual funds, and real estate are capital assets. If a capital asset is sold at a profit, it is taxed at long-term capital gains tax rates, provided it was owned for over one year. Right now and for the next few years, long-term capital gains tax rates are the lowest they have been in many decades.

Taxable Income If Single	Tax Bracket	Long-Term Capital Gains Tax Rate (2006–2009)
Up to $7,550	10%	5%
$7,551 to $30,650	15%	5%
$30,651 to $74,200	25%	15%
$74,201 to $154,800	28%	15%
$154,801 to $336,550	33%	15%
All over $336,550	35%	15%

Children over 18 who are in one of the lowest two tax brackets qualify for the 5% long-term capital gains rate instead of the 15% rate for taxpayers in the higher brackets. To qualify for the long-term capital gains rate, the asset must be owned for over one year. Fortunately, the giver's holding period is added to the holding period of the recipient for this purpose.

EXAMPLE: Milt and Mavis Martin are a married couple with an 18-year-old daughter, Mary. The Martin's purchased 1,000 shares of stock in Acme, Inc., in 2001 for $1 per share. By 2007, it is worth $11 per share. The Martins give the stock to Mary, who is in the 10% income tax bracket. The parents' six-year holding period for the shares is added to Mary's holding period, which is only one month. Mary sells the stock for a $10,000 profit and pays only a 5%

long-term capital gains tax on the profit, for a $500 tax. Had Mary's parents kept the stock in their own names and sold it, they would have had to pay a 15% capital gains tax on the $10,000 profit—a $1,500 tax.

The 5% long-term capital gains tax rate remains in effect so long as your child's taxable income for the year, including capital gains, is within the income ceiling for the 15% tax bracket. As the chart above shows, the income ceiling for singles is $30,650 in 2006. Any capital gains that push the child over the 15% income tax ceiling are taxed at the 15% long-term capital gains rates.

> **EXAMPLE:** Assume that Mary (from the example above) had $25,000 in taxable income from a part-time job and investments. Her $10,000 capital gain puts her total taxable income for the year at $35,000. This is $4,350 more than the income limit for the 15% bracket. As a result, she must pay a 15% long-term capital gains tax on $4,350 of her profit from the Acme stock sale.

From January 1, 2008, through December 31, 2010, the long-term capital gains tax rate for taxpayers in the lowest two brackets will be an incredible, unheard-of, 0%—that's right, zero. However, as explained above, this zero tax rate applies only so long as the taxpayer's taxable income, including income from long-term capital gains, is within the 15% tax bracket. The 15% bracket during 2008 through 2010 will be slightly higher than the 2006 brackets listed above, to adjust for inflation. This all means a child 18 or over could have as much as $30,000 in long-term capital gains in 2008–2010 and pay zero taxes. Obviously, if you have long-term assets that have appreciated in value, transferring them to your children and then selling them during 2008–2010 presents a tremendous, once-in-a-lifetime tax savings opportunity.

> **EXAMPLE:** Vince purchased shares in a mutual fund 10 years ago for $10,000. By 2008, they are worth $40,000. He gives the shares to his 22-year-old granddaughter, Victoria, who is a college student. She immediately sells the shares and pockets the $30,000 profit, which is a long-term capital gain. Victoria's total taxable income for

2008 is $31,000, which places her in the 15% income tax bracket. Thus, the applicable 2008 long-term capital gains rate for her profit is 0%. She gets the $30,000 profit tax free. Had Vince kept the shares and sold them himself, he would have had to pay a 15% long-term capital gains rate on his profit, for a $4,500 tax.

It's doubtful we'll ever see a zero capital gains tax rate again. The long-term capital gains rate for taxpayers in the lowest two tax brackets is scheduled to rise to 10% in 2011.

Because children under 18 are subject to the kiddie tax, you won't benefit nearly as much from the lower capital gains tax rate they pay. Any long-term capital gains that result in a child earning more than $1,700 for the year will be taxed at the parent's capital gains rate, which is usually 15%. So, there will be a tax benefit only if all of the child's unearned income, including income from selling gifted capital assets, is less than $1,700.

Don't Give Away Loser Investments

Don't give your children or others investment property that has declined in value since you purchased it. A person who receives such a gift cannot deduct a loss upon sale of the property, and neither can the person who gives the gift. It's much better to sell the property yourself—that way you can deduct the loss from your own taxes. Then, if you wish, you can make a gift of the money you earned from the sale, plus the amount of tax you saved from your deductible loss.

Your Gift Must Be Real

If you give property to your children or others, the gift must be real and it must be irrevocable—that is, you can never take the property back.

Children who are minors—under age 18—can own money and property, but they cannot manage or control it themselves. An adult must do this for them until they become adults. This means that gifting money or property to a minor is a bit more complicated than giving it to an adult. There are several ways to transfer money or property to minor children.

Custodial account. The easiest and most common way to transfer money or investment assets to minor children is to establish a custodial account. A custodial account is similar to a trust, but much easier to set up and administer. Every state but South Carolina has adopted a version of the Uniform Transfers to Minors Act (UTMA). Under this law, anyone can establish a UTMA account for a minor and contribute assets such as cash, stocks, bonds, mutual funds, real estate, and life insurance. The assets placed in the account become the property of the minor child. The person who establishes the account appoints an adult to manage it, called a custodian. This can be the person who opens the account, or someone else. For example, a parent can establish a UTMA account for a child and appoint himself or his spouse as custodian. However, if you name yourself as custodian for a custodial account for your child, any gifts you make to the account will be included in your estate for estate tax purposes if you die before your child becomes an adult. This may or may not be an important consideration, depending on the size of your estate. You can avoid this by appointing your spouse or another relative or third person to be custodian.

In most states, an UTMA custodianship ends when the beneficiary becomes 21, but a few states end them at 18. A handful of states give you the choice to extend the age to 25; however, this is not a good idea because you can't use the annual gift tax exclusion for your gifts to a custodial account if the custodianship extends beyond age 21 (see below). When the custodianship ends, the child takes over control of the account and can do whatever he or she wants with the money or property it contains.

UTMA accounts are very easy to set up with a bank, mutual fund, or brokerage firm. There are no extra fees to pay. An account can only be for one child. The income from the account is reported to the IRS under the child's Social Security number and is taxed to the child as described above. However, the custodian of the account does not need to file a separate income tax return. Any amount can be contributed to a UTMA account and contributions can be made any time during the year.

The custodian has broad discretion on how to manage the money or property in the account. He or she must act prudently, but they are not required to save all the money in the account, although this is often done. Instead, the custodian can spend the account money on almost anything for the child's benefit—for example, private school tuition, summer camp, travel, music lessons. However, the custodian is not supposed to use account funds to pay for the child's basic living expenses such as food, clothing, and housing—these are the parent's legal obligation. If account funds are used for any of these purposes, the parents may be required to pay income tax on the account income for the year—that is, there will be no income shifting.

Buying U.S. Savings Bonds in Your Child's Name

Ordinarily, a minor child cannot own securities, such as stocks and bonds, in his or her own name and must use a custodial account. However, there is an exception for U.S. savings bonds. You don't need a custodial account to purchase U.S. savings bonds for your child—you simply list the child as the owner when you buy them. Be sure not to name yourself as co-owner along with your child or you'll have to pay tax on the income the bonds earned when they are cashed in. Big exception: The interest is tax free if you use the bonds to pay for your child's higher education, and your adjusted gross income is below an annual ceiling. To accomplish this, the bonds must be purchased in your name, not your child's. See IRS Publication 970, *Tax Benefits for Education*, for more information.

Trusts. When you set up a UTMA account for a child, you can control the funds as custodian of the account until the child reaches age 18 or 21, depending on your state. But then the child takes over control of the account and can do anything he or she wants with it. If you don't want the child to get the property so young, you may want to use a trust instead. A trust is much more complicated and expensive to set up and run than a UTMA account—you'll need a lawyer to do it for you. However, it can give you much more control and flexibility than a UTMA account.

With a trust, you give a person, called a trustee, title to money or property that he or she is required to manage on behalf of your child or other beneficiary. You can set up a trust for a single child (a child's trust) or for several of your children (a family pot trust). Any adult can act as trustee—for example, your spouse, yourself, or another relative.

The trust must be irrevocable for it to be effective for income-shifting purposes. You must create a trust document instructing the trustee how to manage the money. Ordinarily, the trustee is allowed to spend trust money for the child's health, education, and living expenses. However, if you are the trustee and spend trust money on your basic child support obligation, you may be required to pay personal income tax on the trust income. This is similar to the rule for custodial accounts explained above.

When the child reaches the age you specify, the trustee ends the trust and gives the trust property to the beneficiary. Unlike a custodial account, the property does not have to be handed over to the child when he or she reaches 18 or 21. You can specify any age.

The trust itself pays tax on any income earned on the trust property that is not spent on the child or other beneficiary during the year. Thus, the trustee must file annual income tax returns for the trust. Trusts have their own income tax rates, which are somewhat higher than rates for individuals. Trust income spent on the child or other beneficiary during the year is taxed to the child at the child's tax rates. (But, as explained above, because of the kiddie tax, any income over $1,700 is taxed at the parent's tax rate if the child is under 18.)

Education accounts. If your main goal is to save money for your child's college education, neither a custodial account nor trust may be your best option, especially now that the kiddie tax applies to all children under 18. Instead, you should consider establishing an education account—a Coverdell ESA, 529 savings plan, or both. Transferring your money to these accounts also accomplishes income shifting, and they have one other huge advantage: No tax need ever be paid on the income the money in the account earns so long as it is used for educational expenses. This is not the case with a custodial account or trust. In addition, keeping money in these accounts rather than custodial accounts or trusts will make it easier for a child to qualify for college financial aid. If you've already established a custodial account for a child, you can usually switch the money over to a 529 plan. (See Chapter 2 for a detailed discussion of these accounts.)

However, these accounts do have some drawbacks. Higher-income taxpayers are not allowed to contribute to Coverdell ESAs, and the annual contribution limit for those who can contribute is small—only $2,000. 529 plans don't have these limitations, but you have little control over how the money is invested.

In addition, you can only contribute cash to education accounts. You may not contribute property such as stock or mutual funds. This means you cannot enjoy the tax advantages of giving appreciated assets to your children discussed above. If you want to give such assets, you'll have to use a custodial account or trust. This doesn't mean you must forego education accounts. You may have a custodial account, education account, and trust for the same child.

The Gift Tax Bugaboo

There is something called the gift tax, that often frightens and confuses people. They think they'll have to pay taxes on any gifts of money or property they give their children or others. This is not the case. Most people never have to worry about gift taxes. In fact, you have to give away more than $1 million in money or property while you're alive for you or your estate to be subject to any gift taxes at all. Moreover, there are ways to give away even more than $1 million and still incur no gift taxes.

Here's what the gift tax is all about: When you give money away while you're alive, you reduce the size of your estate when you die so you also reduce any estate taxes that will be owed. The gift tax exists to prevent people from avoiding all estate taxes by giving away all their money before they die.

However, there are very generous exclusions from the gift tax. First of all, there is an annual gift tax exclusion of $12,000 per person. This means that you may give up to $12,000 a year in cash or assets to any number of people each year without having to pay any gift tax. Married couples can combine their $12,000 annual exclusions and give, as a couple, a $24,000 gift per year to as many people as they want.

> **EXAMPLE:** Bill and Wanda are a married couple with four children. This year they give each of their children a gift of $24,000, for a total of $96,000. None of these gifts is subject to the gift tax because they each fall within the annual gift tax exclusion.

Even if you give more than $12,000 or $24,000 to a single person in a single year, you're still not likely to incur any gift tax liability because there is a $1 million lifetime gift tax exclusion. Any amounts you give over the annual exclusion are applied toward your lifetime exclusion. You'll only have to pay gift taxes if these gifts exceed $1 million, and then only on the excess amount. However, if you make a gift in excess of your annual exclusion, you will have to file a gift tax return with the IRS. But this is just to let the IRS know about the gift; you won't have to pay any gift tax unless you've exceeded the lifetime exclusion.

> **EXAMPLE:** Assume that Bill and Wanda from the example above gave one of their children $50,000 in a single year. This is $26,000 more than their annual combined gift tax exclusion. Thus, $26,000 is deducted from their $1 million lifetime gift tax exclusion, leaving them with a mere $974,000 lifetime exclusion. The couple must file a gift tax return with the IRS when they do their taxes for the year, but they won't owe any gift taxes.

By the way, spouses can give each other gifts of any size completely gift tax free. The gift tax also does not apply to gifts to qualified charities.

 For more information about gift taxes, see *Plan Your Estate*, by Denis Clifford and Cora Jordan (Nolo).

Give Junior a Job: Employing Your Children to Shift Your Tax Burden

If you own a business, there is another way to shift your income to lower income taxpayers: Hire your children. If your children do legitimate work as employees in your business, you may deduct their salaries from your business income as a business expense. Your children pay tax on their salaries at their own tax rates, which should be lower than yours (unless you earn little or no income). Let's look at just how your children's' income will and will not be taxed.

Can I Make Junior Work In a Salt Mine?

You're probably aware that certain types of child labor are illegal under federal and state law. However, these laws generally don't apply to children under 16 who are employed by their parents, unless the child is employed in mining, manufacturing, or a hazardous occupation. Hazardous occupations include driving a motor vehicle; being an outside helper on a motor vehicle; and operating various power-driven machines.

A child who is at least 16 may be employed in any nonhazardous occupation. Children at least 17 years of age may spend up to 20% of their time driving cars and trucks weighing less than 6,000 pounds as part of their job if they have licenses and no tickets, drive only in daylight hours, and go no more than 30 miles from home. They may not perform dangerous driving maneuvers (such as towing) or do regular route deliveries. For detailed information, see the Department of Labor Website (www.dol.gov).

First of all, there is no kiddie tax on a child's earned income—salaries and other amounts received as pay for work actually done. Regardless of a child's age, all of his or her earned income is subject to taxation at the child's income tax rates, not the parent's. This means that parents can hire their children when they're under 18 years of age and they will not have to pay tax on any part of their salaries at their parent's tax rates.

One of the great tax advantages of hiring your children is that you need not pay FICA (Social Security and Medicare) taxes for your children under age 18 who work in your trade or business or your partnership if it's owned solely by you and your spouse. FICA is a 15.4% tax paid half by the employer and half by the employee, so this is a substantial tax savings. Moreover, you need not pay federal unemployment (FUTA) taxes for services performed by your child who is under 21 years old.

Yet another benefit of a child–employee is that you won't have to withhold any income taxes from your child's pay unless:

- your child has more than $250 in unearned income for the year and his or her total income exceeds $850 (in 2006), or
- your child's pay exceeds the standard deduction for the year.

A child who works can have a much larger standard deduction than a child who just has investment income. A working child gets a standard deduction that is the *larger* of:

- $850, or
- the amount of the child's earned income for the year plus $250 (but this amount can't be more than the standard deduction for single adults—$5,150 in 2006).

Thus, a child can have a standard deduction of as much as $5,150 in 2006 (the deduction for adult single taxpayers), provided that the child had at least $4,900 in earned income from a job.

Let's put all these rules together and see how they can benefit a parent who owns a business.

> **EXAMPLE:** Carol hires Mark, her 16-year-old son, to perform computer inputting services for her medical transcription business during 2006. He works 10 hours per week and she pays him $20 per hour (the going rate for such work). Over the course of a year, she pays him a total of $9,000. She need not pay FICA tax for Mark because he's under 18, but she must withhold income taxes from his salary because he makes more than the standard deduction. When she does her taxes for the year, she may deduct his $9,000 salary from her business income as a business expense. Mark pays income tax only on the portion of his income that exceeds the $5,150 standard deduction—so he pays federal income tax only on $3,850 of his $9,000 salary. With such a small amount of income, he is in the lowest federal income tax bracket—10%. He pays $385 in federal income tax for the year. (Mark gets no personal deduction because he is his mother's dependent.) Had Carol done the transcription work herself and kept the $9,000, she would have had to pay income tax and self-employment tax on it. In her bracket, this amounts to a combined 39.4% tax.
>
> Had Carol paid Mark $5,150 in 2006 (the amount of his standard deduction), his entire income would have been tax free.

A child can get even more tax-free income by opening an IRA and deducting the contribution to the account. If the maximum $4,000 annual contribution is made, up to $9,150 can be earned tax free ($5,150 standard deduction + $4,000 IRA contribution = $9,150). If the child is over 18, this may be both earned and unearned income. But, as described above, children under 18 must pay a kiddie tax on all unearned income over $850 (but not on earned income).

Buy Animal House and Rent It to Your Kids

Here's a tax savings strategy that can work well for families with college age children: Purchase a house, condo, or apartment building near your child's college. Have your child move in—perhaps with one or more roommates—and pay you rent. Hire your child as your employee to manage the building and perform maintenance. The salary you pay your child will be a tax deductible rental expense. You'll also get to deduct mortgage interest, property taxes, depreciation, and repair costs—all of which will reduce or eliminate any tax you must pay on your rental income. Your child will pay income tax on the salary at his or her own lower tax rates. For more information on tax deductions for landlords, see *Every Landlord's Tax Deduction Guide*, by Stephen Fishman (Nolo).

Who Said Never Hire Your Relatives?

You don't get the benefits of income shifting when you employ your spouse in your business because your income is combined when you file a joint tax return. There is usually little or no tax savings if you hire your spouse and both file separate returns—indeed, you could end up paying more tax.

The real advantage of hiring your spouse is in the realm of employee benefits. You can provide your spouse with employee benefits, deduct the cost as a business expense, and your spouse doesn't have to declare the benefit as income provided the IRS requirements are satisfied. This is a particularly valuable tool for health coverage—you can give your spouse health insurance coverage and reimbursements for uninsured expenses as a tax-free employee benefit. (See Chapter 5 for a detailed discussion.)

You don't have the joint tax return issue if you employ relatives other than your spouse. For example, if you're already helping to support your parents, siblings, or other relatives, hiring them to work in your business is a great tax strategy. They'll get the money they need and you'll shift part of your income to a lower-income taxpayer.

Rules to Follow When Employing Your Family

The IRS is well aware of the tax benefits of hiring a child, spouse, or other relative, so it's on the lookout for taxpayers who claim the benefit without really having their family members work in their businesses. If the IRS concludes that a family member isn't really an employee, you'll lose your tax deductions for his or her salary and benefits. To avoid this, you should follow these simple rules.

Rule 1. The family member must be a real employee. First of all, the child or other family member must be a bona fide employee. Their work must be ordinary and necessary for your business, and their pay must be for services actually performed. Their services don't have to be indispensable, only common, accepted, helpful, and appropriate for your business. Any real work for your business can qualify—for example, you could employ your child or other family member to clean your office, answer the phone, perform word processing, do photocopying, stuff envelopes, input data, or do filing. You get no business deductions when you pay your child or other person for personal services, such as babysitting or mowing your lawn at home. On the other hand, money you pay for yard work performed on business property could be deductible as a business expense.

The IRS won't believe that an extremely young child is a legitimate employee. How young is too young? The IRS has accepted that a seven-year-old child may be an employee (*Eller v. Comm'r.*, 77 T.C. 934 (1981)), but probably won't believe that children younger than seven are performing any useful work for your business.

You should keep track of the work and hours your children or other family members perform by having them fill out time sheets or timecards. You can find these in stationery stores or make a timesheet yourself. It should list the date, the services performed, and the time spent performing the services. Although not legally required, it's also a good idea to have the child or other family member sign a written employment agreement specifying his or her job duties and hours. These duties should only be related to your business.

Junior's Timesheet

Date	Time In	Time Out	Total Work Time	Services Performed
1/9/04	3:30 pm	5:30 pm	2 hours	copying, some filing
1/14/04	3:30 pm	5:00 pm	1 1/2 hours	printed out bills and prepared for them for mailing
1/15/04	3:45 pm	5:15 pm	1 1/2 hours	copying and filing
1/24/04	10:00 am	3:00 pm	5 hours	answered phones
1/30/04	3:30 pm	5:30 pm	2 hours	copying, filing
?1/04	10:00 am	2:00 pm	4 hours	cleaned office

Rule 2. Compensation must be reasonable. When you hire your children, it is advantageous (taxwise) to pay them as much as possible. That way, you can shift as much of your income as possible to your children, who are probably in a much lower income tax bracket. Conversely, you want to pay your spouse as little as possible since you get no benefits from income shifting. This is because you and your spouse are in the same income tax bracket (assuming you file a joint return, as the vast majority of married people do). Moreover, your spouse will have to pay a 7.65% Social Security tax on his or her salary—an amount that is not tax deductible. (As your spouse's employer, you'll have to pay employment taxes on your spouse's salary as well, but these taxes are deductible business expenses.) The absolute minimum you can pay your spouse is the minimum wage in your area.

However, you can't just pay any amount you choose: Your spouse's or child's wages must be reasonable. This is determined by comparing the amount paid with the value of the services performed. You should have no problem as long as you pay no more than what you'd pay a stranger for the same work—don't try paying your child $100 per hour for office cleaning just to get a big tax deduction. Find out what workers performing similar services in your area are being paid. For example, if you plan to hire your teenager to do word processing, call an employment agency or temp agency in your area to see what these workers are being paid.

To prove how much you paid (and that you actually paid it), you should pay your child or spouse by check, not cash. Do this once or twice a month as you would for any other employee. The funds should be deposited in a bank account in your child's or spouse's name. Your child's bank account may be a trust account.

Rule 3. Comply with legal requirements for employers. You must comply with most of the same legal requirements when you hire a child, spouse, or other family member as you do when you hire a stranger. This means you must withhold taxes from their pay if required, and file the appropriate tax forms:

- IRS Form W-2, showing how much you paid the employee and how much tax was withheld, if any
- Form 941, *Employer's Quarterly Federal Tax Return*, or Form 944, *Employer's Annual Federal Tax Return*, and
- Form 940 or Form 940-EZ, *Employer's Annual Federal Unemployment (FUTA) Tax Return*.

IRS Circular E, *Employer's Tax Guide*, and Publication 929, *Tax Rules For Children and Dependents*, provide detailed information on these requirements.

Cover the Basics: Making the Most of Your Filing Status and Tax Exemptions

Этот chapter covers two subjects that may not sound exciting, but they can be big money savers—your filing status and tax exemptions. Every tax exemption you qualify for gives you an extra $3,300 tax deduction. And, choosing the best filing status can reduce your top tax rate, which means you owe less in taxes. No one (especially not the IRS) is going to make sure you choose the best filing status and take all the exemptions to which you're entitled. You must figure this out yourself. So, read on. With some planning during the year and an understanding of how it works, you could end up with more tax exemptions and a more favorable filing status.

Choosing the Classification for You

The single most important thing you must decide when you file your taxes is your filing status. There are five possible choices:

- single
- married filing jointly
- married filing separately
- head of household, or
- widow(er) with dependent child.

Why is your filing status so important? Well, for one thing, it determines the income levels for your tax brackets. The income tax brackets are designed so that single people (and married people filing separately) usually pay more tax than married couples filing jointly or heads of households with the same income. You can see how this works in the chart below.

Tax Bracket	Taxable Income If Single	Taxable Income if Married Filing Jointly	Taxable Income if Married Filing Separately	Taxable Income if Head of Household	Taxable Income if Widow(er) with Dependent Child
10%	Up to $7,550	Up to $15,100	Up to $7,550	Up to $10,750	Up to $15,100
15%	$7,551 to $30,650	$15,101 to $61,300	From $7,551 to $30,650	From $10,751 to $41,050	From $15,101 to $61,300
25%	$30,651 to $74,200	$61,301 to $123,700	$30,651 to $61,850	$41,051 to $106,000	$61,301 to $123,700
28%	$74,201 to $154,800	$123,701 to $188,450	$61,851 to $94,225	$106,001 to $171,650	$123,701 to $188,450
33%	$154,801 to $336,550	$188,451 to $336,550	$94,226 to $168,275	$171,651 to $336,550	$188,451 to $336,550
35%	All over $336,550	All over $336,550	All over $168,275	All over $336,550	All over $336,550

Applying these tax brackets, a single person who has $50,000 in taxable income must pay $9,058 in federal income taxes in 2006. A married couple filing jointly with the same taxable income pays only $6,745. This is because you can earn more at a lower rate as a married couple filing jointly than as a single. For example, a single person must start paying income tax at a 25% rate when his or her taxable income exceeds $30,650, but a married couple filing jointly must pay at the 25% rate only when their taxable income is over $61,300.

Married couples filing jointly and widows(ers) with dependent children have the lowest (best) tax brackets. The next best rates go to heads of households, then single people, and finally married people filing separately.

Your filing status is also crucial for calculating your standard deduction, personal exemptions, and income levels for phaseouts of your itemized deductions and personal exemptions. This is shown in the following chart (the numbers are for 2006).

	Single	Married Filing Jointly	Married Filing Separately	Head of Household	Widow(er) with Dependent Child
Personal Exemption	$3,300	$6,600 (two $3,300 deductions)	$3,300	$3,300	$3,300
Standard Deduction	$5,150	$10,300 (two $5,150 deductions)	$5,150	$7,550	$10,300
Income Levels for Deduction Phaseout	$150,500 to $273,000	$225,750 to $348,250	$112,875 to $174,125	$188,150 to $310,650	$225,750 to $348,250

Once again, married couples filing jointly and widow(er)s with dependent children have the most advantageous status, followed by the head of household, single, and then married filing separately.

As you can see by these charts, it's worth making sure you file your taxes with the best filing status possible. In many cases, you'll have a choice as to which status to use. You'll want to choose the one that saves you the most money.

OOPS—I Chose the Wrong Status Last Year

If you discover that you could have paid less tax in a prior year had you chosen a different filing status, you can file an amended return for that year and change your filing status. However, you must do so within three years of the date you filed your original return, including extensions to file. Big exception: If you file a joint return, you cannot later amend your return to file separately (except in some cases where your spouse died). For detailed guidance on how to file amended tax returns, see the IRS publication *Instructions for Form 1040X*.

Filing as a Single Person

If you're not married, have no relatives living with you, and are not supporting your parents, you must file as a single. If relatives live in your home or you support your parents, you should see if you can qualify for head of household status (or widow or widower status if your spouse died), because you would pay less tax with these statuses.

You are considered unmarried for the whole year if, on December 31, you are divorced or legally separated from your spouse under a final divorce decree or separate maintenance decree.

Married Filing Jointly Status

You can choose married filing jointly as your filing status if you are married and both you and your spouse agree to file a joint return. A joint return is a single return for a husband and wife that combines their incomes, exemptions, credits, and deductions. You can file a joint return even if one of you had no income or deductions.

Only a married couple can file a joint return. You are considered married for tax purposes *for the entire year* if, by December 31:

- you are married and living together as husband and wife
- you are living together in a common law marriage recognized in the state where you live or in the state where the common law marriage began
- you are married and living apart, but not legally separated under a decree of divorce or separate maintenance, or
- you are separated under an interlocutory (not final) decree of divorce. (For purposes of filing a joint return, you are not considered divorced.)

For IRS purposes, a marriage is only a legal union between a man and woman as husband and wife. Same-sex marriages and domestic partnerships don't count, although they may be recognized under some state laws (Massachusetts, for example, recognizes same-sex marriages). Couples who live together but are not legally married under their state law cannot file as married. However, it may be possible for one member of an unmarried couple to file as a head of household.

If your spouse dies and you do not remarry in the same year, you may file a joint return for that year. This is the last year for which you may file a joint return with that spouse.

Most married couples file jointly. You'll usually pay the lowest taxes by filing this way, particularly if one spouse earns substantially more than the other. This is because the tax brackets are lower for married people filing jointly and several deductions and tax credits are not allowed for married people filing separately.

EXAMPLE: Jack and Jill are a married couple. Jack had $100,000 of taxable income in 2006. Jill, a stay-at-home mom, had no income. If they file jointly, they will pay $18,115 in income taxes. If they file separately, Jack will have to pay $22,332 in income tax, and Jill will pay no taxes. Filing separately, Jack's top tax rate is 28%. Filing jointly, the top tax rate for Jack and Jill is only 25%.

The so-called marriage penalty—where a couple filing jointly pays more tax than if they filed separately—has for the most part been eliminated by tax law changes that became effective in 2003. Prior to this change, a couple's combined income could push them into a higher tax bracket than they would have been in if they filed separately. This is unlikely to happen anymore under the new tax brackets.

If you are married and don't want to be personally responsible for your spouse's taxes, you should choose the married filing separately status (see "You May Be Married—But Do You Want to File Taxes Together?" below). If your incomes and deductions are about the same, filing separately may not have a significant impact on what you owe in taxes. (But see "Married Filing Separately Status," below, for more on this topic.)

You May Be Married—But Do You Want to File Taxes Together?

As a general rule, when a married couple files a joint return, each spouse is jointly and individually liable for the entire tax owed on the return. This means that either spouse can be required to pay the tax due, plus any interest, penalties, and fines. A spouse can claim "innocent spouse relief" and avoid personally paying the other spouse's taxes if he or she can show the IRS that (1) the understatement of tax was due to the other spouse, and (2) the spouse did not know, or have reason to know, that there was an understatement of tax when he or she signed the joint return. However, both propositions can be hard to prove. You'll avoid being personally responsible for your spouse's taxes if you file a separate return. This is something you should seriously consider if you know your spouse cheats on his or her taxes.

Married Filing Separately Status

If you're married, you always have the option to file your taxes separately. If one of you won't agree to file a joint return, you'll have to file separately, unless you qualify for head of household status. When you file a separate return, you report only your own income, exemptions, credits, and deductions on your individual return.

Filing separately can result in a couple paying the same as, more than, or less than they would pay filing jointly. It all depends on their incomes and deductions. If their incomes are similar and they have similar deductions, there will usually be little or no difference if they file jointly or separately. If one spouse's income is substantially more than the other's, they could end up paying more if they file separately.

If one spouse has large itemized deductions for miscellaneous itemized deductions (such as unreimbursed employee expenses), medical expenses, or casualty losses, for example, they may be better off filing separately. Why? Because you must reduce these deductions by a certain percentage of your adjusted gross income. If filing separately gives the spouse with the deductions a lower AGI, then there would also be a smaller reduction in the spouse's itemized deductions.

> **EXAMPLE:** Marvin and Martha are a married couple. Martha had an adjusted gross income in 2006 of $150,000 and Marvin had an AGI of $50,000. Marvin incurred $20,000 in medical expenses during the year while Martha had $5,000 in medical expenses. Medical expenses are deductible only to the extent they exceed 7.5% of the taxpayer's AGI. If Marvin and Martha file jointly, their combined AGI is $200,000 so they can deduct their medical expenses to the extent they exceed 7.5% of $200,000 (which is $15,000). Their combined medical expenses were $25,000 so they could deduct only $10,000 of this amount. Filing jointly, their total income tax is $42,583. If they file separately, Marvin's AGI is only $50,000—so he can deduct any medical expenses that exceed 7.5% of $50,000 or $3,750. His medical expenses were $20,000, so he gets a $16,250 deduction on his separate return. His separate income tax bill is $4,995. Martha gets no deduction for her medical expenses on her separate return because they were less than 7.5% of her AGI. Her income tax bill is $34,890. They end up saving $2,698 in taxes by filing two separate returns instead of one joint return.

If you live in a community property state, the income you and your spouse earn is split evenly between you, as are your expenses (unless they are paid by one spouse with his or her separate noncommunity funds—for example, money you earned or inherited before marriage). There are nine community property states: Arizona, California, Idaho, Louisiana, Nevada, New Mexico, Texas, Washington, and Wisconsin. In these states, each spouse's taxable income will be similar whether they file separately or jointly, so it usually makes little difference which they choose. However, they may get tax benefits if either or both of their adjusted gross incomes exceed the income threshold for personal exemptions ($112,875 in 2006) and one of them pays for all of their combined medical expenses or miscellaneous itemized deductions from his or her separate funds. That spouse could then deduct the entire amount on his or her separate return.

There are several disadvantages to filing separately that you need to be aware of, however, because these can easily outweigh other benefits:

- You cannot take various tax credits, such as the Hope or Lifetime Learning education credits, earned income tax credit, and, in most cases, the credit for child and dependent care expenses.
- The amount you can exclude from income under an employer's dependent care assistance program is limited to $2,500 (instead of $5,000 if you file a joint return).
- You cannot take the deduction for student loan interest or the tuition and fees deduction.
- You cannot exclude from your income any interest income from qualified U.S. savings bonds that you used for higher education expenses.
- If you live with your spouse at any time during the tax year, you'll have to include in income more (up to 85%) of any Social Security benefits you receive.
- If you live with your spouse at any time during the tax year, you cannot roll over amounts from a traditional IRA into a Roth IRA.
- The following credits and deductions are reduced at income levels that are half of those for a joint return: child tax credit, retirement savings contributions credit, itemized deductions, and the deduction for personal exemptions.
- Your capital loss deduction limit is $1,500 (instead of $3,000 if you filed a joint return).

- You may not be able to deduct all or part of your contributions to a traditional IRA if you or your spouse was covered by an employee retirement plan at work during the year.
- If you own and actively manage rental real estate, it will be more difficult for you to deduct any losses you incur.
- If your spouse itemizes deductions, you cannot claim the standard deduction. If you can claim the standard deduction, your basic standard deduction is half the amount allowed on a joint return.

The only way to know for sure if you'll pay less taxes filing separately or jointly is to figure your taxes both ways. This isn't hard to do if you use tax preparation software.

Head of Household Filing Status

If you're not married, but pay for the upkeep of a home where a relative lives or you support your parents, you may qualify for head of household status. Filing as head of household is better than filing as single because you get a larger standard deduction and the tax brackets are more favorable.

Head of household is the most difficult filing status to understand. However, the basic idea is that you qualify as a head of household if you pay more than half the cost of keeping up a home where you and one or more of your dependents lives.

You can file as head of household if:

- you are unmarried on December 31 of the tax year
- you paid more than half the cost of keeping a home for the year, and
- a dependent child or other dependent relative lived with you in the home for more than half the year (however, a dependent parent does not have to live with you).

It's usually not difficult to tell if you're married or not (see the discussion in the "Married Filing Jointly Status" section, above). The second and third requirements are the hard parts.

First of all, you must have a home where a dependent lives over half the year (temporary absences for things like schooling, medical treatment, vacations, business, or military service are not counted). The home doesn't have to be your main residence, but you must still spend a substantial amount of time there.

A dependent is a person for whom you can claim a dependency exemption (as explained more below in this section). Provided the requirements for the dependent exemption are met, dependents can include:

- **Qualifying children.** Children under 19 years old (or under 24 if full-time students), including your son, daughter, stepchild, adopted child, foster child, brother, sister, stepbrother, stepsister, or a descendant of any of them (for example, your grandchild, niece, or nephew), who lives with you over half the year, and doesn't pay for over half of his or her own support.
- **Qualifying relatives.** No matter what their age, your children who are not qualifying children, parents and stepparents, grandparents, siblings, aunts, uncles, nephews, nieces, and people married to your children, parents, or siblings, who earn less than $3,300 per year, and for whom you provide more than 50% support. People who aren't related to you cannot be qualifying relatives for these purposes, even if you can get a dependency exemption for them.

A dependent parent (or parents) does not have to live in the same home as you; but, then you must pay for more than half the cost of maintaining the home where the parent does live for the entire year. For these purposes, a home includes a rest home or home for the elderly where your parent lives.

You also have to be able to show that you paid for more than half the cost of maintaining the home where the qualifying relative lives. Include in the cost of upkeep expenses such as rent, mortgage interest, real estate taxes, home insurance, repairs, utilities, and food eaten in the home. Do not include expenses for clothing, education, medical treatment, vacations, life insurance, or transportation. You meet the requirement if you paid for over half the total expenses. IRS Publication 501, *Exemptions, Standard Deduction, and Filing Information*, contains a worksheet you can use.

EXAMPLE: Kevin and Kate, who are both unmarried, live together with their 12-year-old son Mike. Because they aren't married, they can't file a joint return. Kevin works full-time and pays 75% of the cost of keeping up the home. Kate works part-time and pays only 25%. Kevin may file as head of household instead of single because he's unmarried and paid for more than half the cost of maintaining the home where his dependent child lived during the year. Kate must file her tax return as single. Filing as head of household gives Kevin a $7,550 standard deduction instead of the $5,150 deduction for singles—$2,400 more. His top tax bracket is 25%, so he saves an extra $600 in tax (25% x $2,400 = $600).

As the above example shows, head of household status may be used by members of many nontraditional families. However, its use in these situations is limited under new rules (adopted in 2005) that a person must be related to you by blood or marriage to be a qualifying relative. Thus, you can't use head of household status if you help maintain a home where someone not related to you lives.

EXAMPLE: Assume that Mike, Kate's son from the previous example, was not fathered by Kevin. Mike is not a qualifying relative of Kevin because he is not related to him by blood or marriage. This means that Kevin cannot qualify for head of household status even though he pays for more than half the cost of maintaining the home where Mike lives. To avoid filing as single, Kevin would have to marry Kate, which would entitle him to file a joint return.

Under the new rules, some people who used to qualify for head of household status no longer qualify. For example, in the past, a single parent qualified as a head of household as long as he or she paid more than half the cost of maintaining the home where his or her child lived. This is no longer enough. The child must also qualify as the parent's dependent—which eliminates this status for some parents.

EXAMPLE: Virginia is a divorced mother of Tom, a 21-year-old, who lives at home and works part-time. Because Tom is over 19 and not a full-time student, he can't qualify as Virginia's qualifying child. Because he earns too much money he can't be her qualifying relative either. Since he doesn't qualify as Virginia's dependent, she cannot file as head of household and must file as single. Virginia has a taxable income of $40,000. She must pay $6,558 in federal income tax filing as single, instead of $5,463 if she could file as head of household.

Head of Household Status for Married People

Even if you're married, you can qualify for head of household status if:

- you don't file a joint return with your spouse
- your spouse was not a member of your household during the last six months of the year, and
- a qualifying child lived in your home for over half the year and you paid more than half the cost of maintaining the home.

If you don't want to file a joint return with your spouse, head of household status will be better than filing as single because you get a larger standard deduction and the tax brackets are more favorable. If you meet the requirements, you don't need your spouse's permission to file as head of household.

Widow or Widower with Dependent Children Status

You may be able to file as a qualifying widow or widower for the two years following the year your spouse died. To do this, you must meet all four of the following tests:

- You were entitled to file a joint return with your spouse for the year he or she died. It doesn't matter whether you actually filed a joint return.
- You didn't remarry in the two years following the year your spouse died.
- You have a child, stepchild, or adopted child for whom you can claim a dependency exemption.
- You paid more than half the cost of maintaining a household that was the principal home for you and the child, for the whole year.

People with this filing status receive the same treatment as married couples filing jointly. So, if you qualify, you should choose this filing status.

Taking All the Tax Exemptions You Deserve

Congress believes that a certain amount of income should not be subject to income tax at all—so it created tax exemptions. A tax exemption is similar to a tax deduction in that it is a sum of money you are allowed to deduct from your income to arrive at your taxable income. Not everyone can take advantage of tax exemptions, however. Both the personal and dependent exemptions are subject to income restrictions and are phased out for taxpayers whose incomes exceed certain levels (see "Phaseout of Exemptions for High-Income Taxpayers," below).

All exemptions are worth the same amount of money—$3,300 in 2006 (the amount is adjusted for inflation each year). For example, if you qualify for three exemptions, you'll be entitled to deduct $9,900 from your income in 2006. As with tax deductions, the amount of taxes an exemption will save you depends on your tax bracket. If you're in the 28% tax bracket, each $3,300 will save you $924 in federal income taxes; if you're in the 10% bracket, it will save you only $330. There are two types of exemptions: personal exemptions for yourself and your spouse (if any) and exemptions for your dependents (typically, your children), but in some cases other relatives as well, such as a parent or sibling. Each type of exemption is worth the same amount of money, but different rules apply to each one.

Personal Exemption for Yourself

You are entitled to one personal exemption for yourself, as long as no one else is entitled to claim you as a dependent. Even if the other taxpayer does not actually claim you as a dependent, you still can't take an exemption for yourself if there's someone else who can claim you.

Personal Exemption for Your Spouse

A spouse is entitled to his or her own personal exemption. If a married couple files jointly, their two personal exemptions are combined on their joint tax return. If you file separately, you can't claim an exemption for your spouse unless he or she had no gross income and was not someone else's dependent.

Joint return. If, like most married couples, you file a joint return, you can claim two personal exemptions—one for yourself and one for your spouse.

Separate return. If you are married and file a separate return, you can claim the exemption for your spouse only if your spouse had no gross income, is not filing a return, and was not another taxpayer's dependent (even if the other taxpayer does not actually claim your spouse as a dependent).

Head of household filing status. If you qualify for head of household filing status because you are considered unmarried (see "Head of Household Status for Married People," above), you can still claim an exemption for your spouse if he or she had no gross income, is not filing a return, and was not another taxpayer's dependent.

Divorced or separated spouse. If you obtained a final decree of divorce or separate maintenance by the end of the year, you cannot take your former spouse's exemption. This rule applies even if you provided all of your former spouse's support.

Dependent Exemptions for Children

One dependent exemption may be claimed on your tax return for each child who meets the requirements of what the IRS calls a "qualifying child." This is where the rules can get tricky. A qualifying child is a child who is:

- **related to you**—your son, daughter, stepchild, adopted child, foster child, brother, sister, stepbrother, stepsister, or a descendant of any of them (for example, your grandchild, niece, or nephew).
- **under age 19 (or student under 24)**—under age 19 at the end of the tax year, or under age 24 if a full-time student for at least five months of the year, or any age if permanently and totally disabled at any time during the year.
- **not self-supporting**—did not pay for over half of his or her own support during the year.
- **lives with you**—lived with you for more than half of the year or is treated as your qualifying child under the special rule for parents who are divorced, separated, or living apart (see below). (Temporary absences for things like schooling, medical treatment, vacations, business, or military service do not count.)

- **a U.S. citizen or resident**—a U.S. citizen, U.S. national, or resident of the United States, Canada, or Mexico for some part of the year.

Most qualifying children are the biological, adopted, or stepchildren of the taxpayers who claim them as dependents, but this doesn't have to be the case. For example, a brother, sister, or grandchild can be your qualifying child if he or she is under 19, lives with you over half the year, provides less than half of his or her own support, and is a U.S. citizen or resident. Moreover, a qualifying child can be as old as 23 if he or she is enrolled in school full-time.

Dependent Children Must Have Social Security Numbers

To obtain an exemption for a dependent child, you must list the child's Social Security number on your tax return. No number, no exemption. This rule is intended to prevent people from claiming exemptions for children who don't really exist. You may obtain a Social Security number for your child by filling out Social Security Form SS-5 and filing it with your local Social Security office or by mail. See the Social Security Administration website at www.ssa.gov for details. It takes about two weeks to get a Social Security number. If you do not have a required SSN by the filing due date, you can file IRS Form 4868, *Application for Automatic Extension of Time to File U.S. Individual Income Tax Return,* for an extension of time to file. If you or your spouse is expecting a child, apply for a Social Security number at the hospital when you apply for your baby's birth certificate. The state agency that issues birth certificates will share your child's information with the Social Security Administration and it will mail the Social Security card to you.

Who supports a qualifying child? Before 2005, you had to provide over half of a child's support to claim a dependent exemption. But the law has changed and now all that is required is that the child must not provide for over half of his or her own support. Thus, as long as a child lives with you for more than half the year, you qualify for the exemptions even if he or she is financially supported primarily by someone other than you—for example, a former spouse. See "Dependent Exemptions for Qualifying Relatives," below, for a discussion of the ins and outs of the support test for the dependent exemption.

Relatives only. Under the definition of a qualifying child, you'll qualify for a dependent exemption only if your child or other dependent is a relative—whether by blood, marriage, or adoption; or a foster child. You can't get a credit for a child who is not related to you, even if you support him or her. However, you can still get an exemption if the person meets the requirements to be your qualifying relative (see the next section).

Divorced or separated parents. If you're divorced or separated, the dependent exemption ordinarily goes to the parent with whom the child lived for the longest time during the year; or, if the time was equal, to the parent with the highest adjusted gross income. This means that a noncustodial parent will not get the exemption, even if he or she pays for the bulk of the child support. However, the parents can agree that the noncustodial parent should get the exemption, or a divorce decree or child support order may require it.

No personal exemption for dependent children. A child who is claimed as a dependent by a parent or anyone else is not entitled to a personal exemption. This matters, of course, only if the child has income he or she must pay tax on.

Dependent Exemptions for Qualifying Relatives

You can also claim a dependent exemption for a person the IRS calls a qualifying relative—for example, a parent or grandparent you support. However, a person doesn't have to be related to you by blood or marriage to be a qualifying relative; and a child who is not your qualifying child can still be your qualifying relative.

These rules are confusing, but they are worth knowing. If you contribute toward the support of a parent or other relative (or even a nonrelative in some cases), you could be entitled to claim a dependent exemption for him or her. Even if you haven't taken a dependency exemption for the person in the past, in some cases paying just a few dollars more to support the person during the year could entitle you to a valuable exemption.

When Not to Claim a Dependent Exemption

If your child attends college, you may be better off not claiming him or her as a dependent. This is because of two tax credits that are available for people who incur education expenses: the Hope tax credit, which is worth up to $1,650 per year, and the Lifetime Learning credit, which is worth up to $2,000 per year. A credit is a dollar-for-dollar reduction in your taxes, so it can be worth more than an exemption. For example, if you're in the 28% bracket, a $3,300 dependent exemption will save you $924 in federal income taxes. A $1,650 Hope credit saves $462 in taxes. A $2,000 Lifetime Learning credit saves $560.

Unfortunately, you cannot claim these credits if your adjusted gross income is $110,000 or more (if you file a joint return), or $55,000 or more (if you're single). In this event, you could be better off if your child claims the credit and uses it to reduce his or her own taxes. Your child can do this only if you don't claim him or her as a dependent. However, it is not necessary that the child pay for education expenses from his or her own money to get the credits. But, the amount of the credit is limited to the child's tax liability for the year. If a child doesn't earn much, there won't be much of a credit.

> **EXAMPLE:** Jon and Karen Smith are married, file jointly, and have an AGI of $120,000. Their daughter, Jane, is in her sophomore year of studies at the local university. Jane earned $25,000 from a job and investments. Jon and Karen paid $4,300 tuition and related fees for Jane in 2006. The Smiths can't claim the Hope or Lifetime Learning credits because they earn too much money. They decide not to claim Jane as their dependent and allow her to claim the Hope credit. Jane's Hope credit can be as much as $1,650, but no more than her tax liability for the year. Her taxes due for the year were $2,128, so she gets the full $1,650 credit. The Smith's lost their $3,300 dependent exemption for Jane, but this would have saved them only $924 in taxes in their 28% tax bracket. Also, Jan would have owed $495 more in taxes on her income because she would not have a received a $3,300 personal deduction.

See Chapter 3 for a detailed discussion of the Hope tax credit and Lifetime Learning credit.

To be your qualifying relative, a person must pass three tests:

Member of household or relationship test. First of all, the person must either be related to you or live with you as a member of your household. A person is related to you for these purposes if he or she is:

- your child, stepchild, eligible foster child, or a descendant of any of them (for example, your grandchild) (a legally adopted child is considered your child)
- your brother, sister, half brother, half sister, stepbrother, or stepsister
- your father, mother, grandparent, or other direct ancestor, but not foster parent
- your stepfather or stepmother
- a son or daughter of your brother or sister
- a brother or sister of your father or mother, or
- your son-in-law, daughter-in-law, father-in-law, mother-in-law, brother-in-law, or sister-in-law.

Any of these relationships that were established by marriage are not ended by death or divorce. However, such a relative may not be your qualifying child or the qualifying child of anyone else.

Confusingly, a person who is not related to you by blood or marriage can still be your qualifying relative for purposes of the dependency exemption. Such a nonrelative must be a member of your household to be qualifying relative—this means he or she must live with you full-time except for temporary absences for things like schooling, medical treatment, vacations, business, or military service. However, this person doesn't help you qualify for head of household filing status.

Gross income test. In addition, the person's taxable income must be very low—no more than the dependent exemption, which is $3,300 in 2006. Income that is not taxable is not included in the person's gross income. This includes Social Security payments (unless the person earns too much money), and tax-free interest from municipal bonds. Tax-free student scholarships also aren't included in income. (See Chapter 2 for a detailed discussion of the types of income that are tax free.)

Support test. Finally, you must pay for over half the person's support during the year (unless there is a multiple support agreement as discussed below). This differs from the qualifying child test which only requires that the child not provide more than half of his or her support, but does not require that the person claiming the exemption pay for more than half of such support.

> ### Your Nonqualifying Child Can Be Your Qualifying Relative
>
> A child who doesn't meet the test to be your qualifying child can be your qualifying relative, entitling you to claim a dependent exemption for the child. Take for example the case of the "boomerang child"—one who is an adult but comes back home to live with his or her parents. Even if he or she is a full-time student, a child over 23 years old can't be a qualifying child unless he or she is totally and permanently disabled. But a child of any age can be a qualifying relative if the support and gross income tests are met.
>
> **EXAMPLE:** Sally quits her job and returns home to live with her parents. She is 25 years old, so she is too old to be her parent's qualifying child. However, she meets the requirements to be their qualifying relative: Her total taxable income for the year is only $3,000, and her parents pay for almost all her support. Sally's parents can claim a dependent exemption for her.

Applying the Support Test for Dependents

When you're dealing with an older child or other person who has income, the support test can easily trip you up. The support tests differ depending on whether a qualifying child or qualifying relative is involved. But for either test you must first determine the total support provided for the person from all sources. Total support includes amounts spent to provide food, lodging, clothing, education, medical and dental care, child care, recreation, transportation, payments to nursing homes, and similar necessities. Things you might not consider necessities may also be included, such as education, music and dance lessons, summer camp, wedding expenses, birthday expenses, toys, vacations, and entertainment such as movies and concerts. However, money used to pay taxes doesn't count as support.

Qualifying relative. You must provide more than half a person's support for that person to be a qualifying relative. You do this by comparing the amount you spent on the person's support with the entire amount of support he or she received from all sources. This includes support the person paid for with his or her own money, including tax-exempt income like Social Security benefits. However, a person's own funds are not support unless they are actually spent for support. Money kept unspent in the bank or elsewhere doesn't count.

> **EXAMPLE:** Your mother received $2,400 in Social Security benefits and $300 in interest. She paid $2,000 for lodging and $400 for recreation. She put $300 in a savings account. Even though your mother received a total of $2,700, she spent only $2,400 for her own support. If you spent more than $2,400 for her support and no other support was received, you have provided more than half of her support.

When you figure how much you spent for a person's support, include the fair market value of any property you give the person—for example, food and clothing. If you provide a person with a place to live, you are considered to provide support equal to the fair rental value of the lodging. Fair rental value includes a reasonable allowance for the use of furniture and appliances, and for heat and other utilities that you pay for.

> **EXAMPLE:** Grace lives with her daughter, Mary, her daughter's husband, Frank, and their two children. Grace gets Social Security benefits of $2,400, which she spends on clothing, transportation, and recreation. Grace has no other income. Frank and Mary's total food expense for the household is $5,200. They pay Grace's medical and drug expenses of $1,200. The fair rental value of the lodging provided to Grace is $1,800 a year, based on the cost of similar rooming facilities. They figure Grace's total support as follows:

Fair rental value of lodging	$1,800
Clothing, transportation, and recreation	2,400
Medical expenses	1,200
Share of food (1/5 of $5,200)	1,040
Total support	$6,440

The support Frank and Mary provide ($1,800 lodging + $1,200 medical expenses + $1,040 food = $4,040) is more than half of Grace's $6,440 total support. Grace, therefore, is a qualifying relative of Frank and Mary and they may claim a dependent exemption for her on their tax return.

If you're contributing to the support of a parent or other person you want to claim as a qualifying relative, you need to keep track of how much money you and they spend on their living expenses. Keep copies of bills, receipts, cancelled checks, and credit card statements. Your goal is to pay at least 51% of the person's total support for the year. If towards the end of the year you are at or below 51%, ask the person to stop spending his or her own money on as many support items as possible until the following year.

Qualifying child. You don't need to be able to prove that you provide more than half of the support for a qualifying child. All that is required is proof that the child didn't pay for more than half of his or her own support.

As is the case with qualifying relatives, only money actually spent by a qualifying child on his or her support counts. Moreover, a child doesn't have to spend any of his money on his support. Money a child keeps in the bank isn't counted, whether a child earns it from a job, or gets it as a gift or from investments. As a general rule, it makes no difference where a child gets the money he or she spends on support. It can be from a job (even if a parent is the employer), cash from parents or other relatives, school loans or other loans, or Social Security benefits. However, a scholarship received by a child who is a full-time student is not taken into account in determining whether the child provided more than half of his or her own support.

> **EXAMPLE:** Jason is an 18-year-old college freshman at Podunk U. This year, he took out a $5,000 school loan to help pay his tuition and earned $5,000 from a part-time job that he spent on his living expenses. His grandfather gave him $5,000, but he spent only $1,000 of it. Jason's total contribution to his support for the year was $11,000. Jason's total expenses for the year included $20,000 for college tuition and another $5,000 for room and board and other living expenses. Because $11,000 is less than 50% of $25,000, Jason did not pay for over half of his own support during the year.

In close cases, remember that money you give a child does not count as support by you, but things you buy for him do. For example, if you give your child $10,000 cash as a gift, it will not count as support you paid for even if the child later spends it for his support. But if you personally pay $10,000 of your child's college tuition, it will count as support you provided.

Multiple Support Agreements

Sometimes no person provides more than half of the support for a qualifying child or qualifying relative. Instead, two or more people, each of whom would be able to take the exemption but for the support test, together provide more than half of the person's support.

> **EXAMPLE:** Wilma is an 80-year-old widow with four children. Each of the children pays for 20% of Wilma's support, with Wilma paying the remaining 20%. Wilma meets the requirements for a qualifying relative, but none of her children pays for over 50% of her support, so none of them satisfies the support test for a dependent exemption for a qualifying relative.

So the question is: Who gets to claim the exemption on his or her tax return? The people providing the support can decide who gets the exemption, but that person must provide over 10% of the support. Each of the others must sign a statement agreeing not to claim the exemption for that year. The person who claims the exemption must keep these signed statements for his or her records. A multiple support declaration identifying each of the others who agreed not to claim the exemption must be attached to the claimant's tax return. IRS Form 2120, Multiple Support Declaration, can be used for this purpose. Each year a different member of the group can claim the exemption by changing the agreement.

> **EXAMPLE:** Wilma's children agree that Bob, her eldest son, should claim the dependent exemption for Wilma because he's in the highest tax bracket. They complete and sign IRS Form 2120, which Bob files with his tax return.

Phaseout of Exemptions for High Income Taxpayers

As your adjusted gross income grows over a certain point, your personal and dependent exemptions are gradually phased out until they are eliminated entirely. The following chart shows the phaseout income ceilings.

Phaseout of Exemptions for High-Income Taxpayers—2006		
Filing Status	Beginning of Phaseout	Exemption Fully Phased Out
Married, filing jointly	$225,750	$348,250
Head of household	$188,150	$310,650
Single (not head of household)	$150,500	$273,000
Married, filing separately	$112,875	$174,125

Calculating how much a phaseout of your exemptions will actually cost you is a bit more complicated than it used to be because the personal exemption phaseout will itself be phased out over the next several years and then eliminated, at least temporarily. It was cut by one-third for tax years 2006 and 2007, by two-thirds for 2008 and 2009, and will then be eliminated entirely in 2010. However, the phaseout will be reinstated in its pristine form starting in 2011, unless Congress acts to eliminate it permanently—something President Bush has requested. These scheduled changes are shown in the following chart.

Year	Phaseout
2006–2007	66.67%
2008–2009	33.33%
2010	0
2011 and later	100%

You begin the phaseout calculation by reducing the dollar amount of your exemptions by 2% for each $2,500, or part of $2,500 ($1,250 if you are married filing separately), that your AGI exceeds the amount shown in the first chart above for your filing status. You then reduce this amount by one-third or two-thirds through 2009, depending on the year, as show in the second chart above.

> **EXAMPLE:** Art and Amy Jones are a married couple with two dependent children in 2006. They are entitled to four exemptions worth $3,300 each, for a total of $13,200. However, the couple's adjusted gross income in 2006 is $300,750—$75,000 more than the $225,750 income ceiling for married people. Thus, they must reduce their dependent exemptions by 60%: ($75,000 ÷ $2,500 = 30; 2% x 30 = 60%). So in 2005 and earlier, they would have had to reduce their exemptions by $7,920 (60% x $13,200 = $7,920). However, for 2006 and 2007, they would reduce it by 66.67% (⅔) instead (66.67% x 7,920 = $5,283). So the dollar value of the Jones's four exemptions is reduced from $13,200 to $7,917 ($13,200–$5,283 = $7,917). In 2008 and 2009, phaseout is at 33.33% (⅓) of the amount it was from the first calculation. In 2010, there will be no phaseout of the Jones's exemption, no matter how high their income.

If you're in the phaseout range, but not too far above it, you can try to cut your AGI. For example, increase your contributions to your retirement accounts, such as a 401(k) or IRA—these contributions reduce your AGI. If you own losing stocks, you can sell them and deduct up to $3,000 of your losses from your AGI. See Chapter 1 for a detailed discussion of AGI.

Another strategy for high-income taxpayers is to ensure that a child fails the support test for the dependent exemption. This way, the child may not be claimed as a dependent by the parents, but may instead claim his or her own personal exemption, which is the same amount as the dependent exemption. The parents lose nothing because they couldn't have gotten a dependent exemption anyway (or would have lost most of it) because their income was too high. The child gets the full exemption instead. This would mean that in 2006, the child could deduct $3,300 from his or her income. The child will also be allowed the full standard deduction for singles ($5,150 in 2006). If the child is in college, he or she may also be able to claim the Hope or Lifetime Learning credits (see Chapter 3).

EXAMPLE: Morgan and Brittany, a married couple, have one son, Dan, who is a 20-year-old college student. The couple had an AGI of $400,000 in 2006, well above the dependent exemption phaseout amount, so they couldn't claim a dependent exemption for Dan. Instead, they give Dan enough money so he could pay for over one-half of his own support. Because he is no longer his parent's dependent, he can claim a personal exemption and full standard deduction on his own tax return. Dan gets $8,450 in deductions from his income for the year.

■

Help Beyond This Book

Thereare many resources available to supplement and explain more fully the tax information covered in this book. Many of these resources are free; others are reasonably priced. The more expensive tax publications for professionals are often available at public libraries or law libraries. And, a lot of tax information is available on the Internet.

Information from the IRS

The IRS has made a huge effort to inform the public about the tax law, creating hundreds of informative publications, an excellent website, and a telephone answering service. However, unlike the regulations and rulings issued by the IRS, these secondary sources of information are for informational purposes only. They are not official IRS pronouncements, and the IRS is not legally bound by them.

Reading IRS publications is a useful way to obtain information on IRS procedures and to get the agency's view of the tax law. But keep in mind that these publications only present the IRS's interpretation of the law, which may be very one-sided and even contrary to court rulings. That's why you shouldn't rely exclusively on IRS publications for information.

IRS Website

The IRS has one of the most useful Internet websites of any federal government agency. Among other things, almost every IRS form and informational publication can be downloaded from the site. The Internet address is www.irs.gov.

IRS Booklets and CD-ROM

The IRS publishes over 350 free booklets explaining the tax code, called IRS publications ("pubs," for short). Many of these publications are referenced in this book. Some are relatively easy to understand, others are incomprehensible or misleading. As with all IRS publications, they only present the IRS's interpretation of the tax laws—which may or may not be upheld by the federal courts.

You can download all of the booklets from the IRS website at www.irs.gov. You can also obtain free copies by calling 800-TAX-FORM (800-829-3676) or by contacting your local IRS office or sending an order form to the IRS.

IRS Telephone Information

The IRS offers a series of prerecorded tapes of information on various tax topics on a toll-free telephone service called TELETAX (800-829-4477). See IRS Publication 910 for a list of topics.

You can talk to an IRS representative on the telephone by calling 800-829-1040. (It is difficult to get though to someone from January through May.) Be sure to double check anything an IRS representative tells you over the phone—the IRS is notorious for giving misleading or outright wrong answers to taxpayers' questions, and the agency will not stand behind oral advice that turns out to be incorrect.

Other Online Tax Resources

In addition to the IRS website, there are hundreds of privately created websites on the Internet that provide tax information and advice. Some of this information is good; some is execrable. A comprehensive collection of web links about all aspects of taxation can be found at www.taxsites.com. Other useful tax Web link pages can be found at:

- www.willyancey.com/tax_internet.htm
- www.abanet.org/taxes
- www.natptax.com/tax_links.html
- www.el.com/elinks/taxes

Some useful tax-related websites include:

- www.accountantsworld.com
- www.unclefed.com
- www.smbiz.com/sbwday.html
- http://aol.smartmoney.com/tax/filing
- www.taxguru.net

> ### Nolo's Website
>
> Nolo maintains a website that is useful for small businesses and the self-employed. The site contains helpful articles, information about new legislation, book excerpts, and the Nolo catalog. The site also includes a legal encyclopedia with specific information for businesspeople, as well as a legal research center you can use to find state and federal statutes, including the Internal Revenue Code. The Internet address is www.nolo.com.

Tax Publications

There are many books (like this one) that attempt to make the tax law comprehensible to the average person. The best known are the paperback tax preparation books published every year. Two of the best are:

- *The Ernst and Young Tax Guide* (John Wiley & Sons), and
- *J.K. Lasser's Your Income Tax* (John Wiley & Sons).

J.K. Lasser publishes many other useful tax guides. You can find a list of these publications at www.wiley.com/WileyCDA/Section/id-103210.html.

Tax guides designed for college courses can also be extremely helpful. Two good guides to all aspects of income taxes that are updated each year are:

- *Prentice Hall's Federal Taxation Comprehensive* (Prentice Hall), and
- *CCH Federal Taxation Comprehensive Topics* (Commerce Clearing House).

Nolo also publishes several books that deal with tax issues:

- *Stand Up to the IRS*, by Frederick W. Daily (Nolo), explains how to handle an IRS audit.
- *Tax Savvy for Small Business*, by Frederick W. Daily (Nolo), provides an overview of the entire subject of taxation, geared to the small business owner.
- *Working With Independent Contractors*, by Stephen Fishman (Nolo), shows small businesses how to hire independent contractors without running afoul of the IRS or other government agencies.
- *Working for Yourself,* by Stephen Fishman (Nolo), covers the whole gamut of legal issues facing the one-person business.

- *Every Landlord's Tax Deduction Guide,* by Stephen Fishman (Nolo) provides detailed guidance on tax deductions for small residential landlords.
- *Creating Your Own Retirement Plan*, by Twila Slesnick and John C. Suttle (Nolo), covers retirement planning for the self-employed.
- *IRAs, 401(k)s, & Other Retirement Plans*, by Twila Slesnick and John C. Suttle (Nolo), covers the tax implications of withdrawing funds from retirement accounts.
- *Inventor's Guide to Law, Business, & Taxes*, by Stephen Fishman (Nolo), covers tax aspects of inventing.

Tax Software

Today, millions of taxpayers use tax preparation software to complete their own income tax returns. The best-known programs are *Turbotax* and *TaxCut*. These programs contain most IRS tax forms, publications, and other tax guidance. Each has a helpful website at www.turbotax.com and www.taxcut.com, respectively.

Consulting a Tax Professional

There are hundreds of thousands of tax professionals (tax pros) in the United States ready and eager to help you—for a price. A tax pro can answer your questions, provide guidance to help you make key tax decisions, prepare your tax returns, and help you deal with the IRS if you get into tax trouble.

Types of Tax Pros

There are several different types of tax pros. They differ widely in training, experience, and cost:

- **Tax preparers.** As the name implies, tax preparers prepare tax returns. The largest tax preparation firm is H & R Block, but many mom and pop operations open for business in storefront offices during tax time. In most states, anybody can be a tax preparer; no licensing is required.
- **Enrolled agents.** Enrolled agents (EAs) are tax advisors and preparers who are licensed by the IRS. They must have at least five

years of experience or pass a difficult IRS test. They can represent taxpayers before the IRS, and in administrative proceedings, circuit court, and, possibly tax court, if they pass the appropriate tests. Enrolled agents are the least expensive of the true tax pros but are reliable for tax return preparation and more routine tax matters.

- **Certified public accountants.** Certified public accountants (CPAs) are licensed and regulated by each state. They undergo lengthy training and must pass a comprehensive exam. CPAs represent the high end of the tax pro spectrum. In addition to preparing tax returns, they perform sophisticated accounting and tax work. CPAs are found in large national firms or in small local outfits. The large national firms are used primarily by large businesses. Some states also license public accountants. These are competent, but are not as highly regarded as CPAs.

- **Tax attorneys.** Tax attorneys are lawyers who specialize in tax matters. The only time you'll ever need a tax attorney is if you get into serious trouble with the IRS or another tax agency and need legal representation before the IRS or in court. Some tax attorneys also give tax advice, but they are usually too expensive for most individuals. You're probably better off hiring a CPA if you need specialized tax help.

Finding a Tax Pro

The best way to find a tax pro is to obtain referrals from a friend or business associates. If none of these sources can give you a suitable lead, try contacting the National Association of Enrolled Agents or one of its state affiliates. You can find a listing of affiliates at the NAEA website at www.naea.org. Local CPA societies can give you referrals to local CPAs. You can also find tax pros in the telephone book under "Accountants, Tax Return." Local bar associations can refer you to a tax attorney. Be aware that CPA societies and local bar associations refer from a list on a rotating basis, so you shouldn't construe a referral as a recommendation or certification of competence.

Be picky about the person you choose. Talk with at least three tax pros before hiring one. You want a tax pro who takes the time to listen to you, answers your questions fully and in plain English, seems knowledgeable, and makes you feel comfortable.

Index

A

"Above the line" deductions, 6, 126. *See also*
Adjustments to income; Business expense
deductions; *specific types*

Accessibility tax credit, 78

Accident insurance proceeds, 57

Accountants, 264

ADA (Americans with Disabilities Act), 78

Adjusted basis, 153, 202. *See also* Basis

Adjusted gross income. *See* AGI

Adjustments to income, 6, 125, 126, 163–165
alimony payments, 165, 178
college tuition and fees, 163, 165, 178, 240
early savings withdrawal penalties, 165
educator expenses, 163, 164, 178
employee moving expenses, 164–165, 178
HSA contributions, 6, 41, 136, 163
planning to maximize, 178–180
retirement account contributions, 27, 88–89,
95–96, 163, 178, 240, 241
self-employed health insurance deduction, 6,
52, 136, 163
self-employed retirement plan contributions,
6, 163, 178
self-employment tax adjustment, 165

Adoption assistance, 49

Adoption credit, 72–73

AGI (adjusted gross income)
defined, 6
reducing, 178, 214, 256
See also Adjustments to income; AGI
limitations

AGI limitations, 126, 131, 175, 178, 214
casualty/theft loss deduction, 152–153
charitable deduction, 142–143, 144, 148
couples' filing status and, 239, 240
high-income itemized deduction limits, 131,
161–163
investment expenses, 159
medical expenses deduction, 131, 132
miscellaneous deductions, 159–160

personal/dependent exemption phaseouts,
255–257
retirement account contribution limits, 97–98
on savings bond interest deduction, 38–39
student loan interest deduction phaseout,
165
unreimbursed job expenses, 156–157

Alimony payments, 165, 178

Alternative fuel vehicle credit, 65

Alternative Minimum Tax (AMT), 9, 179

Amending tax returns, 236

Americans with Disabilities Act (ADA), 78

AMT (Alternative Minimum Tax), 9, 179

Annuities, 93, 116–117

Appraisal expenses, 138, 145, 159

Appreciated assets
donating to charity, 147–148, 206–207
giving to family members, 207–208, 219–221
income shifting and, 212
stepped-up basis for, 23, 111, 112, 185–186

Assets. *See* Appreciated assets; Capital assets;
specific types

Attorneys, 264

Autos. *See* Vehicle *entries*

Averaging methods, securities sales, 204–205

B

Basis, 20–21, 153
calculating, 21, 184–186
carryover basis, gifted property, 185
depreciation and, 200, 202
improvements and, 21, 202
recordkeeping, 202–203
stepped-up basis, 23, 111, 112, 185–186

"Below the line" deductions, 6, 126. *See also*
Deductions; Itemized deductions; *specific
types*

Bonds
donating to charity, 147–148
holding periods, 187
IRS sales reporting, 187

Get the Latest in the Law

Nolo's Legal Updater
We'll send you an email whenever a new edition of your book is published!
Sign up at **www.nolo.com/legalupdater**.

Updates at Nolo.com
Check **www.nolo.com/update** to find recent changes in the law that
affect the current edition of your book.

3

Nolo Customer Service
To make sure that this edition of the book is the most recent one, call us at
800-728-3555 and ask one of our friendly customer service representatives
(7:00 am to 6:00 pm PST, weekdays only). Or find out at **www.nolo.com**.

4

Complete the Registration & Comment Card ...
... and we'll do the work for you! Just indicate your preferences below:

- -

Registration & Comment Card

NAME _____ DATE _____

ADDRESS _____

CITY _____ STATE _____ ZIP _____

PHONE _____ EMAIL _____

COMMENTS _____

WAS THIS BOOK EASY TO USE?   (VERY EASY)   5   4   3   2   1   (VERY DIFFICULT)

☐ Yes, you can quote me in future Nolo promotional materials. *Please include phone number above.*

☐ Yes, send me **Nolo's Legal Updater** via email when a new edition of this book is available.

Yes, I want to sign up for the following email newsletters:

    ☐ **NoloBriefs** (monthly)
    ☐ **Nolo's Special Offer** (monthly)
    ☐ **Nolo's BizBriefs** (monthly)
    ☐ **Every Landlord's Quarterly** (four times a year)

☐ Yes, you can give my contact info to carefully selected
partners whose products may be of interest to me.

LTAX 1.0

Nolo
950 Parker Street
Berkeley, CA 94710-9867
www.nolo.com

YOUR LEGAL COMPANION